Philip Augar worked in investment banking for over twenty years. He led NatWest's global equity and bond business before becoming a Group Managing Director at Schroders. He was a member of the team that negotiated the sale of Schroders investment bank to Citigroup in 2000 before becoming a full-time writer. His first book, *The Death of Gentlemanly Capitalism: The Rise and Fall of London's Investment Banks*, was published in 2000 and was a business bestseller. His co-authored second book, *The Rise of the Player Manager*, was published by Penguin in 2002 and was one of Amazon UK's Business Books of the Year. Philip Augar speaks and broadcasts on business and management issues and has written for many publications including the *Financial Times* and other broadsheets. He can be contacted through his website, www.philipaugar.com.

PHILIP AUGAR

The Greed Merchants

How the Investment Banks Played the Free Market Game

PENGUIN BOOKS

PENGUIN BOOKS

Published by the Penguin Group
Penguin Books Ltd, 80 Strand, London WC2R 0RL, England
Penguin Group (USA) Inc., 375 Hudson Street, New York, New York 10014, USA
Penguin Group (Canada), 90 Eglinton Avenue East, Suite 700, Toronto, Ontario, Canada M4P 2Y3
(a division of Pearson Penguin Canada Inc.)
Penguin Ireland, 25 St Stephen's Green, Dublin 2, Ireland
(a division of Penguin Books Ltd)
Penguin Group (Australia), 250 Camberwell Road, Camberwell, Victoria 3124, Australia
(a division of Pearson Australia Group Pty Ltd)
Penguin Books India Pvt Ltd, 11 Community Centre, Panchsheel Park, New Delhi – 110 017, India
Penguin Group (NZ), cnr Airborne and Rosedale Roads, Albany, Auckland 1310, New Zealand
(a division of Pearson New Zealand Ltd)
Penguin Books (South Africa) (Pty) Ltd, 24 Sturdee Avenue, Rosebank, Johannesburg 2196, South Africa

Penguin Books Ltd, Registered Offices: 80 Strand, London WC2R 0RL, England

www.penguin.com

First published by Allen Lane 2005
Published in Penguin Books 2006
2

Typeset by Rowland Phototypesetting Ltd, Bury St Edmunds, Suffolk
Printed in England by Clays Ltd, St Ives plc

ISBN-13: 978-0-141-01767-9
ISBN-10: 0-141-01767-8

www.greenpenguin.co.uk

Penguin Books is committed to a sustainable future
for our business, our readers and our planet.
The book in your hands is made from paper
certified by the Forest Stewardship Council.

To the three that I admire most

I have never adhered to the view that Wall Street is uniquely evil, just as I have never found it possible to accept with complete confidence the alternative view, rather more palatable in sound financial circles, that it is uniquely wise.

J. K. Galbraith[1]

Contents

PART 4:

Whatever Happened to the Invisible Hand?

Acknowledgements

This book originated in a paper I delivered at a seminar organized by the London School of Economics Financial Markets Group in September 2001. I am grateful to Sir Geoffrey Owen and John Plender for inviting me to speak there, thus getting the ball rolling.

I have carried out a large number of interviews with investment bankers and brokers, their corporate and institutional customers and their regulators in the United States and Britain. Many of these people are still involved with the financial services industry and in most cases I have protected their identity. I should like to thank them all, whether named or not, for being so generous with their time. I also wish to acknowledge the Securities Industry Association for giving me permission to quote from and use their research publications and data.

Several experts on the financial services industry read the draft manuscript. Without exception their input improved its accuracy and clarity. Their comments, together with those of my editors, Stuart Proffitt in London and Adrian Zackheim in New York, have been invaluable. I should also like to thank successive classes of students at Cranfield University who listened to the developing argument during my lectures and shaped it through intelligent and stimulating questions. I am also appreciative of the help given by Adrian Fitz-Gerald and Stephen Sale.

Most of all, however, I am grateful to my immediate family, Denise, William and Rachel. They provided me with support and tolerance when I became grumpy when the writing got tough, they helped with the research and production of the book and they have always been willing to act as a sounding board for ideas and text. I love you all.

Foreword to the paperback edition

Investment banking has moved at its usual hectic pace in the year since the manuscript for the hardback edition of this book was completed. New products, people and protocols have emerged and they are doubtless evolving further as I write. One thing that has not changed, however, is the importance of the investment banks' integrated business model. Conflict of interest – albeit better regulated and managed now – remain inherent in the model. Integration also continues to give powerful investment banks a decisive advantage over other market users. With this in mind, I have resisted the temptation to have a second bite at the cherry. What follows is the original text, updated only for the most significant events and with certain passages moved from the present to the past tense to reflect the passage of time.

Philip Augar
Cambridge, England, 2006

Preface

This book completes a journey that started in 1978 when I took my first job. I worked for over twenty years as an investment analyst, head of research and chief executive with two British securities firms. My work took me round the world. I made frequent visits to Wall Street, reviewing the firms' American subsidiaries and meeting clients. My final task as a full time investment banker was to help my employer, Schroders, sell its investment bank to Citigroup in 2000.

It was a good time to leave. I had become increasingly doubtful about the industry I was in and its role in the economy. During my time, the profession appeared to have moved from putting the client first to putting itself first. We exerted enormous pressure on clients to transact. We helped to raise and recycle lots of capital, yet we employees seemed to benefit more than our clients and shareholders. We never seemed to face up to the truth about what we were really doing.

To start with I thought this was a London problem. My first book, *The Death of Gentlemanly Capitalism*,[1] described how the City of London's investment banks and brokers had lost out to foreign, mainly American, competitors in the years after Big Bang in 1986. I expected that this book would end my interest in finance, but I kept a weather eye on investment banking. Some firms used me as a consultant; others asked my opinion informally; friends in the business kept me in touch with what was happening.

It was hard to ignore: the media was full of the most extraordinary goings-on: the boom and bust of the dot-com bubble, corporate scandal in recession-hit America and lay-offs on Wall Street and in the City. To cap it all, the exposure of uncontrolled conflict of interest at the heart of investment banking came not from the regulators who were meant to be in charge of the investment banks but in the unlikely form of the New York State Attorney General, Eliot Spitzer.

For a year, 2002, Wall Street was on its knees. Then new rules, promises to be more vigilant and rising markets eased the pressure. The investment banking industry regained its equilibrium and the whole episode came to be seen as an unwelcome but inevitable consequence of the 1990s bubble. The consensus appeared to be that Wall Street had received its rap on the knuckles and that capitalism could once again move fairly and squarely forward.

I was less sure. The new rules left intact a business model riddled with conflicts of interest. These are sometimes – in my view incompletely – acknowledged, but even so they are notoriously difficult to manage. I wanted to know whether the integration of so many related activities explained the high profits and regular scandals that have been a feature of the industry for the last twenty years. If so, tackling the symptoms but not the cause of the latest crisis would merely perpetuate the problem.

I wondered where all the money was coming from. I had a sneaking suspicion that if the chain was followed to its logical conclusion Joe Public would emerge as the provider of the rich rewards garnered by the investment banks' employees and shareholders. If so, further questions would need to be asked about how it is all being done and whether capital is finding its most productive home as it passes through the financial markets. I decided to seek the answers, and this book is the result.

Problems in the investment banking system are often seen as an American issue and much of the evidence in this book comes from the USA. Most of the world's top investment banks are American, most investment bankers work in the United States and that's where the most obvious problems have been. But when America sneezes the rest of the world catches a cold and every country with a large capital market is dominated by American investment banks, their business practices and their values.

Britain and other countries that follow the American business model have avoided the most egregious examples of misbehaviour, but do not for a moment think that they are immune from America's cold. If you look hard enough the games that are played in American capital markets can be found wherever you live. And if you look hard enough you will find that you too are paying the price.

Philip Augar
Cambridge, England, 2004

PART I

Introduction

1

The Trusted Adviser Takes a Fall

Millennium Eve, 31 December 1999

'Be Bullish', thundered Merrill Lynch in its report on the year 1999. America expected little else from a firm that sported a bull as its emblem, but this was not just locker-room talk. It was a rallying cry for a new millennium that appeared to offer endless possibilities to commerce in general and to the investment banks in particular.

Investment banks are the powerful firms that provide advice, securities trading and other financial services to the world's corporations and institutions. As we shall see, Goldman Sachs, Morgan Stanley and some half a dozen others stand alongside Merrill Lynch as the leading names in the industry.

On Millennium Eve everything that drove their business looked good. A sound economic foundation had been laid during the previous twenty years. Inflation had been brought under control, interest rates were low, employment was rising and the world's developed economies were delivering solid, reliable growth. From this platform corporations could plan and increase their profits steadily; this, in turn, inspired investor confidence. Beginning in 1982, a virtuous circle had developed, driving stock markets up tenfold. Nearly twenty years later, a few savvy stock market strategists worried about high share prices and the alarming rate at which insiders were selling stocks – but they did not get much air time in the financial news or at the large investment banks. The bull market mentality prevailed and no one wanted to hear otherwise.[1]

The rosy economic scenario was not the only reason for the confidence, optimism and, yes, excitement that pumped through Wall Street on Millennium Eve. Revolution was in the air. The internet promised to alter people's lives as dramatically as had the Industrial Revolution in the nineteenth century. New ways of shopping, communicating and working were turning the world on its head. Dot-com cool threatened established hierarchies, vocabularies and business models. This offered enormous opportunities for the investment banks, who thrived on change. They fell over themselves to proclaim their enthusiasm for, as Morgan Stanley put it, 'the remarkable transformation that is occurring in the world of business generally and with our customers'.[2]

The investment banks had already inserted themselves neatly and profitably between the bright entrepreneurs with businesses to fund and the people and organizations with capital to invest. New share issues in internet-related companies were creating fantastic profits for investors and investment bankers. In 1999 the average Initial Public Offering (IPO) in America opened at a 72 per cent premium to the issue price and the hottest stocks immediately soared to double, treble or even more than what investors had paid for them. Investment banking profits surged on the back of this IPO explosion and the managers and shareholders of Wall Street's top firms could congratulate themselves on successfully riding the new economy wave.

Over the previous two decades there had been a subtle change in the status of investment banking. As leader of the free market economy charge of the 1980s and 1990s, it appeared to have joined the great professions. Markets were in the ascendant and share ownership became a popular passion. In bar rooms, around dinner tables and at cocktail parties, a public eager to make money from the bull market listened to the investment banker's every word.

Their influence was growing. A former director of J. P. Morgan, Alan Greenspan, held the world economy in his thrall as chairman of the Federal Reserve; the outgoing chairman of Goldman Sachs, Jon Corzine, was running for the US Senate; Wall Street was the career of choice for over a third of those graduating from Harvard Business School. When it came to interest rates, exchange rates, regulation, indeed almost any conceivable aspect of government policy, Washington listened to Wall Street: let the market decide appeared to be the answer to every problem.

'Markets Rule' was the headline to a tongue-in-cheek article in *Newsweek* magazine's first edition of the twenty-first century: 'Maybe it's too early for this perpetually rising stock market to join death and taxes as The Only Certain Things in Life. But at this rate, the day is likely to come soon and when it does the next step will seem obvious: the stock market take over of just about every aspect of society.'[3]

Newsweek had summed up Wall Street's newfound importance in the national psyche. Everyone was making money, the economy was strong, American-style capitalism was rampant. Investment bankers appeared to be the miracle workers who made it all happen and by the end of the twentieth century they laid claim to a special place in American life 'fusing the character of a trusted adviser with the capabilities of a global financial intermediary'.[4] Admired by business, fêted in the media and with Washington eating out of its hand, the Trusted Adviser ruled supreme.

A Chequered History

It had not always been like that. In fact for much of its 200-year history investment banking in America had been viewed with suspicion. The tone was set in 1792 when twenty-four brokers and merchants met under a buttonwood tree on Wall Street to form what would become the New York Stock Exchange and signed a pledge to 'give preference to each other in our negotiations'.[5] This shady understanding encouraged the idea that brokers looked after themselves first and their clients second and helps to explain why the American public has never been entirely comfortable with securities and banking people. It was summed up by the distinguished Wall Street economist Henry Kaufman: 'Financiers were held in disrepute by most of the nation's laborers and farmers, who believed that the "money changers" were producing no products of tangible value. Stock trading and bond trading were considered by many to be forms of gambling.'[6]

The power and influence of the so-called robber barons of the first age of American big business – men like John D. Rockefeller, Andrew Carnegie and Jay Gould who put together the giant corporations – were not much liked either. Congress passed the Sherman Anti-Trust

Act of 1890 to curb monopoly power and glared darkly at the investment banks who appeared to aid and abet big business.

The House of Representatives Banking Committee was formed in 1912 to investigate what was disapprovingly called the 'Wall Street Money Trust', and the following year America's central bank, the Federal Reserve, was set up to keep an eye on money markets. True to what would become form, the Federal Reserve Bank of New York was initially headed by a distinguished Wall Streeter, Benjamin Strong. Smouldering suspicion of Wall Street was kindled after 1914 when Louis D. Brandeis, a future Supreme Court Justice, published an influential book, *Other People's Money*, which fingered the private investment banker as the villain of the piece in America's financial system.[7]

Distrust briefly gave way to greed during the 1920s as a speculative bubble built up. Beginning in 1924 and picking up steam in 1927, markets rose in anticipation of the emerging mass market for automobiles, radio and electrical goods, which promised a different and exciting future. Middle-class America wanted a piece of the action and the banks and brokers waded in with easy credit for stock purchases and high pressure sales. Banks such as National City Bank underwrote dud securities, ramped them up and then peddled them through branches to naive investors. The stock market soared, and the broker moved from pariah to provider in one easy jump as the public clamoured for, and got, more and more stock.

Of course it was too good to last. The Great Crash of 1929 began on 23 October, the Dow Jones Index fell 40 per cent in three weeks, the speculative issues collapsed and over-geared private investors were ruined. Panic set into the financial system: over ten thousand banks failed, millions lost their money and Wall Street was back under a cloud.

A Senate inquiry was set up in 1932 under Judge Ferdinand Pecora and for two years pored over the banks' performance. The investment bankers and brokers did not make good witnesses. They looked complacent, greedy and duplicitous: if you had been sold a worthless investment by a National City salesman it did not help much to find out that the bank had been regularly running inter-branch competitions with cash prizes for those who could shift the most stock.[8]

Take for instance the story of Edgar D. Brown of Pottsville, Pennsylvania. In 1927 the ailing Brown was considering a recuperative visit to California. He answered a National City Bank advertisement: 'Are you thinking of a lengthy trip? If you are it will pay you to get in touch with our institution because you will be leaving the advice of your local banker and we will be able to keep you closely guided as regards your investments.' National City Bank switched his $100,000 portfolio from US Government bonds into dubious, high risk stock and bonds and persuaded him to borrow a further $150,000 to invest. Despite the fact that share prices were rising all over the market, Brown's new portfolio went steadily down. Several complaints brought no satisfactory explanation, so he went into the National City branch in Los Angeles and 'asked them to sell out everything'. He told Pecora's inquiry: 'I was surrounded at once by all of the salesmen in the place and made to know that that was a very foolish thing to do.' A few weeks later the market crashed and Brown was wiped out. As he told National City: 'because of my abiding faith in the advice of your company I am today a pauper'.[9]

Pecora heard many similar stories and was not impressed by the banks' explanations. He concluded that they had contributed to the crisis by marketing high risk investments to unsophisticated customers, gambling with clients' deposits, charging excessive fees, favouritism, price manipulation and short selling. The public demanded action.

High profile banking bosses such as Charles Mitchell of National City and Albert Wiggin of Chase resigned in disgrace. The new President, Franklin Roosevelt, introduced a series of laws to tighten up the regulation of the securities and banking industries. A strong national regulator, the Securities and Exchange Commission (SEC), was set up; commercial banking (loans and deposits) was separated from investment banking (securities underwriting and dealing); depositors' funds were insured against bank failure; and investors were to be protected from unscrupulous salesmen.

Despite the comfort of the new rules and a recovery in the economy and the stock market, the Government remained suspicious. President Truman, who took office following the death of Roosevelt in 1945, was no ally of business or high finance and in 1947 the Justice

Department brought an anti-trust case against seventeen leading investment banks. Trusts – concentrations of market power operating against open competition – had been made illegal under the Sherman Act of 1890. The Justice Department now alleged that 'the defendants as a group developed a system to eliminate competition and monopolize the cream of the business of investment banking' by agreeing to share underwriting business amongst themselves.[10] The hearing began in November 1950 and for three years the investment banks were tied up in complex testimony and legal argument. Finally they persuaded the presiding Judge, Harold Medina, that there was no conspiracy and in October 1953 he dismissed the charges, bringing an end to the interventionist approach to financial markets that had prevailed since the New Deal. Wall Street could relax at last.[11]

Investment banking was becoming more respectable and stock broking was even listed as a prestigious occupation by the sociologist Vance Packard in his bestselling book *The Status Seekers* in 1959.[12] The Street enjoyed the conglomerates' merger wave of the sixties and survived the oil crisis of the seventies. But although it was gaining ground, it was not yet a national powerhouse: that change required the major shift in political and economic philosophy that occurred in the last two decades of the twentieth century when free market ideas found favour in Washington. Drawing on the ideas of the eighteenth-century Scottish philosopher Adam Smith, the Chicago School of economists led by Milton Friedman argued that restrictions on trade and business held back growth, heavily influencing the Reagan and subsequent administrations.

Deregulation became the order of the day in the 1980s and 1990s. Many industries – airlines, trucking, utilities, energy, banking, telecommunications in the Telecommunications Act of 1996 – were transformed as governments stood back and exposed them to market forces.[13] In parallel, following the work of Professor Alfred Rappaport at the North Western University Business School, creating 'shareholder value' was elevated above other goals for management. The movement was given added bite by the increasing use of share options to incentivize top executives and they turned to the investment banks to help them grow earnings per share through financial engineering and mergers and acquisitions.[14]

The combination of a strong economy, deregulation and shareholder value created a mountain of corporate finance work for the investment banks as companies merged, demerged and refinanced themselves. Now capital was needed to meet the requirement for corporate finance and a new source unexpectedly appeared in 1980 with amendment 401K of the US tax code. This apparently low key tax break was originally intended to encourage employers and employees to put year-end profit shares into pension plans, but it had unforeseen wider consequences. Benefits experts realized that regular salary could also be sheltered from tax in this way and, as word spread, employees rushed to take advantage, pumping money into the fast rising stock market. Employers encouraged this, seeing an opportunity to reduce their burdensome pension obligations. The amount of money invested in 401K plans quadrupled to nearly $400 billion in the 1980s and then quintupled in the 1990s to almost $2 trillion, helping to drive up share prices through sheer weight of money, giving millions of people an interest in the stock market and providing business with a new pool of capital to tap.[15]

By the middle of the 1980s Wall Street was at the centre of the economic action, serving, on the one hand, the needs of investors with capital to invest and, on the other, companies hell-bent on a dash for shareholder value. As the bull market built in the early 1980s, people on Wall Street began to make serious money. Big deals generated big bonuses. Wall Street became 'Disneyland for adults', in the words of one corporate finance executive eagerly anticipating a $9 million bonus in 1986.

But Wall Street's newfound fame turned sour for a few years in the late 1980s and early 1990s. The huge rewards led to conspicuous consumption, flash spending and growing media interest in life on Wall Street. In the late 1980s Tom Wolfe's bestseller *Bonfire of the Vanities,* Michael Douglas's Oscar-winning portrayal of Gordon Gekko in the movie *Wall Street* and Michael Lewis's tale of the Salomon Brothers jungle, *Liar's Poker*, picked out some not very attractive characteristics of investment banking people.[16]

A crop of insider trading and market manipulation cases – notably the Boesky and Milken affairs in America and the Guinness scandal in the UK – revived old memories of greed and corruption in financial circles.[17] Ivan Boesky was a prominent risk arbitrageur – someone who takes stock market positions in the hope of profiting from takeover bids – who received a prison sentence and a $100 million fine in 1986 after admitting to trading on insiders' tips.[18]

Boesky was well known in financial circles but what shocked the public at large was where the trail led. Boesky turned state's evidence and named Michael Milken as an insider dealer. Milken was the high profile investment banker who had transformed junk bonds – high risk, high yielding securities – from a backwater of the capital markets into a mainstream financial instrument. Under the leadership of Milken and the firm he worked for, Drexel Burnham Lambert, junk bonds were used to underpin the leveraged buy-outs – demergers funded largely by debt – that refinanced corporate America in the eighties. Using the draconian Racketeer-Influenced Corrupt Organizations law (RICO), US Attorney Rudolph Giuliani, who had also prosecuted Boesky, brought a criminal case against Milken and Drexel Burnham Lambert.

A sordid tale of patronage, favouritism and market manipulation emerged. In 1988 Drexel Burnham Lambert agreed to plead guilty to six felony counts of mail, wire and securities fraud, paid $650 million in fines and restitution and went bust a year later. In 1990 Milken was sent to prison and paid close to $1 billion in fines and settlements. Their downfall was a sensation that damaged confidence in US capital markets and precipitated a collapse of the junk bond market in 1990.[19]

The junk bond crisis spread out across Wall Street and corporate America as a number of highly leveraged deals – including 1988's landmark $23 billion takeover of RJR Nabisco by the buy-out specialists Kohlberg Kravis Roberts – struggled under the weight of debt repayments and asset write-downs.[20] Surprising victims included the savings and loans institutions who, following deregulation in 1982, had loaded up with junk bonds with the backing and advice of the investment banks. When the junk bond market crashed, they were left with bucketloads of unmarketable and worthless bonds and US taxpayers were faced with a $500 billion bill to bail them out.[21]

The excesses of the 1980s spilled over into the 1990s. By this time globalization and financial deregulation had spread Wall Street's influence to the UK. Following revelations from Ivan Boesky about an illegal support operation to keep the Guinness share price high at crucial stages of its bid for Distillers Company, three senior financiers and businessmen, including Ernest Saunders, the Guinness CEO, received jail sentences in Britain in 1990.[22] Back in America, Robert Freeman, the head of arbitrage trading at Goldman Sachs, was convicted of insider trading in 1990, fined $1.1 million and given a jail sentence.[23] Soon after, Prudential-Bache Securities had to pay $1.4 billion of compensation to investors defrauded during a limited partnership scam described in a study of the case as 'the most destructive fraud ever perpetrated on investors by Wall Street'.[24]

In 1991 Salomon Brothers was shamed, suspended and fined after rigging the US Government's Treasury bond market. In 1995, without admitting wrongdoing, Goldman Sachs and several other banks settled American and British lawsuits from Maxwell Pension Fund trustees who were facing a £400 million hole following fraud at the parent company.[25]

In the mid nineties, new products, especially derivatives – financial instruments based on movements in other financial assets – led to new scandals. Bank after bank had to admit that they had been tricked by their own derivatives traders and one, the British investment bank Barings, went under.[26] Their clients often fared even worse in the hands of bonus-driven salespeople peddling new and increasingly complex derivative products at rip-off prices to customers who did not understand what they were buying.

In one derivatives affair, the structured notes debacle of 1994, eighteen Ohio municipalities lost $14 million; the Louisiana State Pension Fund lost $50 million; City Colleges of Chicago lost $96 million, nearly wiping out its investment portfolio; and the prosperous Californian municipality Orange County lost $1.7 billion and went into bankruptcy.[27] Bankers Trust, the specialist derivatives house later bought by Deutsche Bank, later settled claims with Gibson Greetings, Procter & Gamble and other aggrieved customers to whom it had sold complex derivatives at this time for over $100 million in total.

The clients were partly to blame but some investment banks cynically exploited their ignorance of this new and complicated product. Belita Ong, a former Bankers Trust managing director and senior derivatives salesperson, recalled that: 'You saw practices that you knew were not good for clients being encouraged by senior managers because they made a lot of money for the bank.' Another salesman reflected: 'Funny business, you know. Lure people into that calm and then just totally fuck 'em.'[28]

Despite this catalogue of greed and corruption, just as in the 1920s, the 1990s saw the public put its doubts about Wall Street's ethics to one side for the opportunity of making a lot of money on the stock market. Share prices, which had been rising steadily since 1982, endured the 1990–1 recession and the setback of an unexpected rise in US interest rates in 1994, but there was no stopping the bull. Between the end of 1994 and Millennium Eve, the Dow Jones Industrial Average and the S&P 500 – both broad indices of traditional 'old economy' American business – trebled and the NASDAQ index – dominated by 'new economy' Technology, Media and Telecommunications companies – quintupled.

Investing, particularly in equities, became a national obsession in the 1990s. The number of American households owning shares rose from under 40 per cent to nearly 50 per cent and equities rose from being a third of household liquid assets to a half.[29] In the second half of the decade new issues – shares in companies coming to the stock market for the first time – got hotter and hotter year by year. Everyone was talking about them. It was the age of wall-to-wall television coverage of the markets, a time when if you were a broker people at parties wanted to talk to you rather than pass on to the interesting looking person in advertising over your shoulder and when investing clubs became as popular as reading groups amongst America's middle-class ladies.[30]

Joseph Stiglitz, Chief Economist at the World Bank for most of the decade, was well placed to assess Wall Street's influence: 'Among our heroes of the Roaring Nineties were the leaders of finance, who themselves became the most ardent missionaries for market economics and the invisible hand. Finance was elevated to new heights. We told ourselves, and we told others, to heed the discipline of financial markets. Finance knew what was best for the economy and accordingly by paying heed to financial markets we would increase growth and prosperity.'[31]

And so on Millennium Eve, with the Dow up 25 per cent for

the year, its ninth straight annual increase, and the NASDAQ up a towering 86 per cent for the year, it seemed good to be alive, good to be an investor and great to be an investment banker, a Master of the Universe. This time, no kidding.

The Smoking Gun

To begin with, the new millennium went according to plan. In January 2000 news broke of the $166 billion merger between AOL, the iconoclastic internet company, and Time Warner, the 'old media' blue chip. Time Warner owned stalwarts of American society such as CNN and the HBO, *Time*, *Fortune* and *Sports Illustrated* magazines, and the Warner Brothers studios. AOL was less than fifteen years old yet already it had 22 million subscribers. The combination excited the pundits, who thought it would create 'a globally powerful company that combines old media power and content with new media speed'.[32] The merger seemed to confirm the convergence of the new and old economies and fired up enthusiasm for internet stocks still further. NASDAQ broke through 5,000 for the first time on 10 March and the IPO market remained strong. Nothing seemed impossible in this best of all possible worlds.

But in the middle of March the internet bubble burst. As often with bear markets, it is hard to identify a single event that precipitated the fall; but once started, it turned into a rout as investors looked hard at the valuations and business plans of the companies they owned. They did not like what they saw. What yesterday had seemed like an exhilarating investment in a bright new future seemed today like a reckless gamble. By the end of the year, the NASDAQ was down to 2,470, bellwether internet stocks like Yahoo virtually halved in a month and a host of once hot new issues dropped 90 per cent in price.

Companies of all kinds, not just those with new economy connections, were left with holes in their finances. Consumer confidence crashed and before you could blink America was officially declared to be in recession in March 2001.[33] Desperately, the Federal Reserve tried to stimulate markets with a string of interest rate cuts, but valuations were too high, too many companies had no earnings and, after 11 September that year, global terrorism added a dreadful new uncertainty. The old economy indices, the S&P 500 and the Dow Jones, had already run out of steam in 1999 and by the end of 2001 a full scale bear market had developed. Fortunes were lost and retirement plans hastily revised. In March 2002, barely two years after the market peak, losses totalled $4 trillion. Almost 30 per cent had been wiped off the value of the stock market holdings of 100 million American investors. Events at AOL-Time Warner summed up the extraordinary change in mood. Barely twelve months after the acclaimed epoch-defining merger, the company announced incredible losses of $54 billion for the first quarter of 2002, having been forced to reassess and write down the value of its over-hyped assets.[34]

The lifeblood of the investment banks dried up as the bear market took hold. Stock market turnover shrivelled and mergers withered. Initial Public Offerings that had offered instant profit opportunities at the rate of two per day in America in 1999 dropped to two per week in 2001 and first-day gains were modest. The investment banks had expanded in the late nineties to cope with the boom. Suddenly they were faced with falling revenues and inflated cost bases. They slashed pay and cut jobs and the industry appeared to be in freefall. In his letter to shareholders at the end of 2002 Philip Purcell of Morgan Stanley characterized the previous thirty months as a period of 'Revenue declines, layoffs, on-the-job deaths and injuries, clients losing major portions of wealth and retirement savings, discouraged and weary colleagues and people working twice as hard for half the pay.' Merrill Lynch saw its net earnings fall from $3.8 billion in 2000 to just $0.6 billion the following year. The bright young things who, when the internet bubble burst, had joked that the acronym 'B2B' no longer stood for 'business to business' but 'back to banking' soon found that there were no jobs in banking either.

The investment banks survived – volatility was something that they had learned to live with in the past and they were able to do so again by cutting costs and piling into the few remaining growth areas – but their reputations did not. It was not just the stock market and economic crisis that gave the Trusted Adviser a beating. There was a related twist, the sudden and dramatic reappearance of business scandal in America in 2001. Denied the camouflage of a rising stock market and economic growth, many companies had to own up to fraud, accounting scandals and weak corporate governance. The names Arthur Andersen, Enron, Tyco, Global Crossing and WorldCom became symbolic of corporate malpractice, 250 large American companies had to restate their accounts in a single year and famous names, including the British companies ICI and Marconi, crashed as their acquisition-led strategies failed. At first the investment banks were able to keep out of the mess as attention focused on the CEOs who had presided over the shambles and the auditors who had signed them off. But there was a time bomb ticking away in the offices of Eliot Spitzer, the New York State Attorney General.

Spitzer, the Democratic son of a wealthy real estate developer, had been elected Attorney General in 1998 at the age of thirty-nine. After two years chasing down environmentalist offenders he turned his attention to the investment banks. If the SEC – the federal agency in charge of regulating the investment banks – and the industry's self regulatory organizations, especially the New York Stock Exchange and the National Association of Securities Dealers, had been up to the mark there would have been little for the state judiciary to do. As it was, prevarication and ineffectiveness left a gaping hole that Spitzer filled. Using 1921 Martin Act powers to investigate securities operations in New York State – effectively the site of America's investment banking industry, since most stock and bond sales pass through Wall Street – Spitzer's inquiry dragged the investment banks into the corporate governance scandals.

The story is well known.[35] The trail began with disgruntled private investors who had lost fortunes in the internet stock crash of 2000. A case brought against Merrill Lynch by one of its clients, a New York doctor, caught the eye of Spitzer's investor protection bureau. Led by Eric Dinallo, the bureau wondered why so many investment banking analysts had maintained 'Buy' recommendations on technology and internet stocks while their share prices collapsed. Were they just incompetent or was there a deeper explanation? Spitzer's team used the Martin Act powers to search investment banks' records and unearthed goings-on that exposed the Trusted Adviser as a sham.

Two departments are at the heart of full service investment banks: brokers, who trade securities for investors, and investment bankers, who advise companies on their financial affairs. The two departments come together when an investment banking client needs to issue securities. Then the broking arm gets involved, using its contacts with investors to distribute the securities, before returning to its routine duties.

This arrangement had always contained the potential for conflict of interest because the investment bank was simultaneously advising buyers and sellers on the same transaction. What might be a good price for the seller was not necessarily a good price for the buyer. If the investment bankers and brokers disagreed, whose view would prevail? Investors were aware that such differences might arise but the banks had always reassured them that these were resolved fairly by internal discussion. This was believable because when securities and investment banking first began working together neither side held the whip hand. Thus both sides were able to portray themselves convincingly as Trusted Advisers.

What the Spitzer investigation revealed was that by the late 1990s any balance of power between the investment bankers representing the issuers and the brokers representing the investors had gone. The late twentieth-century explosion in high margin investment banking work such as mergers and acquisitions and new share offerings gave the bankers and their clients the louder voice. Issuers paid bigger fees than investors and the balance of power swung firmly to them and their banking advisers. With a similar effect to National City Bank's inter-office competitions of the 1920s, big bonuses were on offer for brokers who helped to win and sell deals. Brokers saw which way the land lay and put the investors second. They became cheerleaders for the issuers and told investors what the investment bankers wanted them to hear.

E-mails were the smoking gun that gave away the Trusted Adviser. Since 2001, the SEC had required investment banks to save e-mails for three years. This provided a mountain of evidence for Spitzer's team. E-mails retrieved from the major firms provided some juicy sound bites. Jack Grubman, Citigroup's star telecommunications analyst, was described as a 'poster child for conspicuous conflict of interest' by one aggrieved broker. Grubman evidently grew weary of the balancing act he was required to perform: 'If I so much as hear one more fucking peep out of them we will put the proper rating on this stock which every single smart buysider feels is going to zero.' A Lehman Brothers analyst admitted that: 'The little guy who isn't smart about the nuances may get misled, such is the nature of my business.' So too at UBS Warburg: 'A very important client. We could not go out with a big research call trashing their lead product.' Far from balancing conflict of interest in a 'professional' way, and putting the client first, there appeared to be only one priority. In response to the question 'What are the three most important goals for you in 2000?' a Goldman Sachs analyst replied: '1. Get more investment banking revenue. 2. Get more investment banking revenue. 3. Get more investment banking revenue.'[36]

The suspicion that cynical, biased research was systemic blew the Trusted Adviser out of the water. Client satisfaction ratings dropped to below 50 per cent, but worse news was to come. Spitzer's team alleged commission kickbacks from clients to investment banks in return for favours given during Initial Public Offerings.

During the heady days of the internet bubble, many new share issues opened at a massive premium to the price at which they were originally offered to investors, as we have seen. Those lucky enough to get them could multiply the value of their investment several times over in a matter of minutes, hours or days. The investment banks were in charge of allocating these shares to investors and it seemed that they were looking after their friends. Focusing on two leading investment banks, Salomon Smith Barney and CSFB, Spitzer accused them of using generous allocations of hot new issues to elicit extra business from clients. The process became known as 'spinning and laddering'. Suspicions that an insiders' club operated were raised by the apparent involvement of many top business people.

A class action complaint on behalf of investors in WorldCom Inc., America's second largest long-distance telecommunications carrier before it went bankrupt in July 2002,[37] alleged how spinning worked: 'Since 1996, Salomon repeatedly allocated thousands of hot IPO shares to the same top executives of the same telecommunications companies. In return, these executives, who were all in the position to determine or influence the selection of their company's financial advisers or underwriters, repeatedly directed to Salomon investment banking business worth many millions of dollars.'[38]

Laddering was a variation on the theme. Andy Kessler, a former investment analyst and hedge fund manager, explained how it worked: 'Fund managers promised to buy more IPO shares in the open market on the first day of an IPO to ladder the deal, causing or perhaps just perpetuating the first day pop in the share price.'[39]

As their losses mounted and details emerged of the investment banks' duplicity, the investing public got very angry. The media turned against the investment banks and ran articles such as 'How corrupt is Wall Street?'[40] One of the first books on the subject was called *Wall Street on Trial: A Corrupted State?*[41] Few other commentators were so kind as to give Wall Street the courtesy of the question mark. The same chat show hosts who had lauded the analysts on the way up gave them a kicking on the way down. The investment banks were hauled up before congressional committees, and even President Bush waded in with a speech to Wall Street pledging 'to end the days of cooking the books, shading the truth and breaking our laws' and emphasizing that 'Stock analysts should be trusted advisers, not salesmen with a hidden agenda.'[42]

The analysts had fallen a long way short of Trusted Adviser standards. Those who had covered the hottest sectors, telecommunications and the internet, had made the fanciest forecasts, the biggest bonuses and the most extravagant claims. They were at the nexus of the conflicts of interest and when their sectors crashed they, their managers and the entire investment banking profession were denounced.

And so it seemed that the Trusted Advisers were back where they had been over most of the past two centuries: under a cloud. Low in public esteem, in the regulatory spotlight and in the courts, the investment banker was no longer a hero of the market economy. Modern-day Edgar Browns such as the writer Ed Wasserman ruefully blamed their advisers for financial ruin: 'I lost two-thirds of the money. The market went into free fall. And these guys who I had invested with were paralyzed. I was paying them to manage my money – and they weren't managing. Finally I putted out of that fund on my own.'[43]

The Clean-Up

The clean-up started with the Sarbanes-Oxley Act of 2002, which imposed tougher governance rules on business and auditing and contained a separate section relating to investment banking. The SEC was required to draw up rules to ensure that conflict of interest between analysts and investment bankers was properly managed and disclosed. Faced with damaging allegations, together with mounting regulatory pressure as the SEC and other agencies belatedly joined Spitzer, the investment banks needed to draw a line under the affair. In April 2003 ten of them – Bear Stearns, Credit Suisse First Boston, Goldman Sachs, Lehman Brothers, J. P. Morgan, Merrill Lynch, Morgan Stanley, Citigroup's Salomon Smith Barney, UBS Warburg, and Piper Jaffray – agreed a settlement.

The ten firms, whilst admitting no wrongdoing, agreed to pay $1.4 billion between them and to separate the management of research and investment banking. Analysts were prohibited from receiving compensation for investment banking activities or getting involved in investment banking 'pitches' and 'road shows'. Independent research and investor education were to be provided, and analysts' historical ratings and price target forecasts made publicly available. All ten firms collectively entered into a voluntary agreement restricting allocations of securities in hot IPOs to influential company executive officers and directors. Two further firms, Deutsche Bank and Thomas Weisel, settled on similar terms in 2004 and paid $100 million between them.

Individual penalties were also meted out. Neither admitting nor denying the regulator's allegations, two of the highest profile analysts in the saga, Henry Blodgett, Merrill Lynch's internet analyst, and Jack Grubman, paid $4 million and $15 million respectively to settle the charges and were banned from the securities industry for life. As with previous investment banking scandals, it seemed as though someone had to appear in the dock. This time it was Frank Quattrone, CSFB's king of technology investment banking. Prosecutors said that two days after a CSFB lawyer told him that the bank was under investigation for the way it allocated stock to investors in lucrative IPOs, Quattrone had forwarded to colleagues an e-mail suggesting that staff 'clean up' their computer files. He was found guilty of obstructing justice and received an eighteen-month jail sentence in September 2004. The conviction was later overturned and a retrial ordered.[44]

The bills for the companies were trivial when seen in context. The huge financial services conglomerates Citigroup, Credit Suisse and Merrill Lynch paid the highest shares, $400 million, $200 million and $200 million respectively. These companies had combined group earnings of $15 billion in 2002. The industry-wide settlement of $1,400 million is less than 5 per cent of the profits earned by the investment banking sector during the period that was investigated.

There was, however, a sting in the tail – class actions from disgruntled investors. In 2004 Citigroup's provisions and settled claims for WorldCom and other bubble-related litigation was estimated at $9 billion.[45] The same year J. P. Morgan Chase set aside $2.3 billion for lawsuits related to the corporate scandals.

At the time of writing there are still class actions in the pipeline but the investment banks' reputation bottomed out with the settlement of April 2003. Thereafter new rules, management initiatives and rising markets took the heat off. Profits and portfolios recovered, public anger subsided and the political agenda moved on. The episode seemed to confirm a few home truths. Markets over-react on the upswing and again on the downswing. Investment banking is a volatile business. Bull markets lead to sloppiness in investment banks, regulators and boardrooms. Yes, it would probably happen again, but not until the next bubble had formed and burst. And then, as now, market forces could be relied upon to sort things out. The investment banking industry recovered its poise and moved on, bloodied but unbowed. What happened was written off as a temporary blemish on a capital markets model that, if not perfect, is the least imperfect yet known to man.

If there was any consolation it was that the free market economy had apparently delivered once again, slashing the investment banks' profits and pay. Justice had been done through a combination of regulation, litigation and free market economics. The market's invisible hand, backed up by the long arm of the law, had worked again.

And yet . . .

2

The Age of Deception

This comforting interpretation explains the past, justifies the present and safeguards the future. But it is debatable for three reasons. The first relates to the widespread incidence of scandal. As the previous chapter showed, there had scarcely been a year since 1986 that hadn't seen shoddy business of some description in investment banking. Indeed no part of the system was immune – not even its central institutions.

For example, traders on the electronic stock exchange NASDAQ were accused of price manipulation and in 1998 paid over $1 billion to settle a class action.[1] Elsewhere the board of the New York Stock Exchange blithely approved a $139 million deferred compensation package for Richard Grasso, its chairman and chief executive from 1995 to 2003. Even the SEC, the investment banking industry's lead regulator, wrongfooted by Eliot Spitzer, appeared slow and ineffective.

Capital markets users seemed equally affected. Having dealt with the investment banks, Eliot Spitzer's investigation moved on to their investing clients, the mutual funds, accusing them of dishing out favours to influential 'friends' in the market timing scandal. Corporations had their own dark corners in the form of accounting frauds and excessive compensation for undeserving top executives. The auditing firms who had signed off on bogus accounts had evidently been blinded by revenue generation and one of the leading firms, Arthur Andersen, was ruined in a document shredding scandal.

Every part of the big business machine was tarnished, and the investment banks were in the thick of it. The previous twenty years saw every trick in the book: inside trading, market manipulation, unauthorized dealing, misrepresentation, front running, favouritism and kickbacks, to mention a few. Not every firm was involved in every scam, but none of the major houses kept their noses entirely clean.

Thus investment banks, regulators, investing clients and issuing clients – all seem to have been caught up in the malaise. Most people working in and around financial services are straightforward and honest and the existence of the odd rogue employee is inevitable given the numbers involved. But what happened does not seem to have been merely a few greedy individuals occasionally exploiting a short term opportunity. It looks more like wholesale malpractice that had been going on for years. We need to understand how this situation arose and what damage occurred as a result.

The second reason to look more closely at the investment banks stems from the authorities' response to the crisis. In allowing them to retain their business model, Eliot Spitzer and the other regulators appear to have tackled the symptoms but not the cause of the problem. This model is known as the integrated investment bank and is as old as the American financial services industry itself. It became the accepted global model after 1986 when the British authorities abandoned their system of separate firms carrying out trading, broking and advisory business.

All the leading investment banks operate the integrated structure. Morgan Stanley's Institutional Securities division shows what goes into the mix. This powerhouse offers investment banking services to corporates and governments, and sales and trading services to institutional investors in virtually every financial instrument, and also includes proprietary trading. The conflicts of interest this range of activities creates were clearly set out by Morgan Stanley's then chairman, Philip Purcell, in a speech at the Securities Industry Association annual conference in 2003: 'In our business, we are surrounded by conflicts – not just conflicts between our own interests and those of our clients, but between different parts of our firms, and between the clients in one part of the firm and the clients in another. There is even a conflict in simply acting as an intermediary between a buyer and a seller – the better the price for one, the worse for the other.'[2]

Failure to manage that conflict was at the root of many of the industry's problems of the previous twenty years. Integration created the profits that provided the bonuses that drove otherwise highly professional people to fast talking salesmanship. It created the temptation to misuse the privileged information that flies around every investment bank. It gave investment bankers and brokers the power to favour one client above another and to put the profits of the in-house book before client interests. In many cases, especially when trying to give impartial advice to the buyer and seller in a single transaction, it is impossible to resolve these conflicts. Even *The Economist* magazine, an articulate supporter of free markets and their institutions, described some of these activities as being 'mutually exclusive'.[3]

The authorities preferred new rules and more rigorous enforcement to breaking up the integrated model. The success of this approach depends on the effectiveness of the regulators and management. At the time of writing the new rules and attitudes appear to be holding steady but the record of both parties begs longer term questions. The SEC's performance in regulating the investment banking industry deteriorated in the nineties in the face of budget pressures and an effective investment banking lobby in Washington. Will the arrival of significantly more resources improve the SEC's ability to control the investment banks?

And can the investment banks be trusted to stick permanently to the rules? Although they have finally embraced the need to clean up, their initial response to Spitzer was unconvincing. They argued that not much damage had been done because professional investors could read between the lines of investment-banking-friendly research. A whispering campaign against Eliot Spitzer was started. It was said around lunch tables and bars in financial circles that he was politically motivated and was seeking personal profile to run for even higher office. The implication was that too much was being made of a small thing.

Some senior bankers made the mistake of letting this slip. It was April 2003, just days after the global research settlement, when Philip Purcell commented: 'I don't see anything in the settlement that will concern the retail investor about Morgan Stanley.'[4] Writing in the *Wall Street Journal*, Stanley O'Neal, his counterpart at Merrill Lynch, appeared equally complacent: 'To teach investors . . . that if they lose money in the market they're automatically entitled to be compensated for it does both them and the economy a disservice.'[5] William Donaldson, at the time the Chairman of the Securities and Exchange

Commission immediately criticized comments that showed 'a troubling lack of contrition', but, as we have come to expect, the last word belonged to Eliot Spitzer: 'Some, I'm afraid, probably still don't get it.'[6]

The investment banks did eventually get it. Philip Purcell's speech to the SIA in November 2003 was entitled 'Reconnecting with America' and he listed the measures that Morgan Stanley had taken to manage conflict of interest, including the recruitment of Eric Dinallo from Eliot Spitzer's office to head up the effort. It is an impressive list and other firms have made equally strong efforts to reform. They are policing their business more carefully; they are making politically correct noises and everyone at the investment banks from top to bottom breathes, eats and sleeps compliance. Right now there is no doubt that the mood has changed and the entire industry is trying to be squeaky clean.

But history shows that it pays to be sceptical with the investment banks. Indeed one of the handful of top executives at one of America's leading investment banks told me: 'Going forward, Spitzer's reforms will turn out a complete failure. He could have gone for structure but didn't. Keeping Spitzer away from the model was an extraordinary management achievement.'[7] Andy Kessler, the former analyst and fund manager, was equally forthright: 'It seems to me that Wall Street management reached into the pockets of their shareholders and paid big fines so they could keep the status quo.'[8] The survival of integration beyond the global settlement, the role it played in the scandals during the last years of the twentieth century and the potential it leaves for future problems therefore make it essential to understand fully how it works.

The third reason to review the consensual interpretation of the crisis is the speed and scale of the financial recovery. The industry's volatility – profit collapses, losses and lay-offs in the bad times – diverts attention from its pricing structure, profits and compensation in the good times. Clients, governments and the media do not focus on these matters because they believe that an investment bank that is in profit one year has a significant chance of being in loss the next, and that an investment banker who earns a million-dollar bonus one year could be out on the street soon afterwards.

Coverage of the investment banks at the beginning of the new millennium illustrates this. In 2001 and 2002, as the investment banks cut jobs and pay, headline writers had a field day: 'More lay-offs on Wall Street', 'Deepest job cuts yet', 'Spirits low in eerie London town', 'So long banker', 'Cold Christmas'. But what attracted much less attention was the rebound. The first lay-offs came in the spring of 2001; within three years, over half of those laid off in London had been re-hired. In America, numbers employed dropped in 2001 and 2002, but began to recover in 2003. In the UK, the increase in the City's bonus pool in 2004 exceeded the combined downturn in the two previous years.[9] Compensation was up and guaranteed bonuses were back. In early 2004, firms were reporting rising profits and Morgan Stanley, they of the 'discouraged and weary colleagues', registered a 22 per cent increase in profits for 2003 despite five of the nine items they identified as 'business drivers' being down. Either something had changed about this industry or the conventional high risk, high reward picture was wrong.

Some Tricky Questions

These loose ends give rise to some tricky questions. On the one hand, during the last twenty years of the twentieth century, the Golden Age of Investment Banking, the economies of Britain and America, where the investment banks have the greatest influence, grew strongly. Vast and ever increasing amounts of capital were raised and recycled and the ability of stock markets to absorb shocks appeared limitless. The cost of capital markets transactions apparently fell. Innovation and productivity flourished.

But on the other hand, was this economic miracle achieved because of or in spite of the investment banks? Did their output – the quality of advice that they gave – match their execution skills? Were the prices paid fair? Did they lead to an efficient allocation of capital? Are they the responsible guardians of capitalism that they would have us believe? Or are they something more sinister altogether, vital but potentially dangerous players in the free market economy?

There is one further question that provides a framework for tackling the rest: is there an investment banking cartel? A standard definition is that cartels exist when a few firms dominate their market, act together to keep prices high and competition out, and make excess returns. In the absence of open competition, the quality of output suffers.[10] Testing the investment banks against these criteria thus involves answering five preliminary questions:

- Do a few firms dominate the market?
- Did they make excess returns?
- Did output suffer?
- Did prices remain high?
- Do they act together?

Two chance conversations put me on to this approach. One was with a distinguished American with close connections to the investment banks. When I explained my plans for this book, the level of alarm was like a bird in the garden when the cats are near the nest: 'So you think there's a cartel?' the person asked, visibly anxious. Next I outlined the project to a senior financial journalist. 'Oh, you're writing about the cartel,' he cut in instantly. *Hmm,* I wondered, *you're a smart guy, why haven't you?*

This is a very sensitive matter for the investment banks. The Medina and Pecora inquiries are part of investment banking folklore and the industry is understandably anxious to avoid the risk of a repeat. Investment banks are mindful of anti-trust legislation. The SIA's Anti-trust Compliance booklet warned members that 'Violating the anti-trust laws can be a felony offense. Individuals involved in some antitrust violations can and do go to jail' and outlined the risks in areas such as price fixing, bid rigging and customer allocations.[11] The industry still remembers how in the Drexel Burnham Lambert case the US Government used the Racketeer-Influenced Corrupt Organizations law (RICO), which has been increasingly used against white collar crime and carries severe penalties, including prison sentences, forfeiture of ill-gotten gains and the pre-trial freezing of assets.

It would be a serious matter if there were a cartel in investment banking. Not only are cartels illegal but the existence of such a state at the heart of global capitalism would have profound social and economic influences. How do the investment banks measure up to these criteria?

PART 2

Is There a Cartel?

3

The Blessing of the Leviathans

Do a Few Firms Dominate the Market?

I was sitting with the Chief Financial Officer of one of the world's biggest media companies and we were talking about his relationship with the investment banks. He had dealt with them frequently, having steered the company through several big deals. He described his firm's symbiotic relationship with its financial advisers: 'You cannot move without the blessing of the leviathans. They are extraordinarily powerful organizations. They bestride the planet. In less than twenty years they have established themselves at the crossroads of capitalism.'

He was right. In a very short period of time a group of leading investment banks have made themselves indispensable to big business. Who are they, what do they do, how do they come to be there, and how easy is it to join them? Can they be said to dominate the market?

An Overview of the Leviathans

It is a crowded field. There are some 6,000 securities firms in the USA, approximately 600 members of the American Securities Industry Association and over 50 members of Britain's equivalent, the London Investment Banking Association. These firms range in size from small one-partner operations advising retail investors in Main Street America through mid-sized specialist corporate advisory and broking boutiques to the 'full-service' investment banks. There are less than twenty of these big players, but not all can be regarded as leviathans.

In fact, out of the twenty, most observers would say that only ten make the cut. They are known as 'the bulge bracket', the traditional name for the senior syndicate members that were bracketed together in deal announcements and all were involved in the global research settlement of 2003–4.* Five of the ten bulge-bracket firms are independent publicly listed companies; the other five are part of larger banking groups.

The Independents

Insiders acknowledge Morgan Stanley, Goldman Sachs and Merrill Lynch – MGM or the super bulge, as they are known – as the leading firms. Their business profile is not identical – Merrill Lynch is strongest in retail broking, Morgan Stanley in consumer financial services and Goldman Sachs in trading – and they do not win every league table every year; but they share an unequalled reputation for consistency and market power.

The smaller firms Bear Stearns and Lehman Brothers complete the group of leading independents. Bear Stearns, once a small commission house, has built a consistent profits record, with a strong position in clearing and settling, the pipes and drains of financial services, as well as the more glamorous advisory and broking businesses. Lehman Brothers has emerged from a history of changing owners, financial instability and variable reputation into a strong position.

These five leading independents operate other financial services businesses besides investment banking and they are substantial companies in their own right.† Morgan Stanley, Merrill Lynch, Lehman and Goldman Sachs all rank amongst America's hundred biggest companies. The five firms employed about 150,000 people between them, and made combined profits of over $13 billion on revenues of over $70 billion in 2003.

* Opinions about membership vary. Some would confine membership to a subset of the ten; others would include one or two firms from outside the top ten.

† This book is about investment banking and broking. The banks' other financial services activities are discussed only when they touch on the book's central theme.

The Conglomerates

The remaining five of the top ten are part of financial services conglomerates. Two American and three European commercial banks have bought and built major-league investment banking divisions.

The conglomerates that own these investment banks are enormous. Citigroup, UBS, J. P. Morgan Chase, Credit Suisse and Deutsche Bank are amongst the hundred largest companies in the world. In 2003 their combined profits and revenues were over twice the size of those of the five specialists, at more than $30 billion and $150 billion respectively.

An Overview of the Other Leading Investment Banks

Being a big bank is not always sufficient to gain entry to the investment banking elite: two of the world's largest banks, HSBC and Bank of America, operate investment banks that are just outside the bulge bracket. Bank of America is building out from Montgomery Securities, a mid-sized investment bank acquired in 1997, but it is not yet in the big league in corporate advisory work. HSBC has been dabbling in investment banking for twenty years, but despite strengths in Europe and Asia its gaps in equities and advisory services, especially in America, leave it short of the leading firms. Big European banks such as BNP Paribas, Société Générale, ABN AMRO and Barclays, and European insurance companies such as Allianz and ING, have areas of strength in investment banking, but not right across the waterfront. The Japanese banks have stayed at home and even there have left the investment banking high ground to the Americans.

There are several successful focused businesses such as the British-based advisory bank N. M. Rothschild and Lazards. Lazards' three previously semi-autonomous partnerships in New York, Paris and London were brought together under the leadership of Bruce Wasserstein, a famous Wall Street dealmaker, and the investment banking business was publicly listed in 2005. Although Lazards and Rothschild lack the securities presence to be regarded as full-service investment banks, their good corporate connections make them serious players when it comes to advising on big deals.

Other important focused businesses include the research firm Sanford Bernstein (part of Alliance Capital) and advisory boutiques built around high profile investment bankers such as Eric Gleacher (Gleacher Partners) and Robert Greenhill (Greenhill & Co.). These advisory specialists play a significant role in the industry, frequently being called into big deals by CEOs seeking a counterpoint to the advice of integrated firms.

Where They Are

Full-service investment banking is big, big business. The combined investment banking turnover of the top ten in 2003 was over $100 billion, of which over half was in America, a third in Europe and most of the rest in Asia. Although its customers and staff are widely spread, investment banking is an American business in general and a New York business in particular. Seven of the top ten, along with Credit Suisse's investment bank, have their headquarters in New York. Only UBS and Deutsche Bank are rooted in Europe but they too operate the American business model with securities fully integrated into the investment bank.

Wall Street is still used as the collective term for the investment banks though of the major American firms only Goldman Sachs and Merrill Lynch remain in the traditional financial district of lower Manhattan. Citigroup's investment bank is close by but the others moved to midtown as they expanded, diversified and became more corporate, and most of them are spreading their risk and lowering their costs by opening up secondary sites in New Jersey.

To be competitive the firms have to be global, with deep footprints in the Americas, Europe and Asia and representation in Africa and the Middle East. Global coverage is important both as a business tool and for street credibility. It makes the banks aware of business opportunities, enabling them to know who has businesses to sell and who the buyers might be, and gives them a network to distribute securities. Equally important, their clients and staff expect there to be a global network and those that have it play it up. 'Global' is one of the first words in both the Goldman Sachs IPO prospectus and in Morgan Stanley's Form 10-K. Emphasizing their global capability is a standard feature of investment banks' pitch books and other presentations as they lay claim to be 'unconstrained by national and continental borders' and to 'provide global clients with a global service'.[1]

What They Do

With a global pipeline to fill, the big banks need, and their customers expect, a broad product range. Standard offerings include bank loans, commodities and currency dealing, real estate financing, and prime brokerage services – such as stock lending and financing, clearing and settling – for investors.

Using the firm's own money for proprietary trading in markets and for principal investing in funds and other assets is also considered essential to making the profit numbers meet the expectations of staff and shareholders. But offering these standard items is not sufficient to win leviathan status; for that, a credible presence in three key activities is required. These three 'must have' products are:

- Advice for corporates, financial institutions and governments on debt and equity share issues, mergers and acquisitions, and financial restructuring.
- Equity and equity derivatives research, sales and trading for institutional investors including hedge funds.
- Bond and bond derivatives research, sales and trading for institutional investors including hedge funds.

These three activities come together when a corporation, financial institution or government issues securities. In the USA, the investment bank that leads the underwriting in an issue also leads the distribution through its own securities arm, usually in partnership with the other syndicate members. This is at the heart of the integrated securities and investment banking model. It is an American invention and its evolution helps to explain the shape of today's investment banking leader board.

Evolution of the Industry

There have been two phases in modern investment banking history: 1934–75 and 1975–2005. The Glass Steagall Act of 1934 determined the shape of the first period and influenced the second. In the clean-up after the Great Crash of 1929, financial organizations had to choose between commercial and investment banking. At first the industry was led by firms that dropped lending and focused on investment banking, notably Kuhn Loeb, Dillon Read and Lehman Brothers. Other investment banks were started up by splinter groups from organizations that had decided to remain in traditional banking – firms like Morgan Stanley, which emerged out of J. P. Morgan, and First Boston, which emerged out of First National Bank of Boston – and they progressively made up ground. By the end of the Second World War, Morgan Stanley, Dillon Read, Kuhn Loeb and First Boston were the pre-eminent firms in US investment banking, forming the so-called 'special bracket' of leading underwriters.

The second period was shaped by the abolition of fixed commissions on the New York Stock Exchange on 1 May 1975. The arrival of negotiated commissions caused rates to drop, trading became an increasingly important part of the business and the investment banks and brokers needed more capital, especially after 1982 when bought deals – purchases of blocks of stock with the firm's own capital – were facilitated by an SEC rule change.* As we have seen, in the 1980s and 1990s there was an explosion in capital markets activity,which further increased the need for capital. Partnerships and private companies now seemed too risky and under-capitalized and many investment banks went public – Morgan Stanley in 1986, Bear Stearns in 1985 and Goldman Sachs in 1999 – or merged with stronger partners – Salomon Brothers merged with the commodities trader PhiBro in 1981, Lehman Brothers sold itself to Shearson American Express in 1984, Kidder Peabody was bought by GE in 1986.

* This new rule 415 allowed self-registration for new bond issues, enabling money to be raised at short notice. In these circumstances bought deals replaced underwriting as the method.

The abolition of fixed commissions finally marked the end of the era of 'giving preference to each other' in securities trading that had begun nearly two hundred years earlier under Wall Street's buttonwood tree. Broking now became more competitive and cut-throat. Increased competition in broking soon spread to the hitherto gentlemanly business of corporate advisory work. Most white shoe investment banks still practised relationship banking in that they gave free advice in the knowledge that clients rarely changed adviser and would eventually pay them through underwriting fees when the time came to raise new capital. Relationship bankers did not market to competitors' clients, were not proactive when it came to proposing mergers and many had a policy of not acting in hostile takeovers. Geoffrey Boisi, a former Goldman Sachs partner and co-head of investment banking at J. P. Morgan Chase, recalls: 'The notion that you would raid a company was so ungentlemanly that in the early stages it was almost considered an immoral act. In the late 1960s and early 1970s it was considered improper by the generalist banker to even suggest to a CEO that he consider selling his business. It was like asking him to sell one of his children. It was the worst thing that you could suggest.'[2]

However, by the mid seventies attitudes were shifting. After the stock market crash of 1973–4, and with negotiated commissions on the New York Stock Exchange just around the corner, firms could no longer afford to walk away from lucrative business. The industry became more competitive as the investment banks began to attack each other's client lists and corporations proved willing to drop traditional relationships. The hostile takeover of Electric Storage Battery, then the world's largest battery manufacturer, by the Canadian company International Nickel in 1974 is generally agreed to have been a turning point in the move from relationship to transaction banking. Morgan Stanley advised International Nickel and Goldman Sachs advised Electric Storage, both banks breaking their previous practice of not acting aggressively in hostile bids.

Morgan Stanley was also involved in the second major turning point in the breakdown of relationship banking, IBM's first ever bond issue in October 1979. Morgan Stanley was IBM's traditional banker and as such expected to lead any deals. But on this occasion Salomon Brothers and Merrill Lynch were picked as the lead managers. Morgan

Stanley initially refused to participate in the syndicate until a form of words could be found to enable it to maintain its dignity. It was clear that the world of investment banking was changing fast.[3]

This was reflected in the league tables. By 1980, Kuhn Loeb and Dillon Read, two of the firms that had led the industry for half a century, had given way to the new generation. Morgan Stanley and First Boston remained in the 'special bracket' of underwriters but had been joined by Merrill Lynch, Goldman Sachs and Salomon Brothers, and Lehman Brothers (which bought Kuhn Loeb) was knocking at their door.[4]

Through Hell and High Water: Twenty-five Years at the Top

What is remarkable about the next twenty-five years in terms of market domination is the staying power of this group. The top six firms held on to their leadership position through a revolution in business in general and in the financial services industry in particular. In the last few years they have been joined but not replaced by Bear Stearns and the acquisitive Deutsche Bank, J. P. Morgan Chase and UBS. Their resilience is impressive. They have coped with new products, new markets, new business practices and a growth in the business to proportions that were unimaginable twenty years before, as well as seeing off attacks from scores of firms anxious to join the investment banking elite.

Precise rankings are a matter of intense debate amongst investment bankers. There are so many possible products, geographies, time periods and methodologies that every bank worth its salt can find something to impress its clients. Table 1 shows the author's opinion of the leading global investment banks' overall market position at four points during the last twenty-five years. This opinion is based on business done and market reputation in the principal advisory, underwriting and securities product areas. At each of these dates there were firms not named in the table jostling the leaders – for example, Dean Witter, Kidder Peabody, E. F. Hutton, and Blyth Eastman in 1980 and Prudential-Bache and Paine Webber in 1990 – but six firms stand out for their consistency: Goldman Sachs, Merrill Lynch and Morgan Stanley, followed by CSFB (now called Credit Suisse), Lehman Brothers and Salomon Smith Barney (now called Citigroup).

*Table 1. Leading global investment banks, 1980–2005.**

1980	1990	2000	2005
Merrill Lynch	Merrill Lynch	Merrill Lynch	Goldman Sachs
Salomon Brothers	Goldman Sachs	Goldman Sachs	Morgan Stanley
First Boston	Morgan Stanley	Morgan Stanley	Merrill Lynch
Morgan Stanley	CS First Boston	Citigroup Salomon	Citigroup
Goldman Sachs	Salomon Brothers	CS First Boston	J. P. Morgan Chase
Lehman Brothers	Lehman Brothers	Lehman Brothers	Bear Stearns Credit Suisse† Deutsche Bank Lehman Brothers UBS Warburg

The Super Bulge: Goldman Sachs, Merrill Lynch, Morgan Stanley

For over twenty years Goldman Sachs, Merrill Lynch and Morgan Stanley have stood at the top of the investment banking leader board. They are generally acknowledged as being the firms to beat if you are a competitor, the firms to work for if you are an investment banker and the firms to hire if you are a corporation contemplating a major transaction. These three are the very essence of the leviathans mentioned earlier: you cannot move without their blessing.

Their dominance has not been achieved flawlessly. All three firms have experienced moments of crisis, financial drama and reputational

* Author's opinion based on league table data.

† Renamed in 2005. Historical references to the firm have been left as CSFB in this book.

damage; not only have they survived but they have held on to their leadership position throughout.

Since the days of Gus Levy as senior partner in the seventies, trading and risk-taking have been part of the ***Goldman Sachs*** culture. This has involved periods of profits volatility, for example in the bond market crash of 1994 and again in the emerging markets crisis of 1998, which caused a delay to its IPO; but every time the firm has learned from its mistakes, improved its risk management systems and moved on.

Goldman has been able to withstand these and its share of reputational issues because its team culture is strong, its self-belief never wavers, it is impressive with clients and its risk management is leading edge. As one competitor admiringly told me: 'The people in charge at Goldman Sachs are classy people. They are very aggressive but in an acceptable way. They are not people who would knowingly take on low quality business. They take risk but they want to do things well. Only the best is good enough.'[5]

For much of its history ***Morgan Stanley*** enjoyed a pristine reputation. Until Eliot Spitzer raised the IPO conflict of interest (Morgan Stanley agreed to pay $125 million, the fourth highest amount) and accused it of pushing certain mutual funds to retail investors in return for enhanced commissions, the firm had kept out of the worst of the scandals.

In 2004 I asked a former Morgan Stanley managing director, a person who had headed up one of its big divisions, to look back on the firm's history: 'Morgan Stanley has been on a run of uninterrupted success since the early seventies. The key decision at that time was to retain capital in the firm to build securities rather than distribute it to partners. Then in 1986 the firm went public and was in effect recapitalized. During the eighties we made fewer mistakes than our competitors. We expanded overseas more intelligently, exporting our fixed income skills to Europe and Japan. The loss of Gleacher and Greenhill was an issue but never caused an implosion of the kind that hit First Boston when Wasserstein and Perella left there.* Morgan

* Both pairs of men were their firm's top investment bankers who left to form their own boutiques.

Stanley has longevity of management and consistency of strategy. Parker Gilbert hands over to Dick Fisher, Dick Fisher hands over to John Mack and so on. There is more continuity than disruption. We husbanded our reputation very carefully. First class business in a first class way [the Morgan Stanley corporate motto]: you heard it every day.'[6]

Soon after this conversation events in 2005 jolted that reputation. In a bitter public spat with a group of former senior employees, Philip Purcell was ousted as chairman. Some of the firm's top producers and managers left and former President and Chief Operating Officer John Mack was brought back as Chairman and Chief Executive to pull things together. The public nature of the debate was embarrassing given the firm's discreet, self-effacing reputation and its cherished patina of success. Commentators and competitors wondered if it would cause serious reputational damage but at the time of writing Morgan Stanley appears to have weathered the storm.

The third member of the super bulge, ***Merrill Lynch***, is different in style to its peers. It was the first to go public in 1971; it is big, bold and brassy; and its entire culture is more outgoing. The firm's bull logo was introduced in 1974, 'symbolizing growth, strength, optimism and confidence',[7] characteristics which Goldman Sachs and Morgan Stanley also probably share but keep quiet about. The investment bank grew organically from the retail investor business with a couple of strategic infill acquisitions: White Weld, an old and respected New York investment bank in 1978; Smith New Court, the UK broker in 1995 and Herzog Heine Geduld, the NASDAQ market maker, in 2000.

However, despite cultural differences, it shares with the rest of the super bulge the characteristics of consistency, a preference for promoting from within and good risk management. Like them, it was mixed up in scandal, including Orange County and other derivatives episodes, and it paid $200 million in the 2003 global research settlement, second equal with CSFB. But its reputation for market power has ensured its position at the top.

All three members of the super bulge survived at the top through consistency and good management, and in spite of regular controversies and occasional crises. The endurance of their leading position for over twenty years suggests that, at the very least, these super-bulge firms can be said to have dominated the market. But can the list of dominant firms be stretched still further into the next three firms in the rankings: CSFB, Lehman Brothers and Salomon Brothers?

Impossible to Kill: CSFB, Lehman Brothers and Salomon Brothers

There is almost nothing in the lexicon of mismanagement that did not affect one or other of these firms on occasion: heavy losses, credit concerns, rigging markets, mistreating customers, regulatory problems, reckless acquisitions, staff defections. Yet in 2005, despite various changes in ownership, these three firms were still in touch with the super bulge, having seen off a lot of serious competition over the previous quarter century.

In the early 1980s ***Lehman*** came close to falling apart in a divisive power struggle between investment banking and securities. In 1984 American Express bought Lehman, then principally an investment banking and institutional fixed income firm, and merged it with Shearson, principally a retail firm. The cultures never mixed and in 1993, when American Express decided to get out of the investment business, the retail part was sold to Smith Barney, which was then absorbed by Citigroup. Lehman re-emerged as an independent listed company in 1994. But that year, a bear market in fixed income bond trading hit Lehman's main business. At this time I was in charge of NatWest's debt and equity broking business and Lehman's treasurer came to see me on a mission to keep the firm's credit lines open; we supported them but it was a close call.

Since then, however, under the leadership of Richard Fuld, there has been an impressive recovery. Strict guidelines on costs were imposed and return on equity was made the benchmark for running the business. Team performance was elevated above the individual and this new culture was reinforced by compensation practices. The product range was broadened, and profits and the balance sheet recovered with the help of the bull market. If the clients harbour any thoughts about Lehman's brush with financial death they keep them well concealed, for the firm is once again back in the top six.

But at least Lehman's problems were financial rather than ethical. ***Salomon Brothers***, by contrast, contrived to get itself into a financial mess that was equal to Lehman's and compounded the problem by a series of scandals. The first financial mess came in 1987 when volatile trading profits left it vulnerable to takeover. It escaped the clutches of the financier Ronald Perelman when Warren Buffett pumped in $750 million in return for high yielding convertible preferred stock.

Next the firm's reputation took a dent in 1989 with the publication of *Liar's Poker*, Michel Lewis's unflattering account of its trading room culture, an image which seemed to be confirmed in 1991 when the Treasury bond scandal broke. Under the rules of the auction for US Treasury notes, no single dealer was permitted to control more than 35 per cent of each issue; Salomon submitted false bids on behalf of clients and ended up with 86 per cent of one issue. This was a scandal that struck at the heart of the capital markets: if the T-bond market was rigged, was there anything that clients could trust? John Gutfreund, the firm's CEO, resigned and agreed not to run an investment bank in future without SEC approval; Paul Mozer, the trader responsible, went to jail and Salomon paid fines and settlements totalling $290 million. Morale slipped, key traders defected and for a while the investment bank was unprofitable.[8] It is hard to disagree with Frank Partnoy's summary of Salomon at this time: 'A close examination of Salomon's practices from the mid-1980s until 1994 reveals that the firm was completely out of control.'[9]

There was a partial recovery following the bond market collapse of 1994, but it was clear that Salomon needed help. Warren Buffett encouraged a merger and in 1997 Travelers, the financial conglomerate then run by Sandy Weill, paid $9 billion in stock for Salomon and merged it with its retail broker Smith Barney. Travelers was shortly to merge with Citigroup, but the investment bank by then known as Salomon Smith Barney lived on.

Salomon Smith Barney now seemed to be in a strong position as part of the world's largest bank, especially after the Gramm-Leach-Bliley Act of 1999 pulled down the last of the Glass Steagall restrictions. The investment bank took on the parent's name and all it needed to do now was to keep its nose clean and exploit Citigroup's financial strength and corporate connections. Under the leadership of Michael Carpenter it seemed to recover, but scandal and Salomon appeared to have a close affinity and it was heavily implicated in the next wave.

The firm agreed to pay the largest share of the industry's $1.4 billion conflict of interest settlement with the regulators in 2003 and several of its clients were involved in the accounting scams that emerged in 2001–2. Congressional Banking Committee hearings suggested that Citigroup had played a leading role in designing the special purpose entities and structured finance deals that had made it so hard for investors to spot what was going on at Enron. A senior Citigroup official was asked in Washington whether the bank's actions had facilitated the deception. He thought carefully before answering: 'It depends on what you mean by deception.'[10]

Clients of Salomon Brothers could be forgiven for concluding from this litany of mismanagement and corruption, stretching back fifteen years through three different owners and any number of senior managers, that there was something wrong with its culture. Robert Rubin, a former Goldman Sachs senior partner and Secretary of the US Treasury, was hired in 1999 to strengthen Citigroup's senior management. In his autobiography he discusses Citigroup's merger with the UK investment bank Schroders in 2000: 'The merger ran into trouble over the Schroders people's concerns that Salomon might still resemble the Salomon Brothers of the *Liar's Poker* era . . . The Schroders people asked me to fly to London for a Saturday night dinner to discuss the Salomon culture with them and to satisfy themselves that Salomon now functioned in a more civilized, client-focused manner – all of which I was comfortable doing.'[11] I attended that dinner and sat next to Rubin: he did a fine job at laying our concerns to rest. But this was before Enron, before WorldCom and before the IPO scandals. I sometimes wonder how, if he had known then what he knows now, he would have played the conversation.

Throughout Salomon's recent history, bad news regularly changed shape but its reappearance seemed embedded in the corporate profile. Customers might well have dropped the firm in the belief that whatever the investment banks were currently up to, there was a more than average chance that Salomon would be involved. But they are evidently a trusting lot, for in the author's opinion Citigroup is currently the big three's closest competitor.

The durability of *CSFB*'s position close to the top is, if anything, even more remarkable. First Boston was an early success amongst the new firms that emerged from Glass Steagall but lost its way in the 1970s, formed an alliance with Credit Suisse in 1978 and changed its name to Credit Suisse First Boston shortly after. Then it recovered, heading the mergers and acquisitions charge of the eighties and, despite big losses in bonds in 1986 and in equities in 1987,[12] ended that year in a powerful position. One of the firm's senior investment bankers told me of that time: 'We stood eye to eye with Morgan Stanley and Goldman Sachs, up there as the blue blooded merger and acquisition investment banks. Then our paths diverged.' And how.

The divergence started when Bruce Wasserstein and Joseph Perella, the inspirations behind the mergers and acquisitions business, left to form their own boutique in 1988. The following year, CSFB lost $1 billion on its corporate-loan book and Credit Suisse had to bail it out with a $300 million injection. Profits recovered in the early nineties as a result of the success of its derivatives business, Credit Suisse Financial Products and, in the late nineties, from the arrival of Frank Quattrone's internet IPO revenues. However, many corners were cut in the dash for profits. Regulatory problems seemed inevitable and they duly occurred in Japan, India and the USA. It was no surprise to find CSFB deeply involved in the Spitzer investigation.

The regulators alleged that, along with Salomon, CSFB had been involved in the practice known as spinning. According to the SEC, influential executives were allocated hot IPO shares 'with the belief and expectation that the executives would steer investment banking business to CSFB'.[13] Like the other firms involved in the settlement, CSFB neither admitted nor denied the allegations. Its share of the $1.4 billion settlement was $200 million, half that paid by Salomon but equal second with Merrill Lynch in a league table where the winners came last.

CSFB's regulatory problems were compounded by cost issues arising from the decision in the middle of 2000 to pay $12 billion for another large investment bank, Donaldson, Lufkin & Jenrette, in a top of the market deal. With regulatory issues breaking out across the globe, Credit Suisse fired Allen Wheat, who had been running the investment bank, and brought in John Mack, formerly President and Chief Operating Officer of Morgan Stanley.[14]

Mack's reconstruction of CSFB is dealt with in another chapter, but it is amazing that there was anything left to revive. Reckless trading, regulatory ill discipline, problems in derivatives, accepting kickbacks in return for IPO allocations, serious staff defections. It is difficult to think of more events or accusations that could have damaged the firm's reputation. Yet survive it did. And indeed it restored its reputation to such a degree that when in 2004 the founders of Google decided to list their company in a groundbreaking way, with all sorts of ethical objectives about the way they wanted ownership to work, guess who they chose to co-lead the issue?

No Way In

This background of financial volatility, staff turnover and scandal at Lehman, Salomon and CSFB should have provided ideal circumstances for other firms to join the top six. Drexel, Burnham in fact did so in the mid eighties on the back of Michael Milken's junk bond revolution, but by 1990 it had collapsed when Milken was dragged into the Boesky insider dealing affair.

Bankers Trust was another star that burned brightly for a while. It was eighth in 1990 and for the next three years its derivatives business helped to make it the most profitable major bank in the USA. Its business was damaged in 1994 by its involvement in the Gibson's Greetings and Procter & Gamble derivatives scandals, and then in 1998 it got a mauling in the emerging markets crisis of that year. It disappeared into Deutsche Bank in 1999.

Kidder Peabody had been one of the most reputable investment banks for fifty years. GE had bought the firm for $600 million in 1986, but then suffered nearly a decade of financial scandals, waning profits at Kidder and a $350 million loss through the activities of the bond trader Joseph Jett before thankfully baling out in 1994 in return for a 25 per cent stake in Paine Webber. GE finally got some payback from investment banking when UBS bought Paine Webber, giving it nearly $2 billion profit on its stake. Jack Welch, chief executive of GE, sounded relieved to be out of it: 'Anyone who knows GE's history in the brokerage business knows we weren't so good at the game.'[15]

The failure of new entrants to break into the top group is not for want of trying. A whole host of American and European financial institutions tried and failed. Many of the leading American commercial banks thought they saw their chance with the relaxation of the Glass Steagall Act, which they were successful in getting progressively dismantled in the 1990s through powerful lobbying. There was a wave of buying and selling as the banks jostled for position – there were fifty-four merger and acquisition deals in the US investment banking and broking industry between 1997 and 2001 with a total value of $232 billion.[16]

The difficulties of breaking in to the leading group were illustrated by the progress of Chase Manhattan and J. P. Morgan. Chase Manhattan had tried a mixture of buy and build strategies before making a step jump in 2000 with the purchase of J. P. Morgan, which had been ready to talk having failed to build a top-ranked full-service investment bank on its own. These were two substantial and otherwise successful organizations that finally resorted to getting together in order to enter the inner sanctum of investment banking.

Setting its Own Agenda

Bear Stearns is the only firm in modern times that has worked its way up the top ten as an independent. It went public in 1985 and has continued to emphasize partnership virtues and sound business management. In an industry best known for profligacy and flash spending – just count the limos waiting outside any investment bank's office on any working day – Ace Greenberg ran a tight ship, famously ordering the re-use of paper clips and envelopes 'to make our people conscious of expenses'.[17] The firm sets its own agenda, developing its business at its own pace and refusing to be sucked into the expansionist games that many others play.

Continuity of management is important. In 1969 Greenberg interviewed a young man with an interesting résumé. A former professional bridge player and a scrap iron salesman for six years, James Cayne was hired as a broker and worked his way up the firm, becoming Greenberg's right-hand man and eventually his successor as chairman and CEO. The firm's solid organic growth strategy has kept it in the top ten, albeit in the lower reaches, whilst managing to maintain a strong financial position and generally keeping clear of reputational damage.

Bear Stearns' success shows that breaking into the top ten can be done but that it requires exceptional management. Breaking into the top six is much harder, and into the top three harder still, and no firm has done it for twenty-five years. This pack is chasing the leaders hard, and maybe some are in terminal decline. Perhaps one of the conglomerates will buy one of the independents. But do not bank on it. To judge from history, it is just as likely that they will decide that the hoped-for synergies between commercial and investment banking are not there, that the perceived volatility of investment banking is damaging their share price and that the best strategy is to exit the business.

Market Concentration

It is one thing to show that the same firms appear at the top of the league tables every year but it is something else to say that they dominate their industry. Even though – year in, year out – they appear able to see off the competition, do the leading banks dominate the industry through market share?

The number of products on offer, and the multiplicity of regions in which they have to do business, are such that no single bank or group of banks dominates in all of them. Local banks score better than the global leviathans in parts of their home markets and global specialists top a few league tables in their niches.

There are also some products such as loans, securitized bonds – securities backed by the cash flow from a pool of financial assets such as credit card receivables – and foreign exchange that favour the firms with the biggest balance sheets. Customers for these products want liquidity not advice and the big money centre banks win out over the investment banks. For example, in global currency dealing the biggest player, UBS, recently had a market share more than double that of Goldman Sachs, the highest placed investment bank in sixth place;[18] and in credit derivatives, a vast and rapidly growing area that involves repackaging and swapping corporate debt, the big financial conglomerates are the market leaders.

However, as we have already seen, corporate advisory work and underwriting are the key investment banking products in terms of deal flow and prestige. These remain dominated by the top investment banks. With at least a dozen global investment banks theoretically able to carry out most transactions, the customer clearly has plenty of choice. Yet when it comes to exercising that choice there has been an increasing tendency for customers to go with the leading players. For big ticket, prestigious deals in the core investment banking areas the top firms steadily increased their grip. According to research presented to the SIA, the big three investment banks increased their share of globally announced mergers from 10 per cent in 1992 to a peak of over 50 per cent in 1999. The same report showed that their share of IPOs in America grew from 30 per cent in 1991 to 50 per cent in 2001.[19] Other research shows that the market share of the next seven largest firms also increased.[20]

Compared to other professions this is a moderate to strong degree of concentration. At the beginning of this century, in the US legal profession the top *ten* firms accounted for 32 per cent of the total fees earned by the fifty largest firms – less than the core market share of the top *three* investment banks.[21] Compared to auditing, the investment banking market is less concentrated. Whereas the top 90 per cent of the world's largest companies use the big four auditors,[22] lead adviser status is spread across ten investment banks.[23] Market concentration in investment banking therefore appears to be midway between the narrow focus seen in auditing and the wide dispersal seen in law. This confirms what investment bankers say: 'If you ask boards of directors which investment banks they would use for high profile deals, only five or six major firms would be mentioned and perhaps two or three boutiques.'[24]

It Depends What You Mean by Domination

The modern history of investment banking shows that nearly every outcome is possible in nearly every situation. You can throw your huge balance sheet behind it and still fail – like several top American financial institutions, and some of the biggest banks in Europe. You can throw a huge balance sheet at it and succeed – like Deutsche Bank and UBS. You can be one of the world's best managed businesses and fail at investment banking – like GE. You can be old guard and blow it – like Kidder Peabody. You can be brash, aggressive and successful but still blow it – like Drexel and Bankers Trust. You can be Steady Eddie and flourish – like Bear Stearns. You can be a bulge-bracket firm and periodically damage your clients, shareholders and reputation and stay up there – like most of the top six.

The one outcome that never occurred was the permanent entry of a newcomer to the circle. Aspiring investment banks found it hard to mount a sustained assault on the bulge bracket, requiring skill, deep pockets and shareholders that had the patience to tolerate years, maybe even decades, of poor returns. The leading firms may not control every part of the business, but they dominate the strategically important advisory and underwriting businesses, minimizing competitors' access to these high profile gateway areas. Later chapters will show how this most subtle, most effective kind of market domination was achieved and maintained.

4

Heads We Win

Did the Investment Banks Make Excess Returns?

Like Monty Python's merchant banker struggling to comprehend charitable giving – 'No, no, no, I don't follow this at all, I mean, I don't want to seem stupid but it looks to me as though I'm a pound down on the whole deal'[1] – twenty-first-century investment bankers would find it hard to grasp the idea that they might be making too much money. Achieving a high return is considered so important, so fundamental to their existence, that challenging it would be greeted with incredulity, as if they had been asked whether they believe in looking after the sick and elderly or being kind to animals.

Such a response would be perfectly understandable. The high priests of capitalism eat, breathe and sleep making money – it's their product as well as their objective – and they genuinely believe themselves to be in a business that is risky, volatile, under pressure and getting more so. A report for the Securities Industry Association, one of the investment banks' most influential trade organizations, summed this up in a paper in 2002 called 'Large Investment Bank Margin and Return on Equity Trends: The Twenty-Year Downtrend to Continue'. It presented an industry being squeezed by steady declines in margins, more competition, commoditization of core products and ever increasing capital requirements. It forecast 'a war of attrition for market share driving lower peak cycle returns on equity going forward'.[2]

Other leading commentators had the same opinion. The *Wall Street Journal* portrayed an industry in secular decline: 'New banking products have shorter shelf lives – made obsolete by fast changing markets or swiftly copied by rivals. Corporate clients are wringing as much savings as they can out of their competition stressed bankers.'[3] The respected industry analysts Freeman & Co described the investment banks as 'Under Siege' in 2002 in the face of declining revenues and deteriorating profit margins.[4] In January 2004 the *Financial Times* reported that: 'The volatility of investment banking earnings is, if anything, rising as margins fall on straightforward activities such as investment grade debt underwriting and trading.'[5] *The Economist* agreed: 'Returns have fallen as fast as markets have risen. Yields on corporate debt of all types, for example, have fallen dramatically, and commissions for all sorts of businesses have also dropped. So banks are having to bet more of their own money to continue generating huge profits.'[6]

So when the investment banks are downbeat about their own business they are reflecting a widely shared perception. Goldman Sachs's warning to prospective investors at the time of its IPO – 'The financial services industry is intensely competitive and rapidly consolidating'[7] – fairly reflects opinion inside the industry. Investment bankers have to fight the good fight every day. They know that for every deal there are half a dozen capable competitors on the long list, and two or three on the short list, with massive intellectual and financial resources and steely resolve. They have lived through years when profits were down, bonuses were cut and colleagues were laid off. Many of them, perhaps the majority, work in product areas such as equity and bond sales that are steadily falling towards commodity status. In their terms, measured by their subjective experience, it is a tough business that is getting tougher: 'Excess returns? Forget it. We are lucky if we can make any returns at all these days. It's lethal out there.'[8]

However, 'how it feels' is not always the same as 'how it really is'. In a volatile, fast-changing business the underlying profits trend is difficult to discern and requires analysis to complement gut reaction. When results are good they are very, very good, but when they are bad they are horrid – so they must be measured over a period of time. New products come along so fast, and have such an impact, that declining old businesses may be balanced by profitable new ones. The whole portfolio needs to be considered before reaching a judgement on the returns being made.

It is also important to see the investment banks in a wider context. Profits and compensation have been so high for so long in investment banking that it is hard for insiders to stay in touch with how the rest of the world fares. Comparisons need to be made between compensation and profits in investment banking and those in other businesses and professions. Only when we have this broader perspective can we determine the appropriate risk premium for investment banking and whether extra returns are required to compensate.

Profits

Discussion of how to deal with profits volatility has been around ever since investment analysis came of age in 1934 with the publication of *Security Analysis* by Benjamin Graham and David L. Dodd. Use of their moving average technique to iron out the effects of the business cycle[9] helps us to understand the performance of the modern investment banks, allowing us to look beyond the volatility that deflects the eye from the industry's underlying profitability.

After the modern age of investment banking began in America in 1975 with the abolition of fixed commissions, profits in the securities industry, the most volatile part of the investment banking business, fell on average one year in three.[10] This is more than twice as often as the average for the American economy and nearly double the volatility of other financial services institutions such as commercial banks.*

But smoothing the results brings out the underlying pattern to the volatility.† Between 1975 and 2004 there was never a five-year period when the industry's profits were below those of the previous five. Using a shorter time, three years, to bring out the volatility, reveals only two intervals, 1987–9 and 2002–4, when profits were down on the previous period.[11] The volatility was there but the upswings were

* In ten of the twenty-nine sets of annual results after 1974, profits were below those of the previous year. Real annual American GDP fell on only four occasions during that period, and commercial banks' profits fell in only five of the twenty-nine years.

† Graham and Dodd averaged out over ten years but modern investment banking is too young, requiring a shorter period to be used.

always bigger than the downswings and successively took the industry onto higher levels.

Profits in the American securities industry grew by a towering twenty-six times, from $804 million in 1975 to the peak of $21 billion in 2000, quadruple the increase in America's corporate profits and GDP over the same period. Smoothing helps in working out the underlying rate of growth. Taking a smoothed 1975 as the base year* and a smoothed 2004† as the finishing year, securities industry profits before tax grew at a compound rate of more than 10 per cent per annum. This compares with a compound growth rate of 7 per cent per annum in both US nominal GDP and corporate profits and 4 per cent per annum consumer price inflation.

Thus even allowing for the fact that one year in three was a down year for profits, this most volatile part of the investment banking industry outperformed the bulk of American business by a country mile for nearly thirty years. Whilst the industry's nervousness is understandable because of the volatility, it remained highly profitable by most reasonable measures.

Margins

The paper produced for the Securities Industry Association in 2002 opened with the headline 'Margin Trends Heading South' and summed up twenty years of investment banking history as follows: 'In the early 1980s, the average pre-tax margin for the large investment banks[12] was 28.9%. In the mid-1990s the pre-tax margin had dropped to as low as 11.2%. During the peak of the TMT boom, margins recovered to 16–17% before declining again in 2000–01.'[13] The trend line (the upper dotted line in Figure 1) through the peaks since 1980 indeed points down.

But as with all analysis of time series, the interpretation depends on the starting point and a different picture emerges if 1990 is used as the base. The use of 1980 as a base year meant starting the analysis at a time when margins were astronomically high as the capital markets

* Average profits, 1975–9.

† Average profits, 2000–2004.

exploded and the merger wave offered rich pickings to those few investment banks lucky and smart enough to be in the right place at the right time. Inevitably, as the new capital markets matured, other players woke up to the opportunities, clients forced prices down, market conditions got choppy and margins fell.

But in the 1990s bull market another cycle developed as the investment banks invented new products, improved their risk management and margins were rebuilt. By the second half of the nineties, and even into the bear market of the twenty-first century, margins were comparable with those of any period except the new frontier years of the early eighties. In fact, drawing a trend line from the 1990 nadir through the subsequent peaks and troughs (the lower dotted line below) and extending it to 2003 suggests that for this period it was more a case of 'Margin Trends Heading North'.

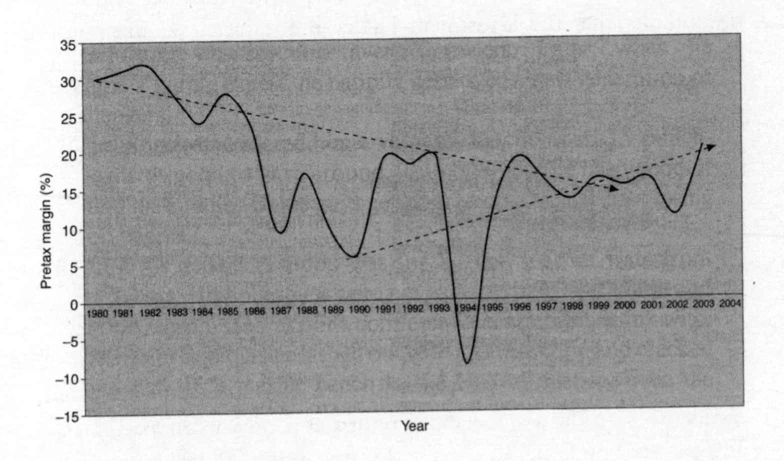

Figure 1. Large investment bank pre-tax margins, per cent[14]

Returns

Return on Equity

Profit and margin analysis provides only part of the story for, as Peter Drucker said in a *Harvard Business Review* article, 'Until a business returns a profit that is greater than its cost of capital, it operates at a loss.'[15] Capital comes in two forms: equity capital, which belongs to the shareholders, and debt capital, which is borrowed in return for an interest payment, deployed in the business and then returned to the creditor at the end of the loan's term. Debt capital is a means of enabling the business to operate for the benefit of equity shareholders. The return on the equity capital invested is widely used as the fundamental measure of a business's profitability.

Return on equity (ROE, profits as a percentage of equity capital) is the number that the investment banks and industry commentators and analysts watch. Every single bank gives prominence to it in its financial statements and most include an ROE target amongst their business objectives. A Lehman Brothers banker recalls how return on equity was a top business aim: 'The firm lived and died for its ROE. We were shown our ROE quarterly and also that of our competitors, adjusted where necessary by stripping out their non-investment banking businesses. There were profits and there was ROE; we had to hit both targets.'[16]

A discussion in a recent Morgan Stanley annual report is typical of how management views this ratio: 'Our return on equity (ROE) of 14.1 percent in 2002 was significantly better than almost all our competitors and is a satisfactory return at a time when 10-year US government bonds yield 4 percent. Even so, our ROE target continues to be 18–20 percent over the course of the business cycle. While we clearly cannot always expect the 30 percent ROE of two years ago, we also do not regard last year's 14 percent as a permanent condition.'[17] Morgan Stanley's approach suggests a number of questions.

- What is the overall trend: is it rising or falling?
- How does the ROE achieved compare with that earned by other companies? This is an important check for investors: why put up capital for

an investment bank if you could get a better return by investing in a candy store?

- How does the ROE compare with low risk or risk free returns such as bank deposits or Government bond yields? This is relevant because investors demand a premium for putting money into risky business enterprises when they could get guaranteed returns elsewhere.
- How does the return on equity capital invested compare with the rate of inflation? A return of 5 per cent in a year when inflation is running at 10 per cent represents an erosion of real capital; if that trend continued for a long time the capital invested in the business would be worth very little.

Measured against these questions the investment banks achieved extraordinarily strong returns in the period under review. The SIA databank goes back to 1980 and is an excellent source for analysis of the large investment banks, revealing what an outstanding business it has been for the owners of the securities business.[18]

Table 2 shows the long term trend in the large investment banks' ROE compared to American interest rates and the annual rate of inflation. In absolute terms, the large investment banks' ROE is declining: in five-year blocks, it averaged 48 per cent 1980–84, 22 per cent 1985–9, and 14 per cent 1990–94. However, the late nineties boom

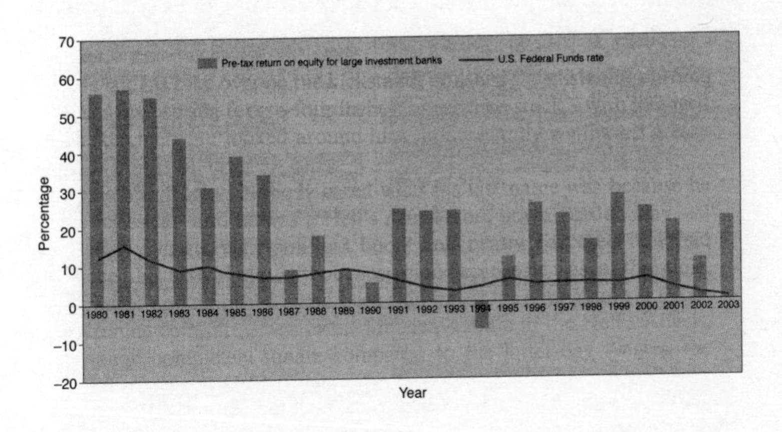

Figure 2. Return on equity for large investment banks.[19]

saw a recovery to 21 per cent in 1995–9, and even when returns dipped to 19 per cent in the following 'bear market' period they were still higher than they had been a decade earlier. The figure shows the ROE data in graphic form.

*Table 2. Large investment banks' real ROE.**

Time	Actual return %	Interest rates %	Risk premium %	Inflation %	Real return %
1980–84	48	12	36	6	42
1985–9	22	8	14	4	18
1990–94	14	5	9	3	11
1995–9	21	5	16	2	19
2000–2002	19	4	15	2	17

The fall from the peaks of the early eighties is not just the industry maturing out of the zesty early years of free market economics. ROEs were adjusting to falling interest rates and lower inflation. Lower returns were sufficient to preserve the real value of capital and compensate for risk in this new era and when, as in Table 2, this is taken into account, the investment banks' returns can be seen to have remained very high.

Comparisons with the returns of America's non-financial corporate sector confirm the investment banks' strong performance, for they achieved a higher ROE in twenty out of twenty-five years. Indeed, even in 2002, in the depths of the bear market, the investment banks' ROE was still where it had been for most of the previous two decades: sitting at a handsome premium to the non-financial sector.

The investment banks operating in the securities industry have an enviable financial record. Although it is true that 'the ROE performance of the industry's large investment bank sector has steadily declined despite cyclical rebounds',[20] the falling absolute return is

* Risk premium is actual return less interest rates; real return is actual return less inflation. Federal funds rate for interest rates; US consumer price index for inflation.

entirely consistent with falling inflation rates and tumbling bond yields. The crucial thing is that the premium over inflation, risk free investments and other business activities remained high in this period.

Cost of Equity Capital

Drawing on the work of the consultants Stern Stewart and their economic value added model, the investment banks always set their ROE targets by reference to their cost of equity. The cost of equity capital is derived from a complex and controversial calculation called the Capital Asset Pricing Model.[21]

In the early stages of my research one of the elite banks told me that, using the CAPM, their cost of equity was 15 per cent. At the time they were making an ROE of about 20 per cent, which seemed reasonable against this benchmark. But the more I thought about it, the less convinced I became. In the real world, why should an institution pay 15 per cent for equity capital when it could borrow for 5 per cent? I realized that cost of equity is an accounting game that bears very little relation to the real world yet operates rather nicely for investment banks seeking to justify their profits.

This is because the volatility of the company's share price is an important input to the CAPM. If the company's share price performs in a more volatile fashion than the stock market as a whole, its theoretical cost of equity will be increased. As we have already seen, the investment banks have volatile profits and a reputation for being high risk. Their share prices are therefore very sensitive to changes in sentiment.

However, much of the volatility that surrounds the investment banks' share prices is more to do with perception than reality. If investors did Graham and Dodd-style smoothing they would see that the investment banks' ups are bigger than their downs. This would create a more stable perception, a less volatile share price and a more realistic cost of equity.

Basing cost of equity on swings in market sentiment is a debatable exercise neatly summed up by Roger Lowenstein: 'This theory that the cost of equity capital varies with the volatility of a company's stock price is one of the oldest canards of finance. It is known as the capital asset pricing model. Intellectually it has no merit, and, in practical terms, it has been discredited by numerous academic studies.'[22] Using cost of equity calculated this way to justify super returns has little merit either. It is circular to argue that a high return on equity is justified because the cost of equity is high. It's like saying that the price of a hotel room is expensive because hotels charge a lot of money for the room.

In analysing the investment banking industry's returns, more straightforward comparisons are preferred. If an industry outperformed inflation, the risk free return and the rest of the business community by a wide margin, it seems reasonable to regard its returns as having been abnormally high. The investment banks' performance over twenty-five years met all of these criteria.

Compensation

As a result of rising markets, the unimaginable explosion in capital markets activity after 1982 and the accepted practice of the employees taking half of revenues, compensation in investment banking started high and got even higher. When we assess the total returns from investment banking, therefore, we need to consider these very high levels of employee compensation, some large part of which, in other professions, would have gone to shareholders.

The investment banks are in effect joint ventures between shareholders and staff. The client franchise of the individual is often as great or greater in the clients' eyes as that of the firm. All investment banking managers are aware of this, and know that when star names move, much business goes with them. Except in a bear market, when the demand for staff abates, the investment banks are more beholden to their stars than their stars are beholden to them.

The joint venture is reinforced by practices that grew up in the old partnership days when the firms' principals shared the risks and the rewards between them. Employees were cut in on the joint venture through a variable bonus that depended on the firm's results. This culture survived incorporation and sale and is encouraged by management.

Both aspects of the joint venture contrived to make investment banking a very well paid profession during the late twentieth century. An unwritten understanding developed that there would be a more or less equal split in revenues between the shareholders and the employees. The shareholders were left to meet the other costs of the business out of their half of the revenues and their profit was what was left over; the employees got to share their half amongst themselves.

The persistence of the revenue-sharing principle at a time of rising markets, and therefore rising revenues, sent compensation through the roof. Even better for employees, as capital markets business took off firms competed for each other's staff, bidding up pay in a lucrative spiral. The ratio of compensation to revenues at the large investment banks crept up, rising from 44 per cent in the early eighties to 50 per cent in the mid nineties and peaking at 52 per cent early this century.[23]

The effect on individuals' pay was dramatic. An occupation that was already very well rewarded became even more so. Many – the author included – could scarcely believe their luck. In 1998, Allen Wheat, the CEO of CSFB, admitted to the journalist Helen Dunne: 'OK. If I am being honest with you then, yes, let's whisper it, but the truth of the matter is that all of us are overpaid. There is nothing magical about what we do. Anybody can do it.'[24]

Salaries for even the most senior bankers, traders, salespeople and analysts were kept to around the $100,000 level – low by the standards of other professions – but after bonuses, average compensation for the several thousand managing directors in the investment banks reached $3.2 million in 2000 and remained well above $1 million even during the bear market of 2002. The recipients were not managing directors in the literal sense because they did not direct the business and the firm's directors. They were very important senior practitioners akin to the partners in law firms and auditors; but their compensation left these counterparts in other professional services firms trailing. In 2002 the average partner's profit share at only one in four of America's top law firms exceeded $1 million; the average managing director in investment banking received more than that despite the bear market.[25]

Junior investment bankers shared in the riches. Average compensation for associates with just one foot on the professional ladder was

$240,000 in 2000 and bottomed out at $150,000.[26] This compared with the average starting salary for a graduate of a good business school of $70,000. In between were the middling ranks of directors and vice-presidents who also earned a premium compared to their counterparts in other professions.

The investment banking industry's reported profits would have looked very different if compensation had been pegged back to the rate of inflation, as happened to the pay of the average worker in the United States in the last quarter of the twentieth century. The simplest of calculations reveals that the investment banking industry's profits would have increased enormously if compensation had kept pace with what was going on in the rest of America. For consistency with other calculations, 1980 is taken as the base year. It was neither a particularly bad nor particularly good year for investment bankers. Equity markets rose for the third year on the run, a record amount of corporate capital was raised, securities industry employment rose and investment bankers seemed like they usually do: content and well paid. Between then and the year 2000, average compensation for an American securities professional tripled; for the average American worker it doubled.

Taking 1980s average compensation for a securities professional, grossing it up for inflation, and multiplying it out for the number of people working in the industry year by year, gives a total wage bill for 1980–2000 of $422 billion; the actual figure was $542 billion. That is an extra $120 billion that was diverted from shareholders and customers to the employees in two decades. Given that the total profits of the US securities industry 1980–2000 was $127 billion on SIA data, adjusting the actual returns made for this $120 billion of extra compensation pretty nearly doubles everything: profits, margins and ROE.[27]

The Best Business in the World

I recently attended a retirement party for an investment banker. He made a charming and at times moving speech looking back on his career in what he described as 'the best business in the world'. The analysis given in this chapter is not necessarily what he had in mind, but anyone looking at profits and returns might just as easily choose the same words.

This is confirmed by what happened to the securities industry in the 2002 bear market. In one sense, 2002 was a shockingly bad year. Profits were only one third of those achieved in the peak year, 2000. The large investment banks' margins were down to 10.6 per cent, having peaked at 16.3 per cent in 1999, and return on equity was 10.8 per cent, down from 28 per cent in the peak year, also 1999. Forty thousand people had left the industry in 2001–2, nearly 5 per cent of the total.

Individual firms took some very big hits. Morgan Stanley's return on equity had plunged from a peak of 33 per cent in 1999 to 14 per cent in 2002. One in four of the people working for Merrill Lynch in 2000 no longer did so by the end of 2002. Pre-tax earnings at Goldman Sachs dropped from over $5 billion to little more than $3 billion in the space of two years. And these firms were the best in the business; their weaker competitors saw their results deteriorate even more sharply.

But viewed another way the industry's results were not shockingly bad: they were shockingly good. Many other businesses do not earn a margin of over 10 per cent at the top of their cycle let alone the bottom. The numbers employed in the industry in 2002 were still 4 per cent up on 1999 despite the shake out. And the return on equity number, depressed though it was compared to previous years, was still ahead of inflation, Government bond yields and America's non-financial corporate sector.

As we have seen, 2003 was even more interesting. Although capital markets activity was still depressed, the results from the investment banks came bouncing back up towards record levels. Net earnings at Goldman Sachs exceeded $3 billion and were within a whisker of the record year 2000. Morgan Stanley saw a recovery of no less than 27 per cent in net earnings and return on equity climbed from 14.1 per cent to 16.5 per cent. Net income at Lehman Brothers was nearly back up to 2000's highs, whilst Bear Stearns posted a new record. Over at Merrill Lynch, chief executive Stan O'Neal reported best-ever earnings, 'disciplined growth and superior shareholder returns'. All round the track a strong recovery was under way and total profits of New York Stock Exchange member firms were close to the top of the previous cycle.

The industry, of course, remains volatile, and conditions turned choppy again in 2004 before recovering in 2005. But the shallowness and brevity of the recession and the rapid bounce back confirmed what the data on the investment banks have been telling us for twenty-five years: it really is 'the best business in the world'. The published numbers show that profits were strong despite the volatility, especially in the context of inflation, interest rates and what other businesses achieved. Adjusting them for 'normalized' compensation – rebasing investment bankers' pay to 1980s levels adjusted for inflation – further increases this already stupendous profitability. Whether this profitability can be termed 'excessive' depends on the value it created and the potential for it to be eroded through competition and customer choice. The results of this analysis will determine whether we are looking at an exceptionally important and skilled industry that deserved its returns because of the value it created or at an organizational form that kept returns high by other means.

5

Tails You Lose

Measuring the quality of the investment banks' output helps to establish whether the industry merited the high returns it made. It is a difficult piece of analysis to perform. Not only is the product range diverse but the value created by the investment banks needs to be disentangled from the other effects of free market economics, for the two are intricately entwined.

During the last quarter of a century, America and Britain have achieved near-perfect economic conditions: reassuringly steady growth, productivity gains, rising employment, low interest rates and – at least for the foreseeable future – the elimination of inflation as a threat. Potential pitfalls have been avoided: deflation has not materialized, recessions have been minimized and economies have not generally overheated.

The effect of free market economics and the allied movements of globalization and shareholder value have been widely praised: in 'the period since 1980 – the age vilified for its rush into globalization – both global inequality and the proportion of the world's population and number of the world's people in extreme poverty have fallen.'[1] Former US Treasury Secretary Lawrence Summers had no doubt who was responsible: 'It was impatient, value-focused shareholders who did America a great favour by forcing capital out of its traditional companies and thereby making it available to fund the venture capitalists and the Ciscos and the Microsofts that are now in a position to propel our economy very rapidly forward.'[2]

The growth, liquidity and ability of capital markets to withstand all kinds of shock were crucial as America led the world's stock markets to a tenfold increase in capitalization in just two decades.

There seemed to be nothing that governments, investors or issuers could not do. The annual total capital raised by US business and government quadrupled during the course of the 1990s from $1 trillion in 1990 to nearly $4 trillion in 2001. Corporate underwriting increased eightfold over the same period, the global value of mergers and acquisitions quintupled and daily share volume on America's stock exchanges grew nearly fortyfold. In 1982, at the start of the bull market, the combined value of America's stock exchanges was less than half of GDP; at the peak in 2000, it exceeded GDP by more than 50 per cent.[3]

The investment banks were responsible for much of the development of capital markets. They evolved, flexed and grew with the markets and if they had not, growth would surely have been impeded. They were responsible for many product innovations, especially in derivatives and other forms of structured finance. They expanded their own balance sheets from $7 billion in 1980 to $157 billion in 2003, which eased capital flows, and they grew their infrastructures, which enabled them to handle the massive increase in volume. They also pioneered the advances in risk management that kept markets open through nearly every kind of political and economic turmoil.*

In the years immediately before the bubble burst in 2000, the role of the investment banks in the economic miracle was admired by governments and seldom questioned. Investment banking seemed to be not only a profession that worked but one that enabled everyone else to work too. Whatever price was paid, however much the investment banks made, seemed justified by the bull market. After all, everyone was gaining and so what if the Wall Street people took a little more than their fair share? Maybe they even deserved it. The prevailing view was summed up wryly by Joseph Stiglitz, a critic of globalization and free market economics as played out in the 1990s: 'The rich rewards that financial markets were reaping for themselves all seemed well deserved, for they were taking but a small share of what they were contributing to all of us.'[4]

The bear market, the corporate scandals and the Spitzer revelations

* The only time in recent history that US markets closed for any length of time was in the few days after the terrorist attacks on 11 September 2001.

prompted a rethink. Suddenly Wall Street's performance was an issue. Initial shock gave way to anger and the public wanted to know why it had all happened.

The most popular explanation has been behavioural rather than institutional: just as markets overshoot on the upside, so too with the investment banks, whose behaviour degenerates as the prizes rise. In the opinion of people such as Jon Corzine, formerly CEO of Goldman Sachs, occasional malpractice at the financial institutions is an inevitable but temporary by-product of rising markets: 'At the conclusion of any bull market there are always elements of excess that get washed out or cause the system to evolve. But the fact is that we are coming out of the most shallow recession in post-war history and the outlook is good.'[5]

A rarely heard alternative explanation is that the activities and products of the investment banks had been institutionally flawed for many years. This would be consistent with the outcome expected of cartels where, in the absence of perfect competition or anything approaching it, output suffers. Through lack of alternative, the customer has no choice but to accept the inadequate output of a ring, and the producers have no incentive to improve their own performance. Four areas that are representative of their business – fund manager services, mergers and acquisitions, initial public offerings and derivatives – will now be considered as a testing ground for this alternative thesis.

Fund Manager Services

Guests will not easily forget the annual *Institutional Investor* awards dinner on 12 November 2002. The function was to honour the winners of the magazine's prestigious poll for the analysts of the year – 'first teamers', as the top analyst in each category is known – and the guest speaker was Eliot Spitzer. It was the height of his investigation into conflict of interest and the audience expected some barbed comments. Spitzer did not disappoint – 'it's wonderful to be here because I really want to put faces to all of those e-mails' – but went way beyond gentle ribbing:

More than 40 per cent of this year's first team all-stars did not perform as well as the average analyst for their sector. The same is true of the 2000 and 2001 first team all-stars whose performance was reviewed . . . Alen Abelson and Michael Lewis – two supposedly staunch advocates for the banks and the market – both have written that there is no need for regulation because every investor ought to recognize that analyst stock recommendations are useless.[6]

Spitzer's concern was to protect unwary private investors, but his remarks also raised important issues for mutual funds, unit trusts, investment trusts, pension funds, insurance companies and even hedge funds, the vibrant force in the market that target high returns through aggressive trading strategies. These institutions manage the pooled assets of millions of savers, policy holders, pensioners and workers investing for retirement. They range in size from top firms like UBS, Fidelity, State Street, and Barclays Global Investors, which manage over a trillion dollars apiece, to small hedge funds looking after a few million dollars.

They rely heavily on brokers whose job is to provide them with advice, information and share dealing: 'Our best brokers have a great appetite for information retrieval and dissemination. We get our first Bloomberg messages at 5.20 a.m., it's an information game. We pay brokers $60 million of commission out of a $3 billion fund and most goes to those that phone us most often. They are fast ten-second conversations, often Bloomberg driven. I get a thousand e-mails a day and I read them all.'[7] The broking divisions of the top investment banks flood their clients with information: 'We give them a view on every single price movement; it's all about short term momentum. We have a team of people who get the analysts to comment every time a share price moves and they then pass it on to the hedge funds.'[8]

The brokers' analysts are central to this buy-side and sell-side relationship.* At the peak of the bull market the leading bulge-bracket banks were spending half a billion dollars a year each on their broking research departments. Teams of highly qualified people were employed to analyse stocks, bonds, derivatives, markets, economies and currencies. Their output, especially that of the stock analysts, has been

* Fund managers are known as the buy side, brokers as the sell side.

studied carefully by academics in America and Britain since the job was established in the late 1970s.

The Securities Industry Association summarized the findings of a series of academic studies encompassing 500,000 recommendations made by analysts during the period 1985–2000:

> Although investors would have outperformed the market indexes following the consensus recommendations of analysts, to implement this trading strategy would require buying and selling stocks frequently – since so many analysts were included in the study and they changed their recommendations frequently – with turnover rates at times in excess of 400 per cent annually would produce significant transaction costs.* In other words analysts do a good job picking stocks but an investor following all their recommendations would incur commissions and other costs such as taxes that could reduce the investor's performance to that of the market indices.[9]

In Britain an academic study of leading brokers' recommendations in the mid nineties came up with a similar conclusion: 'High trading levels are required to capture the excess returns generated by the strategies analysed, entailing substantial transaction costs and leading to abnormal returns for these strategies that are not reliably greater than zero.'[10] The evidence from Britain and America is consistent in finding that the total returns from following analysts' recommendations in these years were not sufficient to cover trading and other costs. Sell recommendations were more accurate than Buys, but they were outnumbered five to one in the early 1990s and fifty to one by the end of the decade.†

The hidden agenda of investment banking partly explains this poor performance. In the nineties, IPO and other forms of investment banking work diverted analysts from their original function of providing investment advice to fund managers. But as one study of analysts'

* Transaction costs are commissions, taxes, financing and deal processing expenses.

† Analysts mark the companies they follow on a five-point scale, from 'strong buy' at the top to 'strong sell' at the bottom, over two time periods, usually three months and two years. Companies often react badly to criticism from analysts and during the IPO boom of the 1990s an investment bank whose analyst had a negative rating on a stock could expect to be excluded from any capital markets business that was in the offing. The analysts knew which side their bread was buttered and virtually stopped making negative recommendations.

forecasts 1996–2002 showed, analysts faced all sorts of bullish influences, ranging from sensitive CEOs who got angry if they were criticized to the commercial reality that the audience for Buy stories was limitless while only existing shareholders were interested in Sells.[11]

The plain fact is that investment research is a difficult job at the best of times. Back in the thirties, Graham and Dodd identified three problems in analysis – incomplete data, random events and irrationality in markets – and when late twentieth-century commercial pressures were added to the list the job became nearly impossible. It is little wonder that during the eighties and nineties the theoretical gains to be made from following analysts' recommendations would have been wiped out by trading costs and other practical constraints.

The poor performance of the analysts' recommendations need not necessarily invalidate their role. John Rogers, chief executive of the UK Society of Investment Professionals, said: 'It would be a problem if the investment market was full of naive people who relied on the recommendations of analysts whose analysis was not independent. But we are operating in the world's largest international financial centre which is full of buy-side firms that can differentiate this chatter from good recommendations.'[12] Investing institutions say that they value the information flow and fundamental business analysis that investment research provides. If this is correct, some, at least, of these fund managers should have been able to demonstrate this through consistently superior performance.

The actual results are disappointing. The average fund manager should perform in line with the market, since 'the market' is the sum of everyone's investment decisions; but in the ten years to 1999, America's actively managed funds returned 10.9 per cent annually compared to 12.4 per cent for the S&P 500 index, most of the difference being trading costs. If fund managers, and by association brokers, were really adding value it should have been possible to identify a statistically significant group of consistent out-performers. In fact, repeat winners did occur but were rare, and picking fund managers was generally a lottery: 'Just 2 out of 65 balanced pension funds outperformed the sector average each year over the last five years. That is no better than chance would suggest – a coin tossed five times would keep landing heads up on 2 out of 64 occasions.'[13]

Even hedge funds, which have the advantage of flexibility and agility and of being managed by highly incentivised people, did not perform all that well. In ten years, the CSFB Tremont Hedge Fund Index's overall return was only slightly better than the return on the S&P 500 on a risk adjusted basis, and probably no better at all if the performance of failed hedge funds were to be included.[14]

Some commentators say that not only are analysts and active fund managers failing at present, they are doomed to fail for evermore. These supporters of the efficient market theory believe that security prices fully reflect all available information and that future movements are entirely random. It seems more accurate to say that capital markets are competitive but not perfectly efficient due to institutional constraints on participants, behavioural biases and other market imperfections.

This ought to leave room for intelligent research to add value, and a few funds do actually manage to achieve regular out-performance over the longer term. But worryingly for the brokers, two of the best, Capital Group and Berkshire Hathaway, do so by relying on their own research more than brokers' advice.[15]

The record of the vast majority of fund managers during the last quarter of the century supports the comment of the British economist John Kay: 'The efficient market hypothesis is 90 per cent true and you will lose money by ignoring it. The search for the elusive 10 per cent, like the search for discarded $10 bills, attracts greater effort than the rewards.'[16] The brokers' role in that search was unconvincing. They were efficient purveyors of information and opinion but the evidence shows that the value added by their advice was marginal, hardly justifying the effort or expense.

Initial Public Offerings

The ultimate function of capital markets is to raise capital efficiently and the explosion of activity suggests that the rise of the IPO as a means of raising capital was one of the key economic developments of the late twentieth century. The investment banks were quick to connect private companies needing capital with the growing amount of institutional money looking for investment opportunities and put the two together by promoting IPOs.

In the year 2000, the peak of the cycle, US initial public offerings totalled $76 billion and the number of companies being floated had risen steadily during two decades: one per day in the 1980s, two per day in the early 1990s, three per day in the later 1990s. Although when the internet bubble burst, share prices collapsed and capital markets were in effect 'closed' to new issuers, by then going public had become a mainstream route to new capital.

Credit, then, where credit is due. Many others were involved – lawyers, consultants, auditors, regulators, investors – but without the investment banks none of this would have happened. However, the evidence is also that a good idea was spoiled in implementation. An efficient IPO market would have three features:

- For the issuer a small premium over the offer price indicating that something but not too much had been left on the table for new investors.
- For the investors an initial premium in the share price followed by long term out-performance.
- For the capital markets as a whole evidence of transparency and fair dealing to encourage smooth and efficient functioning in future.

What Was Left on the Table

Setting the issue price for an IPO is a part of the investment bankers' job that requires great judgement and helps to justify the fees. IPO shares are issued at a discount to the price at which they are expected to trade in order to attract buyers. A delicate balancing act is required, for the discount needs to be narrow enough for issuers to believe that they have received a fair price and for investors to believe that the shares offer further growth prospects.

Once the IPO market took off, the discount to the price at the close of first-day dealings steadily widened from 7 per cent over the period 1980–89 and then up to 11 per cent from 1990–94. In the second half of the nineties the discount crept up further to 18 per cent 1995–8 before soaring to 72 per cent in 1999 and 56 per cent in 2000[17] as the internet bubble formed.

These figures suggest that the investment banks were getting their pricing wrong, but they had a difficult job. Most of the hot new issues in the late nineties were young internet firms with a lot of potential but no earnings, and in some cases no revenues either. Valuation was further complicated by the fact that no one knew what the coming internet age would look like.

Investors got overexcited at the prospect of short term profits and what they thought might be a second Industrial Revolution: 'We brought the company to market at $15; the price at the close of the first day was $35. There wasn't a book at $35 or $25 or even $20. The public took over: thousands of people sitting at terminals buying 100-share lots. That demand was invisible and irrelevant to book building. The public was materially and in large part responsible for the bubble. Wall Street was merely responding to what its clients demanded, not selling a point of view.'[18]

There is some truth in this as an explanation. The speaker, a managing director with a West Coast investment bank that specialized in the technology sector, knew that if his firm priced the deal too high, investors would have shunned it, there would have been no order 'book' of demand and the issue would have failed. So the deal was priced low enough to attract the institutional investors and the investment bank was able to build a book of orders to get the deal done. However, once that occurred, punters piled in, gambling that the frenetic mood of the bubble would persuade others to follow, thus driving the opening price up way beyond the issue price. The investment banks certainly had a difficult balance to strike and did not hold all the cards, but they cannot be entirely absolved from responsibility for creating the euphoria. They were relentless in talking things up, particularly their cheerleaders in research who encouraged investors to chase shares almost regardless of their valuation.

Professor Jay Ritter, the academic who has done much to initiate the debate on IPOs, used the case of Corvis to illustrate over-bullish research. CSFB took the firm public in 2000 and the shares went to a first-day premium of 135 per cent. After the end of the twenty-five working-day quiet period during which underwriters are not allowed to make recommendations, the five co-managing underwriters all put out 'Buy' recommendations and the lead manager initiated coverage of Corvis with a 'Strong Buy' recommendation. By then the stock was trading at a premium of 150 per cent to the offer price and Corvis had a market capitalization of $30 billion, despite never having earned any revenue; little over a year later, after the bubble had burst, its market valuation was less than $1 billion.[19]

Corvis was no one-off. An academic survey of analyst initiations at the end of the quiet period between 1996 and 2000 revealed that 96 per cent were 'strong buys'.[20] If ever there was a moment when the investment banks could have justified their fees and returns by dampening speculation, this was it. Instead, they could not bear to jeopardize lucrative new issues and fanned the flames by cynically encouraging investors to keep buying.

I interviewed the head of research at an investment bank that had been a major player in the IPO boom: 'There was such largesse at stake that everyone's head was turned and no one was cognizant of ethics. When I got there I asked each analyst, "What do you get paid for?" They all answered, "Banking revenues."'

In the gold rush, training and fundamental analysis were forgotten: 'There was so much business out there that unqualified people were lured in for a fast buck. No one was interested in quality research, merely in form and quantity. These new people were told to visit private companies, win business and write reports, so they did because they had no training or ethical framework.

'I asked the analysts what role return on capital plays in evaluating the companies you follow. Only one understood the question. I held classes trying to teach them how to be an analyst. The second highest earner in the department was very resistant. I brought him into my office and asked him how he valued companies. He told me: "If a company has good management, a good product and a good record, I like it." I said, "What if the price goes up $10?" "Yes, I still like it." "$20?" "Yes." "$50?" "Yes." "$200?" Finally he got the point. He was a smart guy but he had no clue.'[21]

Wiser heads might have prevailed but they were blinded by greed: 'The older analysts should have known better because they had seen what happened at the end of the eighties. These people were just bought; they couldn't resist temptation. Anyone who said no was simply replaced; in 2000 one analyst at the firm made

$12 million, several were at $10 million and several more were at $8 million.'

Long Term Performance

Investors would have been better off buying an index tracker fund than adopting a buy and hold strategy for IPOs. Between 1980 and 2001, based on the first day closing price, the total return of US IPOs was 23 per cent less than the value-weighted market index and 5 per cent less than a sample of similar sized and styled stocks. In other words, apart from the first day opening premium of 19 per cent, the IPOs underperformed. The best strategy would have been to sell them after the opening day.[22]

As I shall discuss in a later chapter, the longer term underperformance of IPOs helps to explain why issuers did not complain at leaving so much on the table. As insiders, they knew best what the stocks were really worth and were prepared to see the share price adjust as investors came to the same conclusion. The bankers and analysts should have known too.

But the mature judgement that might have said 'enough is enough' was lost in a desire to keep the IPO pot boiling. There is something wrong about a market that discounts so much of future returns into the first day of dealing. It certainly is one way of redistributing capital, but it looks more like a lottery than an efficient market.

Market Reputation

Trust in the market depends on investors being able to rely on fair dealing, transparency and on the financial statements of listed companies. The fate of Germany's Neuer Markt shows what happens if confidence goes: the market disappears. This Frankfurt-based stock exchange set relatively undemanding criteria for companies wanting to list their shares and attracted a lot of fledgling technology companies in the late 1990s. But from its peak in March 2000 to its trough in September 2001, it lost 94 per cent of its value and was closed down the following year. This is an extreme case, but there are shades of it in the long downturn in the US IPO market.[23]

The IPO drought of 2001, 2002 and 2003 – when the number dropped year after year to below the levels seen in any year since 1980 – was no doubt partly due to issuers preferring to wait for recovery following the calamitous fall in share prices. But it was also due to a buyers' strike as investors were scared off by the recent collapse of so many IPOs.[24] They stayed away for a long time suggesting that something more than market timing was at work. This is understandable. In an environment where research recommendations were shown to have been biased and where there was a record of favouritism in allocations, giving rise to suspicions that an insiders' club operated, investors could scarcely be expected to rush back to the new issue market.

A Good Idea Spoiled

At the beginning of this section we identified three criteria for measuring the investment banks' output in IPOs. A mixed message emerges. A previously little used means of raising capital was developed and expanded into a mass market that worked well for issuers. But for investors it was little better than a casino requiring caution and a disciplined approach to cashing in when they were ahead.

After the advances in the IPO market in the eighties and nineties, its reputation was damaged by the Spitzer scandals and by the bubble. The investment banks have to bear some responsibility. Their staff talked and wrote things up and they used hot IPO shares as currency to curry favour with influential clients. This reduced customers' confidence in the market and may have been a factor in it remaining depressed for so long.

Mergers and Acquisitions

The merger movement was not a late twentieth-century invention but during the eighties and nineties it was transformed from a cottage industry into a big business. Even after the merger wave of the sixties, top advisers such as Morgan Stanley had only about four merger and acquisition specialist investment bankers.[25] The senior partner of Goldman Sachs 'would say that he *was* the original merger department, in the sense that the bottom left-hand drawer held the buyers and the bottom right-hand drawer the sellers'.[26] There were only three hundred bulge bracket investment bankers in America in total in 1965 and only 1,500 in 1978.[27]

It was the leverage-based corporate raiders of the eighties such as Carl Icahn and Ronald Perelman and the mega-mergers of the nineties such as Travelers-Citicorp and Vodafone-Mannesmann that signified the arrival of mergers and acquisitions as a mainstream activity for the investment banks. In 1980 there were only 106 M&A deals announced in America and 97 in the rest of the world; in 1998, the peak year, there were nearly 12,000 in America and over 30,000 elsewhere. The value of US deals rose from $234 billion in 1990 to $1.75 trillion in 1998, and the average deal size quadrupled to $150 million. The investment banks fed and watered this movement, seizing on new business theories and ideas and urging managements to merge or die.

There is no doubt that it is a great business for the investment banks, but economists and other academics debate whether mergers benefit the economy as a whole. On one side, market economists argue that an active mechanism for changes in corporate control encourages the efficient allocation of capital. It acts as an incentive for new start-up businesses by offering the owners the prospect of cashing out through sale. It enables businesses in need of development to be placed in the hands of owners with the means to do so. Advocates believe that exposing companies to the markets test protects shareholders against underperformance because businesses get taken over and managers get sacked if they underperform. According to such theories, an active merger market is therefore essential to the operation of the free market economy.

On the other side, critics believe that the merger movement does not work. They argue that fear of takeover and the need to show immediate results from acquisitions precipitate short term actions such as cutting down on research and development work or laying off too many people. They point to the after-effects of the leveraged buy-out boom of the 1980s, which left companies struggling to keep up with interest payments and deferring long term expenditure. Social consequences are perceived in job losses, which frequently accompany mergers and which have devastating effects on communities and individuals. Critics challenge the economic benefits of mergers, arguing that they achieve wealth redistribution from buyer to seller rather than efficient capital allocation. Most importantly, they argue that mergers destroy rather than create value.

The critics' arguments are persuasive. Many reviews of acquisitions in the USA, the UK and Europe show that shareholders of acquirers on average experienced wealth losses and that in many cases there was a sharp deterioration in acquirer performance several years after deal completion. Most large acquirers – between 50 per cent and 80 per cent according to several studies, such as those published by PricewaterhouseCoopers, KPMG and A. T. Kearney, 1999–2000 – failed to match the companies' previous organic performance.[28] Professor Sudi Sudarsanam's review of merger literature over the longer term also reaches a stark conclusion: 'Numerous studies from the US, UK and some continental European countries provide clear evidence that shareholders of acquirers experience wealth losses on average or at best break even . . . The odds of positive and significant value creation for acquirer shareholders may even be less than 50%, which is what one would get with the toss of a fair coin. Thus M & A transactions are high risk corporate transactions. The cost of failure is egregious when one considers the value of M & A transactions especially during merger waves.'[29]

Evidence from the dot.com era makes especially bleak reading. A study of the acquisitions of 4,136 American companies during the period 1998–2001 found that the announcement of the bids reduced the combined stock market value of the merging firms by $158 billion. Shareholders of the buying firms saw their wealth reduced by $240 billion, representing 12 per cent of the purchase price. The wealth destruction was concentrated amongst the biggest equity-financed deals; the bigger the deal, the worse the results.[30] Often there was a sharp deterioration in acquirer performance for several years after the deal is done.[31] The merger of AOL and Time Warner in 2000 is a case in point. As we saw in Chapter 1, the deal was intended to create a world-class modern media company but instead led to the largest losses in corporate history.

Bankers such as the legendary dealmaker Bruce Wasserstein are dismissive of the value-destroying arguments: 'The problem with many academic studies is that they make questionable assumptions to squeeze untidy data points into a pristine statistical model.'[32] But the weight of evidence from the late-twentieth-century merger wave seems to show that the handsome profits made by the selling shareholders were usually offset by subsequent losses for the acquirers.

This would suggest that many mergers were not well thought out and were attempted by managers that lacked the skills and techniques to make them work. CEOs and their boards are not exactly babes in the wood, but investment bankers were the driving force behind many mergers. With over $10 billion dollars of fees paid out for global merger advice in some years, much of it payable on success only, they and other advisers wound up the pressure to transact at a time when many of their clients would have been better off tending their own back yards. As Sir Peter Job observed after his years as CEO of Reuters: 'As asset prices went up, fees became too tempting, too lucrative, for the investment bankers to resist.'[33]

Derivatives

Derivatives – financial contracts based on other financial assets – are simple products that grew more complex as they evolved. The three basic derivatives are: futures (agreements to buy an asset at a set future date at a fixed price); options (the right but not the obligation to buy or sell an asset in the future at an agreed price); and swaps (agreements to exchange foreign currencies or interest payments at agreed prices). These basic forms are easy to calculate and evaluate and have been successfully used to trade commodities for centuries and financial assets for decades.

Three developments in the last quarter of the twentieth century complicated matters. The first was the growth of over-the-counter derivatives arranged by dealers between buyers and sellers without going through a central exchange. The derivatives exchanges and regulators do not play a role – they might not even know about the trading – but these lightly regulated over-the-counter markets now account for 85 per cent of all derivatives trading.

The second important development was the cross-linking of the three basic derivative mechanisms and the blending of all sorts of different assets into interconnected, interdependent securities known as exotic or complex derivatives. These first came to prominence in the structured notes scandal of 1994 described in Chapter 1 and have evolved into a major part of the modern derivatives industry.

Bankers Trust and Credit Suisse Financial Products (CSFP), a specially created AAA-rated subsidiary of CSFB, are the firms best known for pioneering these products in the early 1990s, but the other investment banks rapidly became involved. A description of one of CSFP's structured notes illustrates how complex derivatives had become: 'Unlike a typical bond, which has a series of standard coupon payments and then a fixed principal repayment, a structured note's returns might vary wildly, based on different variables. In other words, the bond – or note – was structured so that its payments were based on any conceivable financial instrument or index. One structured note was even linked to the number of victories by the Utah Jazz, a professional basketball team, although more typical variables were interest rates or currencies.'[34] This basic principle – linking the returns on a security to movements in several other variables – is at the heart of complex or 'exotic' derivatives that make up a large part of the over-the-counter markets.

The third development stemmed from securitization, the process of transferring certain receivables (such as interest on mortgage loans or credit card payments) to a newly created company or trust which then issues shares. Because these vehicles are stand alone entities and are backed with assets, they are given a high rating by the credit agencies. These special purpose entities (SPEs as they became known) were ideal for issuing complex derivatives, especially if based off-shore, and became an essential link in the chain.

Opinions about derivatives are sharply divided into two camps. In the blue corner, former Chairman of the Federal Reserve, Mr Markets himself, Alan Greenspan. Greenspan believes derivatives are good for the global economy. They make the financial system more flexible, increase growth and allow banks, businesses and governments to control risk. In support of Mr Greenspan: nine out of every ten of the world's top five hundred companies who regularly use derivatives of one kind or another; the Basel Committee on Banking Supervision; an army of academics led by the Nobel Prize winner, the late Merton Miller; and most financial institutions.

In the red corner, America's most famous investor, the Sage of Omaha, Warren Buffett, who in 2003 described derivatives as 'financial weapons of mass destruction'. In support of Mr Buffett: Bill Gross, the manager of PIMCO, one of the world's largest bond funds; shareholders in Procter & Gamble; Gibson Greetings; 'Freddie Mac' and Enron; the citizens of Orange County; and countless others who have lost huge amounts of value through derivatives and who believe that the $218 trillion of global derivatives contracts presently outstanding contains hidden losses that will in due course come to haunt their owners.

The enormous size of the market – $201 trillion in interest rate derivatives, $12 trillion in credit derivatives and $5 trillion in equity derivatives, according to a recent survey by the International Swaps and Derivatives Association[35] – illustrates both sides of the argument. If anything went wrong, the consequences could be life threatening to the organization or country involved; on the other hand a market this size would not exist and flourish if it served no purpose.

As it is, derivatives are used by many different organizations for many different things. Governments use them for raising funds in bond markets, for managing foreign currency reserves and in designing government-sponsored savings products.[36] Corporations use them to hedge interest rate, foreign exchange and other exposures and to raise capital efficiently. Financial institutions use them to manage liability risk, to add value to portfolios and to provide customers with products such as fixed rate mortgages and guaranteed return investment products. Banks, including investment banks, use derivatives strategies as a risk management tool to hedge and leverage market positions for customer and proprietary business and to spread counterparty and credit risk. They also sell derivatives to customers providing governments, corporations and other financial institutions with the products to meet their needs as outlined above.

Heads We Win, Tails You Lose

Time will tell which of these two powerful opinions is correct but it is already clear that, like real weapons of mass destruction, in the wrong hands derivatives can cause great damage whilst in the right hands they can stabilize volatile situations. The other thing that they have in common with real weapons of mass destruction is that those who provide them usually walk away enriched and unharmed.

There were some spectacular derivatives losses during the past fifteen years. Risk never rests and the hideous mistakes of the early nineties were replaced by different but no less painful ways to lose money in derivatives. Treasurers have come a long way since the days of Procter & Gamble, Gibson's Greetings and Orange County, but not as far as you might think. In 2003, one in three big company treasurers still felt uncomfortable with derivatives, which is frightening considering that nine out of every ten used them.[37] London's Centre for the Study of Financial Innovation 2003 survey on business risk found that Complex Financial Instruments were regarded as being the biggest threat to the banking system.

Mistakes were still being made. They were different and less naive than those of the nineties but could still be very damaging. General Electric, regarded by many as the model of a well-managed company, reduced its 2001 earnings by $502 million and cut shareholder equity by $1.3 billion because of changes in the way it accounted for derivatives. The Federal Home Loan Mortgage Corporation, 'Freddie Mac', had been in business for three decades and had earned a second nickname, 'Steady Freddie', until in 2003 it announced it would have to restate earnings by $4.5 billion because of incorrect accounting in its derivatives portfolio.[38] Another government-sponsored mortgage finance company, 'Fannie Mae', said it would have to restate previous years' earnings – by $9 billion according to some estimates – because of incorrect accounting on its derivatives book.[39] Its regulator, the Office of Federal Housing Enterprise Oversight, said this raised 'serious doubts' about 'the overall safety and soundness of the business'; the company contested this view but made management changes.[40] Even the experts can get it wrong, as we saw when Long-Term Capital Management's sophisticated investment bankers, Nobel Prize-winning economists and rocket-scientist traders, lost nearly all their clients' money in 1998.

The losses came from several sources. Complex derivatives are hard to understand and hard to value. Frequently there is no external market in which to test valuations and holders can be surprised when they try. Misrepresentation was behind many derivatives losses. Derivatives encourage misrepresentation by helping organizations get round rules and regulations, avoid taxes and mislead shareholders, analysts and other observers. Although some free market economists follow Merton Miller in arguing that finding ways to avoid regulation is a positive and desirable stimulus to financial innovation, rules are usually there to protect against excessive risk-taking and it is no surprise that some institutions tripped up in their attempts to avoid them.

Misrepresentation was encouraged by the unreported, unregulated nature of over-the-counter trades, the off balance-sheet status of many SPEs and the fiendish complexity of structured derivatives. Deceitful organizations relied on the fact that they were often concealed from public scrutiny, and even if they were visible the chances were that they would be too complicated for most analysts to understand. Enron, for example, used derivatives to make itself look bigger and better than it was. It created special purpose entity partnerships that enabled it to borrow money without showing the debt. Provided Enron controlled less than 50 per cent of the partnerships, they did not have to be consolidated under accounting rules. Any debts were the partnership's, not Enron's, and were disclosed only as a footnote to Enron's financial statements, not in the balance sheet. But Enron stretched the definition of outside investors by allowing employees and other related parties to invest and by, in effect, protecting them against losses. When the outside world finally realized that many of the 'outside investors' were really inside investors or Enron itself, its share price went into a tailspin and triggered off a sequence of events that brought the company down.

Enron was not the only company around the turn of the twentieth century that was punished by investors once they realized what was being done with derivatives. The stock prices of US energy corporations Dynegy, El Paso and Williams Companies all suffered from such problems. So too PNC Financial, a major bank, which settled SEC charges that, as a result of off balance sheet deals, its 2001 earnings had been overstated by half.[41] Telecommunications companies were adept at selling capacity to each other using derivatives contracts to make costs look like revenue. Global Crossing used bandwidth swaps to create earnings that met analysts' expectations before filing for bankruptcy in 2002. Qwest restated its earnings by $1 billion having used a similar derivatives trick.

Credit derivatives, which have become a massive market tripped up many users. They were initially developed by Bankers Trust and CSFP in the early 1990s and in little more than a decade the market was worth $12 trillion. Banks seeking to improve their balance sheets packaged up their loan portfolios and put them into SPEs. The SPE got an investment grade rating and its bonds (drawing on the high income of the sub-investment grade pieces of the whole portfolio) offered extra yield compared to other AAA-rated securities. Income-seeking investors such as insurance companies that were prohibited from investing directly into high risk, high income bonds were able to do so indirectly by buying shares in the new highly rated entities to secure the yield they need. However, the early twenty-first-century corporate crisis caused many of the underlying companies to default on their loans and triggered losses in the SPEs. One of the biggest losers from the defaults of 2002 was Prudential plc, which announced losses of half a billion dollars on credit related derivatives.

Heads we win, tails you lose continued into the twenty-first century in derivatives. In 2001, Wall Street's banks made an estimated $1 billion buying and selling credit derivatives just prior to the wave of corporate failures that made many of them worthless. Citigroup hedged its entire $1.2 billion exposure to Enron and lost nothing when Enron defaulted in 2001 leaving investors in Citigroup's SPEs to pick up the tab.[42]

Having looked at five of Enron's structured finance transactions involving Merrill Lynch, Citigroup and J. P. Morgan Chase, the US General Accounting Office concluded that: 'Certain investment banks facilitated and participated in complex financial transactions with Enron despite allegedly knowing that the intent of the transactions was to manipulate and obscure Enron's true financial condition.'[43]

Top banks received several hundred million dollars in fees from Enron to work on structured finance and co-invested in its partnerships, and yet none pointed out to investors the derivatives problems. As late as October 2001, sixteen out of the seventeen analysts covering Enron rated it a buy or above.[44] Enron generated a reported $323 million in underwriting fees between 1986 and 2001, over half of which went to Goldman Sachs, Salomon Smith Barney and CSFB.[45] Although the investment banks cannot be held directly responsible for what happened, the *Wall Street Journal* aptly headlined a major article on the subject, 'How Wall Street greased Enron's money machine'.[46]

The use of derivatives to misrepresent companies' true financial position happened all over the world. In 1999 the Financial Supervisory Agency in Japan discovered that CSFB's derivatives trading company in Tokyo had been marketing trading strategies to help Japanese banks conceal their losses.[47] Parmalat, the Italian food company that collapsed in 2003, used SPVs to hide the money that was being siphoned out of shareholders' funds. The *Financial Times* summed up the situation as follows: 'Parmalat abused the capital markets for years by raising money under false pretences. Money was siphoned off for family purposes and the whole mess hidden in a complex structure of 200-plus subsidiaries and special purpose vehicles scattered across the globe, including in tax havens such as the Cayman Islands, the Dutch Antilles and Cyprus.'[48]

Although scarcely a quarter went by without a new derivatives loss emerging, it is important to balance this by remembering that the latest recession and bear market passed off without any large scale bank failure. The financial services system showed itself able to absorb great volatility and kept working throughout, in part because derivatives helped institutions to ride the volatility. Ruth Kelly, then the British minister responsible for financial markets, noted that the collapse of Parmalat 'passed with relatively few repercussions at least in part due to the increasingly widespread use of default swaps', and in a balanced comment on the Buffett–Greenspan derivatives debate she concluded that: 'If used carefully [derivatives] have the power to spread risk. More has been lost from bad real estate investments than from derivatives.'[49]

This may be so, but what about the role of derivatives and the investment banks in causing the problems in the first place? Parmalat's investment banks included J. P. Morgan, Merrill Lynch, Morgan Stanley and Citigroup, who between them took $45 million-worth of fees for arranging its biggest bond and equity issues. Little over a year before Parmalat collapsed, Morgan Stanley led an equity-linked bond issue for a subsidiary of Parmalat, despite the fact that its accounts had been qualified by the auditors for the three previous years.[50] At the time of writing, Parmalat is suing several other banks either to win damages or force them to repay the fees. One suit alleged that Citigroup helped Parmalat obscure the state of its finances while encouraging investors to buy its bonds; all the banks are contesting the cases.[51]

Overall, the investment banks' record in complex derivatives is mixed. They invented and expanded something that enabled many sophisticated customers to hedge risks, enhance growth and improve shareholder returns. Yet they also turned a blind eye to misrepresentation and used their own superior knowledge to make huge profits and pass the risk on to others. Customers thinking of using complex derivatives might be well advised to remember one recent comment: 'The only people well equipped to assess the value of these instruments are the people selling them.'[52]

There is one leading investment bank that has presented its derivatives strategies with a slide showing investment banks on one side and clients on the other linked by a box labelled 'risk transformation', the argument being that as they are repackaging risks they are reducing them.[53] But derivatives strategies comprise a series of linked transactions in which there are going to be winners and losers; only one side of the trade can be successful. Risk transformation involves handing over the risk from those in the know – often the investment banks – to those not in the know, or to those taking a different and maybe less informed view. History will judge the financial weapons of mass destruction debate when more evidence emerges; meanwhile it is already clear that for some users they became weapons of mass deception.

What Goes Around Comes Around

So while the investment banks certainly enabled their clients to transact in size, the quality of the advice that they gave was variable. Whether it was analysts' recommendations, suggested mergers and acquisitions or structured derivatives, the course recommended by the investment banks brought no guarantee of success and sometimes damaged the financial position of the recipient.

We know that the investment banks do many things very well and we also know that in nearly efficient markets predicting is very difficult. But to judge from the four product categories surveyed, the output of the investment banks could and, in my opinion, should have been better in the years under review.

On balance, the high returns made by the investment banks sit uneasily alongside such indifferent output. In recollecting his inquiry into the Great Crash of 1929, Judge Ferdinand Pecora described the investment bankers of the day as having 'heads I win, tails you lose ethics'. Three-quarters of a century later it seemed that everything and nothing had changed.[54]

6

The Sound of Silence

Whenever people of the same trade meet together, wrote Adam Smith, 'the conversation ends in a conspiracy against the public or in some contrivance to raise prices'. Were investment banks involved in such conspiracies or, as Smith expected would occur, did open market forces keep prices down?[1]

Did Prices Remain High?

It is conventional wisdom in and around investment banking circles that prices are being squeezed. Commentators describe 'the commoditisation of core products',[2] and Goldman Sachs warned potential investors: 'We have experienced intense price competition in some of our businesses in recent years, such as underwriting fees on investment grade debt offerings and privatizations. We believe we may experience pricing pressures in these and other areas in the future as some of our competitors seek to obtain market share by reducing prices.'[3] The New York and London financial press shared this view, the *Wall Street Journal* reporting that 'fees have been slipping on an assortment of Wall Street offerings'[4] and the *Financial Times* stating that capital markets business has 'also become increasingly commoditised' and that 'the price has moved south very dramatically'.[5]

Testing the accuracy of these views is complicated by the diversity of the investment banking business. There is no single product that is representative of the entire range. The pricing basket needs to include activities such as loans, currency and interest rate trading, where margins have been low for a long time; others such as equities and exchange-traded derivatives, which have come under pressure relatively recently, and certain areas – for example complex derivatives and IPOs – where prices and margins have been buoyant. The overall picture on price, therefore, needs to take account of price competition in commodity areas and also the favourable pricing structure that prevails in other parts of the business.

Equities Trading and the Dog that Did not Bark

The strongest evidence of price competition appears in share trading. On the New York Stock Exchange, where charges are set in cents per share traded, commission rates have been falling ever since fixed rates were abolished on large lots in 1971 and on all trades in 1975.[6] Since 1980 average commissions on shares listed on the NYSE have dropped from nearly 40 cents per share to less than five cents.[7] For shares listed on over-the-counter markets such as NASDAQ, spreads fell from over 30 cents per share to below four cents per share. If anything, the trend is accelerating, with rates down a third in the past few years and the proportion of net – commission free – trades rising steadily.

Block trades – big deals in a single stock – and programme trades – big deals in a number of stocks traded simultaneously for a single client – are particularly competitive. Corporate or institutional clients wishing to buy or sell shares in this way ask two or three brokers for prices at which they would deal. The brokers quote a premium or discount to the prevailing price and sometimes a commission rate, depending on market conditions and the nature of the trade. It is a high risk and keenly contested activity that has become increasingly common. Programme trading now makes up over a half of NYSE volume compared to less than 10 per cent fifteen years ago and large single stock block trades, once a rarity, are now an everyday occurrence.

A good example of a block trade occurred in 2004 when, according to reports, after outbidding other banks Citigroup bought €1.8 billion-worth of shares in the German stock Infineon from Siemens AG. It paid €12 per share, which was just below the listed price, and hoped to sell them for about 10 cents more. Instead Infineon's price dropped and Citigroup could only get out at prices between €11.50 and €12.[8] This experience was not unusual; it is generally reckoned that 30 per cent of any commission on block trading is lost in getting out of the positions.

Falling commission rates, the increased proportion of net trades and the growing popularity of programme trading have combined to make trading equity stocks for customers a precarious business. When commentators and people in the business speak of commoditization, this is one of the main areas that they have in mind. Yet the authoritative paper 'Large Investment Bank Margin and ROE Trends', written for the Securities Industry Association by Brad Hintz, a respected analyst with the broking firm Sanford Bernstein and a former CFO of Lehman and Treasurer of Morgan Stanley, contains some surprising results. Hintz used the SIA Databank to establish margins on individual business lines. In contrast to the apparently bleak picture outlined above, Hintz's analysis showed that in equities – defined as commission-bearing agency business as well as proprietary and other trading and derivatives – the margins were very high:

Table 3. Pre-tax margins in equities: large US investment banks.[9]

Year	1991	1992	1993	1994	1995	1996	1997	1998	1999	2000	2001
Margin %	17.5	17.2	14.6	11.3	16.8	29.2	45.0	44.9	59.6	59.9	43.2

How can this be reconciled with equities' reputation as a product line that is under intense margin pressure? Hintz himself gave the answer, explaining that the commoditization of the straight equities business has been offset by an important new area: 'These pricing trends have been offset since the late 1990s by the rapid growth of high margin equity derivative books in the business during the past several years. Some firms have cited that up to 30 per cent of their net revenues are now coming from derivative activities.'[10]

Derivatives are the dog that did not bark during the debate on pricing, a discussion that has not kept pace with changes in the industry. The many words that are written about falling margins in stock and bond trading divert us from looking in the right area. The profit story is no longer about cash equities and bonds. Instead it is about the opaque world of derivatives: unregulated, unreported, unseen and offering unbelievably high margins.

We are speaking about over-the-counter derivatives – trades arranged dealer to dealer and not going through a central exchange – in particular, for exchange-traded derivatives – deals that are carried out and reported on a central exchange – have been subject to the same pricing pressures as cash equities. One derivatives expert explained that on standard exchange-traded products 'Everyone uses the same model to price options. You know the life of the option, the current price, the strike price and the historic volatility. Only the premium for volatility is unknown, but it is easy to calculate and to compare quotes, so the bid–offer spread has fallen over time.'[11]

But complex customized derivatives are harder to price and, because they do not get reported on official exchanges, harder to track: 'As you get more exotic and esoteric, the deals are complex and there are so few of them that it is hard for clients to evaluate the price. There is no public record and the range of prices is very high.'[12] Another derivatives expert told me: 'The price is based around the client's need. For a client insuring a $10 billion portfolio the banks can have a very wide bid–offer spread.'[13]

The pricing game has moved on. The old businesses – cash equities, plain vanilla derivatives – have become traded commodities, but rip-roaring prices have been switched into new areas. As ever with the investment banks, it is as well to be aware of what they are not talking about. When the effects of pricing pressure in the old businesses are offset by the high prices in the new, it is clear that the investment bank pricing cocktail is more sophisticated and attractive than at first appears.

Underwriting

Academic work by Professor Jay Ritter and others has drawn attention to the persistence of high spreads in the US IPO market and to the increasingly common use of 7 per cent as the standard fee. They observed that: 'In the period from 1995 to 1998, for the 1,111 IPOs raising between $20 and $80 million in the United States, more than

90 per cent of issuers paid gross spreads of exactly 7 per cent. This clustering of spreads at 7 per cent has not always been present. There is much more clustering at 7 per cent now than a decade ago, although the average spread on IPOs has not changed during this period.'[14]

Although average equity IPO spreads in the United States dipped slightly from just under 7 per cent in the first half of the nineties to just under 6 per cent a decade later they remained remarkably high, especially in comparison with other markets. Spreads on IPOs were about half of the levels charged in America in Australia, North Asia and Europe.[15] Larger deals get lower spreads than smaller deals, but even at the top end of the market prices held up very well. Spreads on the Google IPO, initially forecast to be a cartel-breaking issue, turned out to be 3 per cent, only half a point down on what might have been the price five years earlier.

Chen and Ritter also showed that there was less clustering in other parts of the capital markets than in equity IPOs. This suggests that there was a certain amount of underwriting price competition in some product areas, a suggestion confirmed by evidence of price erosion in American follow-on equity offerings,[16] European IPOs,[17] and fixed income underwriting.[18] In these areas, the conventional view of investment banking as an industry under margin pressure had some foundation.

But the American IPO market was different, not being price competitive or price sensitive. The IPO market represented a third of all the new equity raised in American capital markets during the 1990s and the price resilience of this important area means that the conventional blanket view of investment banking as an industry suffering severe price pressure needs to be modified. Possible explanations for this are discussed later.

Advisory Work

The prices charged by the investment banks for advisory work are often related to financings and it is difficult for outsiders to disaggregate the pure 'advice' element. As a result, opinion about pricing trends varies. According to the consultants Freeman & Co., the prices charged for mergers and acquisitions may actually have increased in the later nineties from 1.1 per cent in 1994 to over 1.5 per cent by 2000.[19] Senior investment bankers disagree with this, insisting that competition has forced prices down: 'There is always a discussion about fees. We negotiate the best we can get. In fifteen years I have never known a deal where there hasn't been a discussion.'[20] Other sources appear to confirm that on prestigious or strategically important deals the investment banks sometimes compete with each other on price. The *Wall Street Journal* reported the case of Southern Peru Copper Corp, which needed an investment bank to fend off an unwelcome takeover approach. Reportedly Merrill Lynch cut its price from $3m to $2m in an attempt to win the business but still lost out to Goldman Sachs, which offered an even lower price.[21]

But whatever the outcome of the debate between the consultants and the practitioners, any such discussion misses the point unless it tackles the issue of how the advisory fees are calculated. The most significant feature of the fee rates quoted on advisory work is not the absolute numbers but the fact that they are based on deal size. In times of rising asset prices, such as the 1980s and 1990s, this was a very effective mechanism for increasing prices.

The Big Bazooka: Basis Point Pricing

The investment banks based their charges for underwriting, advisory work and securities trading in many overseas markets on a percentage of the consideration. Provided the underlying market price rose and volumes held up, income grew with little impact on costs.

Basis point pricing was particularly important on advisory work, sending investment bankers' revenues soaring. The value of the average global merger doubled in the nineties, generating enormous fees for the investment banks. For example, advisers in the £8.5 billion takeover of Britain's Abbey National by the Spanish bank Santander Central Hispano shared £121 million between them, a payout described by one Madrid banker as 'the big bazooka for us'.[22]

For the investment banks basis point pricing at a time when stock prices increased tenfold in just twenty five years made the bull market a stairway to heaven. In IPOs and mergers and acquisitions, the rise in deal size more than made up for the slight fall in basis point rates.

The average sized IPO in 1980 raised about $10 million, earning the underwriters $700,000 at a spread of 7 per cent. In 2000 the average IPO raised $165 million; the price charged by the underwriters appeared to have fallen because the spread was down to 6 per cent. But the actual dollar price paid for the underwriting had risen to $10 million.

Drilling this down to a single hypothetical example of a medium sized company listing on the New York Stock Exchange for the first time in 2004 at a share price of $50 shows how the 'big bazooka' of basis point pricing worked. The gross spread taken out by the underwriters would probably have been 5 per cent, equivalent to $2.50 per share. If the company had come to the market ten years earlier the spread on a company this size would have been 6 per cent. However, during that decade share prices had doubled. If the company had come to the market then, with an identical record, its share price would have been not $50 but $25. The 6 per cent spread would have earned the underwriters $1.50 per share. The apparent price reduction from 6 per cent to 5 per cent, if market inflation is taken into account, is actually a price increase from $1.50 to $2.50.

Bankers argue that underwriting is a risk business which therefore merits basis point charging. It used to be a risk business but as a result of sophisticated book-building techniques over the last twenty years the underwriting risk is now much reduced. Book building is based on talking to potential investors and establishing their demand under various 'what if' scenarios. Using an algorithm model to adjust price and size for external factors such as the behaviour of other investors, the investment banks can build up a clear picture of where the demand might come from and at what price. If it looks as though demand will not be there, the price is reduced or the issue is pulled. The only real risk is of a cataclysmic collapse in markets and there the underwriters are protected by *force majeur* clauses and by hedging. Underwriting became more of a process than a risk operation and basis point charging seems anachronistic.

Nor is basis point charging justified by any increase in the costs of doing bigger deals. Although it takes more resources to distribute a big deal than a small one, the economies of scale are significant. This is clear from the ability of quite small numbers of securities people to distribute very large amounts of shares. The number of shares traded in America in 2002 was 132 times more than in 1975, yet the number of securities people needed to handle that volume was only five times more. As the academic experts on the subject pointed out, 'there is widespread agreement that fixed costs exist in underwriting IPOs yet investment bankers charge the same seven per cent spread on $20 million deals as they do on $80 million deals'.[23]

The effect of basis point charging in an era of rising asset prices, the high margins still available on complex derivatives and the price resilience of American IPOs show that the conventional picture of an industry under pressure needs to be tempered. Margin pressure, falling prices and increased risk in some parts of the investment banking business were offset by high prices in others. Whether the glass then looks half full or half empty depends entirely on your mindset.

Do They Act Together?

Standard definitions of a cartel require the participants to act together: without collusion there is no cartel. In many areas of investment banking there is clearly no collusion and therefore no cartel. As one expert on the industry told me: 'The top gorillas in this business . . . all hate each other and want to steal each other's business whenever they can and they are paid big bonuses for doing so. Business is done deal by deal and deals are copied instantly and offered at lower rates. It is hard to imagine how price fixing would work.'

Equity and bond markets are indeed very price competitive and the brokers are constantly at each other's throats. Exotic derivatives are so complex and opaque that high margins come not from collusion, but from baffling the customer with science. If there was an investment banking cartel it is most likely to have occurred in advisory work and American IPOs, where, as we have seen, despite the intense head-to-head competition between banks to win deals, the pricing structure had some curious features.

It is the pattern of IPO prices, as well as their resilience, that looks suspicious. The US Department of Justice took a look at alleged price fixing in domestic IPOs in 2000 before dropping the case a year later, but many questions remain unanswered.[24] There were great differences in the fees charged by investment banks for identical products in different parts of the world, and when US firms were involved the fees tended to be higher than if local or regional firms were used. It appears that prices were set by reference to custom, bearing little relation to the cost of production. Why else would the price of an identical service, involving many of the same people, be less in smaller, diverse and more complex European and Asian markets than in the United States? Why else would the price of issuing high yield bonds, which many consider to be quasi-equity, be half the equity equivalent? Why else would American IPO spreads have clustered round the 7 per cent figure?

The explanation is unlikely to be explicit collusion, which would be simply too risky. Conspirators would be too fearful of the word leaking out and of the serious consequences. It is impossible to believe senior bankers would be so unwise as to sit round a table and reach a modern-day buttonwood tree agreement: 'We do hereby solemnly promise and pledge ourselves to each other that we will not work on any initial public offering from this date, for any person whatsoever, at a spread less than 7 per cent of the total capital being raised and that we will give preference to each other in our negotiations.' As Chen and Ritter point out: 'With literally scores of people involved in setting spreads at investment banking firms, the ability to explicitly collude and keep it a secret strains credibility. Legal liability is also a deterrent.'[25]

They suggest that a more likely explanation is implicit collusion or strategic pricing. The participants in the IPO and advisory markets had the shared objective of keeping prices high for as long as possible. The established players did so well that there was no incentive to disrupt the show by cutting prices and they competed with each other by other means. How and why they were able to achieve this is the subject of the second half of this book.

Drawing on game theory, Chen and Ritter explained that the firms involved in strategic pricing understood the long term strategic advantages of maintaining high prices and placed them above the short term gains that might come from winning deals by cutting prices: 'Strategic pricing requires that each underwriter realizes that high spreads result in large year end bonuses that would be jeopardized if spreads get driven down to competitive levels due to cut-throat competition.' Similar considerations applied to advisory work, except on high profile deals where the participants elevated strategic above financial considerations.

The success of strategic pricing depends on the market not being very price sensitive. The reasons for this being so in investment banking are discussed later, but one way to preserve this is to avoid drawing attention to profitability. Talking a lot about margin pressures and depressing published profits by paying high compensation has the side effect of keeping the industry's true profits out of the limelight. So too does tapering down the basis point rates on larger deals: 'If the profits on a deal are too large, each underwriter has an incentive to undercut the competition, even if it means jeopardizing all of the future profits from high spreads. In order to forestall a price war breaking out, underwriters must limit the economic profits earned on any given deal to a "reasonable" level.'[26]

Insiders acknowledged that they did whatever they could to keep prices up: 'Investment bankers readily admit that the IPO business is very profitable and that they avoid competing on fees because they "don't want to turn it into a commodity business".' Another investment banker has been quoted as saying: 'The fact is, we'd be cutting our own throats to compete on price.'[27]

Clients who tried to get the investment banks to budge on price found that they played a hard ball game. A former investment banker now working in private equity recalls one such case: 'We had a billion dollars of equity to place, a follow-on tranche of a company we had already floated. The lead underwriter quoted 4.5 per cent. Because of my background I was asked to negotiate with them. I asked them if they could do better on price; they came back with 4 per cent. I asked them to justify the 4 per cent; they handed to me a sheet showing that's what they had charged on their last thirty deals. I said that's not a justification; they said that's the price. I said, "That's not good enough"; they said, "We'll pay your expenses." It was a pitiful gesture but I sensed it was time to let it drop. Later I heard that the underwriter had almost walked away from the deal. They would rather have lost the business than cut their fee, which would have ruined everyone's business. They were prepared to pay our expenses because they could still have advertised 4 per cent as the going rate – that's the number that would have appeared on the sheet they showed to the next guy. If we had sought bids as a bought deal someone would have bid 6 cents a share because they could have kept the price secret. Some product lines are very competitive but when it comes to high profile initial public offerings and merger advice, top firms say, "If you want us, that's the price." It's a matter of mystique and they perpetuate it. Do they sit around the table and collude? Of course they do not. Do they try to keep prices up? Of course they do.'[28]

There is evidence of a similar approach with corporate advisory clients: 'We were planning a takeover of another company in our sector. It was our idea but it was a complicated situation. There were issues as to how to structure the offer and where to pitch it. We needed an investment bank and we brought in a firm who were experts on the sector. Despite having initiated the fee discussion at the start of the process, we made little progress and we were ultimately put in a position where we had little choice. With about a week to go we pressed them to say what they would be charging. Bear in mind that we had originated this deal ourselves and we were really only using them for technical details of the offer and for a view on how the market would react. They said $2 million. We were taken aback. It was about one per cent of the consideration. They had spent very little time on the job and preparing the offer documents was a boilerplate operation. We told them that was ridiculous. There were no other deals going on in the sector at that time. They would look good by being involved in a high profile deal at a quiet time. They absolutely refused to budge. They said that they could not justify working on a project that paid less than $2 million. We got the impression that they were prepared to walk away rather than cut their price. In the end we decided that it wasn't worth the hassle of pursuing and we accepted their price.'[29]

Retired investment bankers confirm the efforts that were made to protect prices. A former head of Equity Capital Markets at a European investment bank told me how middle managers on American competitors' syndicate desks were concerned that others should not wreck their party: 'The prices for US domestic convertible deals are higher than for Euromarkets deals. We once did a convertible deal in the Euromarkets and sold it back to the US. A couple of the top US firms got very aggressive with us, made a fuss all the way up to the top of our bank. The noise came from their capital markets desk and got supported up to quite a high level. Eventually someone very senior told them to forget it.'[30]

Another investment banker told me how they dealt with customers who asked about price: 'If they do query the price, and that's rare, we will make a gesture but it depends on how busy we are. In peak times we would not really look at work with a ticket below $2 million; now times are quieter, that's changed. There's a famous story about a client of a well-known takeover lawyer who received a one-line bill: "For services rendered: $3 million." The client asked him to justify the charges and received another one-line reply: "Pay whatever you think is fair but don't call me again." '[31]

The Sound of Silence

It is possible to argue both ways when it comes to pricing. The old product areas of cash equity and bond trading have seen commissions driven down in the face of competition and client pressure. Plain vanilla futures and options went the same way because they are transparent, relatively simple and became commodities relatively quickly. This was more than offset by the investment banks' ability to make high prices stick on the new derivatives products. Exotic over-the-counter derivatives stayed profitable because, being unreported and complex, it is difficult for clients to benchmark the market price. The overall picture on trading was therefore much healthier than the weight of published opinion would suggest.

In corporate business bought deals for certain kinds of issues became increasingly common and competitive. But in other primary business areas the market was not very price sensitive and the investment banks took full advantage of this. IPOs and advisory work were priced at what the market will bear and, in the knowledge that price cutting rarely wins market share, the investment banks stuck to their guns on pricing. The use of basis point pricing was a further hidden form of price protection.

As for collusion, the investment banks displayed a strategic understanding that high prices meant good business for all. Price cutting is most common in areas characterized by frequent and transparent transactions. Clients view these as commodity activities, show little brand loyalty and are prepared to go for the cheapest price offered by any respectable counterparties.

It is in the high value areas, where clients value the relationship more than the price, that strategic pricing was most evident. Bulge-bracket banks cut prices on strategically important deals but evidence from smaller and medium sized advisory and IPO deals suggests that, in general, they were able to keep prices high.

Perhaps the most striking example of implicit collusion occurred outside the pricing arena. It helps to explain how mismanaged conflicts of interest were allowed to go on for so long in the IPO market. Any senior banker stopping for a moment would surely have realized that it was wrong to ask an analyst to favour one client while pretending to serve another, but, as with pricing, no one wanted to spoil the party. Whether it is called strategic pricing or implicit collusion, the suspicion remains that in modern investment banking the only real conspiracy was the sound of silence.

Is There an Investment Banking Cartel?

The first half of this book has weighed up the investment banks' performance for over two decades against five generally accepted criteria for cartels. On a strict definition, the investment banks are not operating a cartel in any part of their business. However, the results for each of the five criteria contain some anomalies that require explanation.

Do a Few Firms Dominate the Market?

In straightforward market share terms, investment banking is not like auditing, where a handful of firms dominate the market, nor is it like law, where a large number of firms share the pie. But the top investment banks have such prestige and market power that they are able to set a pace that the rest of the industry finds it hard to follow.

Despite an often volatile performance in profits and reputation, the leading firms have been able to hold on to their pre-eminent position. Having been through changes in ownership, loss of independence and conversion from partnership to limited liability company, the top six brand names of a quarter of a century ago are still recognizable today and remain at the top of the ladder. A few large financial conglomerates are now challenging them, but they seem more likely to join rather than replace the top six. At the very top, the members of the super-bulge tightened their grip. The market share of the top three rose throughout the nineties, peaking at close to 50 per cent of high margin investment banking business at the height of the bull market.[32]

Did They Make Excess Returns?

Applying the principles of investment analysis to a subject that usually goes with the shout of the crowd – 'Profits are up? It must be a great business. Profits are down? It's a terrible business' – shows that the investment banks' returns were generous, to say the least. Smoothing profits to iron out the volatility shows a healthy progression that compared favourably with the performance of other participants in the American economy. Margins had to come down from unreasonably high levels during the eighties and early nineties, but the trend turned in the mid nineties and they rebuilt nicely for several years.

Over this period, return on equity, the figure the industry likes to use to judge itself, compared very favourably with the risk-free rate of return available in government bond markets and with the returns achieved in corporate America at large. When adjusted for inflation, real returns were very high. There is one further important adjustment to make: compensation. In practice, investment banking is still a partnership between the owners of the business and the staff. It is a partnership that has seen both groups do well, sending investment banking compensation into the stratosphere. It is a way of dividing the spoils that also disguises the returns. Adjusting profits to reflect normal levels of compensation as seen in other comparable professions, and adding back the savings into Return on Equity calculations, produces rates that could have caused a client revolt or government inquiries. Paying staff generously kept returns down to acceptable levels. The industry's total returns were high in the context of other sectors of American business; whether they are considered excessive depends on the view that is taken of the value they generate.

Did Output Suffer?

At the headline level, investment banking works. The banks are the intermediaries between capital seekers and investors, a connection that has been crucial to the march of the market economy. Although they have used shareholder value, deregulation and market forces – and used them to their own advantage – these doctrines have also helped to create good economic conditions in America and Britain. It is only when the detail of the investment banks' output is examined that the flaws appear. Research recommendations, the power that sustains stock market turnover, produced results that were to all practical intents and purposes little better than those achieved by tossing a coin. The IPO market worked well for sellers, but for investors the outcome was like stumbling into a casino, winning with the first stake and then blowing the lot, and more, over the next several years. Mergers often produced a similar effect of instant wealth for the owners of the businesses being acquired but a winners' curse for the acquirers as they struggled to achieve the synergies they and their advisers promised.

Derivatives, the instrument that the investment bankers like to call risk transformation, are not that at all. Risk cannot be transformed: it can only be spread. Risk transfer is a better description for an activity that can involve passing on overpriced assets from those in the know to those who should know better. The investment banks claim, and their clients accept, the principle of caveat emptor – buyer beware – as a health warning on their products, but the investment banks were too smart and too powerful for some clients.

Did Prices Remain High?

Investment banking products have segmented into two groups: commodity and value added. In the commodity areas such as equity and bond trading, plain vanilla futures and options and syndicated loans, prices are falling. These markets may eventually resemble the foreign exchange market, where no commission is paid and the bid–offer spread is very tight. But these traditional areas have been supplemented by new and exciting products, especially over-the-counter-derivatives where prices are protected by their complexity and opacity. Price protection also came from the use of basis point pricing, the investment banks' stairway to heaven. This brought them price increases in bull markets yet looked like price cutting because they were able to show reductions in the percentage rates charged. The investment banks' pricing basket contains many items. Viewed in the round, these prices were more complex and more price resistant than might be inferred from a superficial glance at commission rates and spreads in securities trading.

Do They Act Together?

There are some parts of the investment banking business, such as IPOs and areas of corporate advisory work, where historically the clients have not been price sensitive. They put a high value on the advice that they received and tended not to ask the investment banks to cut prices. When they did, the investment banks did their best to resist such pressure. As commercial enterprises with a mission to make money, they can scarcely be blamed for that. However, when competing amongst themselves for business, the leading group rarely cut prices and it has been suggested that the clustering of rates in the American IPO market pointed to implicit collusion. This impression was strengthened by the American investment banks' willingness to carry out identical IPO work for lower prices in other countries. Not spoiling the party is consistent with the investment banks' decade-long silence while they were mismanaging conflict of interest during the IPO boom years.

Is There a Cartel?

Pulling this together, a fair conclusion is that the industry is dominated by a few firms in influence, if not in market share. They achieved unusually high returns; even though the whole was greater than the sum of the parts, their output was patchy; and in certain products their prices remained higher than open competition would suggest. But, crucially, there is no evidence that the firms deliberately acted together to keep prices up and competitors out. In my opinion, there is no deliberate investment banking cartel in any significant part of the business.

But that is not the end of the story. There was no explicit collusion yet no one spoiled the party. The high returns and same old players lingered on and the banks were rarely held accountable for poor advice. It may not be a cartel, but what is it?

In economic theory there are three basic states of competition. Perfect competition exists where there are low barriers to entry, falling prices and many suppliers for customers to choose from. It does not appear to fit the investment banking industry as a whole, although it applies to a few product segments within fixed income and currency trading. The second state, monopoly, exists where there is only one dominant supplier. It exists in investment banking only for brief moments early in a new product's history before competitors replicate the product.

The third state is oligopoly, which occurs 'when a few firms dominate a market. Often they can together behave as if they were a single monopoly, perhaps by forming a cartel. They may collude informally, by preferring gentle non-price competition to a bloody price war. Because what one firm can do depends on what the other firms do, the behaviour of oligopolists is hard to predict. When they do compete on price, they may produce as much and charge as little as if they were in a market with perfect competition.'[33]

Other terms that are synonymous with oligopoly are 'monopolistic or imperfect competition', where 'there are fewer firms than in a perfectly competitive market and each can differentiate its products from the rest. These small differences form barriers to entry. As a result, firms can earn some excess profits, although not as much as a pure monopoly, without a new entrant being able to reduce prices through competition. Prices are higher and output lower than under perfect competition.'[34] In the period under review, this description seems to fit the case of investment banking best. Freeman & Co. have gone so far as to say that 'An "oligopoly" has emerged, with the top firms getting stronger and capturing a larger proportion of fees.'[35]

A senior financial services practitioner speaking to my MBA students summed it up very neatly: 'There is a lot of competition, you can't deny it. But is there good competition? I doubt it. There is a cartel of sorts out there. They quote cartel prices for merger work and IPOs. The oligarchy is protected by brand name and reputation. The top corporate names revert to Goldman Sachs, Merrill Lynch, Morgan Stanley and one or two others every time. There is so much comfort in choosing the big brand – especially if the deal goes wrong.'[36] It was a good summary: the investment banks used their power to protect their position and keep others out and the clients went along with it. This had the effect of raising barriers to entry and, in turn, protecting indifferent output from the full blast of open competition. Existing players and aspiring new entrants fought hard to win more business, but with price cutting taboo and ineffective they resorted to other less conventional means of competing.

The second half of this book will see how it was all done.

PART 3

What Really Goes On

7

The Edge

There is a paragraph in James B. Stewart's Wall Street classic *Den of Thieves* which says a lot about the investment banks' business methods in the 1980s. Stewart describes a conversation between Robert Freeman, head of arbitrage at Goldman Sachs, and another trader. Freeman reflects 'that when he was younger, he loved to go to Las Vegas to gamble. But now, he says, he doesn't like casino odds. "It's not fun anymore. I guess I've been in this business too long," he says. "I'm used to having an edge."'[1]

It's a telling comment. The odds in a casino are loaded in favour of the operator. Freeman preferred his own business where the odds favoured the trader. That's what Freeman meant by 'having an edge': the house always wins.

Nearly twenty years on, some things have changed, if not before Spitzer, Enron and Sarbanes-Oxley, then certainly afterwards. But although the investment banks have accepted that they have to police the new rules and keep to the old ones, they still have an edge that gives them a devastating advantage over other market users.

Wall Street's edge is knowledge and integration. The large investment banks know more than any other institution or organization about the world's economy. They know more than their clients, more than their smaller competitors, more than the central banks, more than Congress, more than Parliament, more than the Chancellor of the Exchequer and more than the Secretary of the United States Treasury.

Every line of market related business that is tradable, conceivable and legitimate – equities, bonds, derivatives, foreign exchange, commodities and mortgages – flows through their dealing rooms. They are giant stock exchanges with global reach and multi-product inventories. Through their asset management and retail investor arms they can sense the mood of savers before it translates into marketplace action. Through their broker-dealer businesses they have their fingers on the pulse of market movements as they happen, tracking price formation and customer flows. Through their corporate advisory departments they can learn of strategic changes in the way the business world is thinking. Through diverse group businesses such as consumer credit and insurance they are able to anticipate significant changes in the real economy.

Integration as practised by the world's big investment banks is what converts knowledge into the Edge. The veteran Wall Street analyst Jim Hanbury explains how this worked: 'In such an organization sales, research, trading, underwriting, advisory, asset management and brokerage are under one roof and the professionals work together smoothly. Some easy examples include analysts proposing candidates for M&A or financing; sales and trading informing bankers of client needs, bankers introducing clients to high net worth brokers and so on. In the great firms this generates a lot of revenues.'[2]

Following the global settlement of 2003, the link between research analysts and investment banking has been broken and more care is being taken to manage other conflicts of interest. But the integrated, diversified investment banks remain in an unbeatable position compared to other market users. Their superior market knowledge and power stack the odds in their favour. From their privileged vantage point, provided that compliance procedures are followed, they are uniquely placed and legally entitled to use this information for profit – and they do.

Not everyone agrees. When I was in the early stages of my research I explained the Edge to a top American fund manager. The breadth and depth of the investment banks' activities and their integration did not concern him because, as he put it, 'even though they have all the information, they don't join up the dots'. He thinks that the investment banks are not smart enough or sufficiently well organized to take advantage. He is a person whose views I respect and someone who knows the investment banks both as an institutional investor and as the head of an organization that had used them for corporate restructuring. I decided to look further.

The Traders

In the Flow

Trading is where the investment banks collect most of the revenues from the Edge. It has become a huge business for the investment banks. In 1980 when the American securities industry was still adjusting to the new era of negotiated commissions on equities, and had not yet developed fully alternative revenues, trading income was half that of commissions; twenty years later, at the top of the cycle, trading income was a third bigger than commissions.[3] Amongst the large investment banks, trading accounts for about half of group revenues at Lehman Brothers, Bear Stearns and Goldman Sachs, and about a quarter at Morgan Stanley and Merrill Lynch.

The trading advantage that comes from the Edge starts with market share. A typical leading firm might have over 10 per cent of the market in global equity underwritings, global debt issues and global IPOs, and slightly smaller but still significant market shares in secondary stocks and bonds trading, individual investor accounts, foreign exchange, over-the-counter derivatives and exchange-traded derivatives. They are in the flow and know what is going on within each product.

The Edge is sustained by the range of their activities. Equities, bonds, foreign exchange, derivatives, precious metals, oil, other commodities and property: the safe assumption to make is that if it is traded and legal, the investment banks are involved. World markets are working twenty-four hours a day and are increasingly interlinked. As a result of the breadth of their business they have a view of the world that is better than anyone else's. They trade more products than the stock exchanges; they are more real time than the central banks; they know more than their corporate clients, who have a narrower focus; and they know more than their investing clients.

Such timely knowledge is vital in trading businesses. Knowing what is happening or is about to happen ahead of the rest of the market is a priceless advantage. Making the most of that advantage requires skill and good organization on and off the trading floor.

A day on the floor in a typical trading business has a familiar pattern to it no matter what product is being traded. The dealers get to their desks at about 6 a.m. and, depending on their time zone, review European markets or Asian markets with their colleagues who work there. About an hour later there is a meeting at which the researchers give their views on the economic and company data expected that day and the salespeople exchange news and key information about what their clients are doing. Based on what they have heard, together with their personal reading of markets and what their individual contacts are saying, the firm's traders start to make the opening prices.

It's only a little after 7 a.m. and already the Edge has given the big investment bank an advantage over their clients and smaller competitors. On the basis of information collected from their global networks, and an informed knowledge of what clients might do, they have been able to position their books in readiness for the day.

The salespeople start to call their clients and once orders start to flow they get a feel for market direction. Every day is different in a trading room. As news breaks, order patterns emerge and moods change. Experienced people can tell whether the market is going up by the sound and body language of a trading room; they can smell it a mile off. The firm's traders are party to all this. They sit in the same room, listen to many of the same meetings, see many of the same internal message boards and hear the same messages over the squawk boxes as the sales staff who talk to clients. They will be able to anticipate client demand as it builds and accumulate the necessary positions – long or short – to enable business to be transacted profitably.

On the trading floor the Edge comes from sensing what the client-base is doing a moment before it becomes public knowledge and being able to do something about it. The higher the market share, the more the information flows in. Firms need to have good traders and good systems to convert the information to profit, but knowledge is a priceless weapon and the more of it the better. Their big market share is a virtuous circle for the largest firms. It puts them in the driving seat, they have the business to show other clients, they have the axe, and they are in the flow. And the more they are in the flow the more they know and the bigger the Edge becomes.

Customer flow is a nice unthreatening phrase but properly defined it takes on a more potent meaning. In the nineties 'Salomon and

Goldman, publicly boasted of exploiting their knowledge of the "customer flow". Translated this means that when a Salomon or a Goldman got wind of which way its customers were running, it often ran there too – and fast."[4] Analysts of the investment banks speak of 'the information they gain from looking at the flow going through their desk. The proprietary trading profits of the big investment banks are testimony to that.'[5]

In most countries, dealing ahead of client orders – known as front running – is illegal in equities and frowned on or forbidden in other products, but there are many legitimate ways to benefit from knowing the customers' intentions. Traders know from their experience and from what their analytics are telling them that a big deal in one stock will soon have knock-on consequences in others and can position their books accordingly. Traders can devise and implement structured derivative trades, make futures and options bets and run software programs that will alert them to arbitrage opportunities. It requires smart people, sophisticated information technology, great risk management skills and lots of capital, but it would not even get started without customer flow. The effects of joining the dots can be dramatic. When Goldman Sachs integrated its fixed income and equities sales, trading and research teams, the *Financial Times* reported that the new arrangements contributed to a 77 per cent rise in equity trading revenues in the first half of 2003–4.[6]

Risk management

What happens on the trading floor is only the tip of the iceberg. The real power of the Edge takes place in quiet meeting rooms, over video conferences or in front of computer screens in product managers' offices. In these places, the product heads at the investment banks gather with their risk managers to assess their firm's risk positions. Learning painful lessons from the stock market crash of 1987, the bond market collapse of 1994 and the emerging markets crisis of 1998, the large investment banks powered up their risk analytics and risk management departments and tightened their risk assessment structures.

Committees attended by all of the important business heads as well as the independent risk managers were set up, strengthened and empowered. Their role is described with reassuring words like 'monitoring excessive concentration', 'measurement, management and analysis of risk profile' and 'responsible risk management' in the annual reports and detailed financial filings made on Form 10-K (10Ks). Intelligent, responsible risk management is essential to the success of a modern investment bank and the existence of a comprehensive system of communication and committees shows shareholders that good corporate governance is in place. But good corporate governance cuts both ways: risk management means capturing profit as well as protecting against loss.

The descriptions of these committees make it very clear that the investment banks are joining up the dots. Morgan Stanley manages trading risk 'on a Company-wide basis, on a worldwide trading division level, and on an individual product basis'.[7] Bear Stearns described 'constant communication between trading department management and senior management concerning inventory positions and market risk profile', including 'formal reports of positions, profits and losses and certain trading strategies' to a committee 'which comprises senior managing directors from each trading department as well as the Risk Management Department'.[8] A committee at Lehman Brothers that includes the key business heads 'meets weekly and reviews all risk exposures, position concentrations and risk taking activities'. The company's Capital Markets Committee, which included the CEO, the global head of risk, the chief economist and strategist as well as the business heads, served 'to frame the company's risk opinion in the context of the global market environment'.[9] Merrill Lynch ensures that 'risk taking is consistent with business strategy, capital structure and current and anticipated market conditions'.[10]

At Goldman Sachs an interdisciplinary risk committee was established in 1995 after the firm lost money in the previous year's bond market collapse. The situation in the late nineties was described as follows: 'Every Wednesday at 7.30 a.m. New York time, the committee convenes by teleconference and examines all of the firm's major exposures, including the risks related to the market, individual operations, credit, new products and businesses, and the firm's reputation. Any trader wanting to put a substantial amount of the firm's capital at risk must defend his action before this group, explaining the rationale and proposed course of action. No one is exempt.'[11]

The recently retired head of risk at one of Goldman Sachs's competitors told me about similar meetings at his firm: 'The head of the investment bank chaired them. I attended along with the heads of fixed income, foreign exchange, equities and debt and various other business heads. We discussed the market view and the credit view. If there were two different opinions on any issue both sides would get a chance to state their case and everyone else would air their views. He wanted to know what it would cost us if the view was wrong and how much we could make if it was right. When it came to risk decisions, client considerations would never be allowed to justify taking unacceptable amounts of risk on to the bank's balance sheet. We drilled down to every single large position.'[12]

At the large investment banks these are extraordinarily powerful meetings. Seated round the table are people who have got to the top of their product speciality at the world's biggest financial players. These people know what they are doing and they know everything there is to know about their product area. They get together daily; they are not discussing the weather or the sports scores, they are discussing business threats and opportunities, 'anticipated market movements' to use one of their favourite phrases. These are real life, dynamic meetings not dull bureaucratic risk-control affairs. These are firms in a state of 'constant communication', as Bear Stearns put it, not just in the meetings but outside too, using the informal networks that the organizational structure develops. When a firm like Morgan Stanley writes in its Form 10-K of managing the business 'on a Company-wide basis, on a worldwide trading division basis, and on an individual product basis' it is referring to this constant sharing of information upwards, downwards, sideways and crossways. With the benefits of global communications, modern technology and a big market position, it is a heady brew. This is an industry taking a great deal of trouble to join up the dots at every conceivable permitted level.

Proprietary Trading

Money gets made in trading by taking a turn out of client business and from deliberately taking positions in the hope of making a profit. Both ways involve proprietary trading.

Lisa Endlich's insider–outsider account of Goldman Sachs published in 1999 shows how it worked in the nineties: 'Goldman Sachs's service to its clients over the years had yielded an enormous flow of business. Slowly it became clear that this flow was in itself a source of valuable market information, an early indication of developing trends. It would provide a real edge if the firm was willing to risk some of its own capital. This proprietary activity was seen as "leveraging the franchise" and an opportunity to take advantage of and supplement the firm's established client business . . . Because of the breadth and depth of its client relationships, the firm also had a unique window on global capital movements.'[13]

It's unusual to get such a full account: 'Proprietary trading went forward because it provides the firm with a sizable and diversified stream of revenue and can be complementary to its client businesses. When market conditions are inhospitable to underwriting and sales activities (for example in a bear market for bonds and stocks) proprietary trading can be a source of substantial profits for the firm . . . As Goldman Sachs provided clients with more innovative products and investment opportunities, it invested its own capital alongside them. Throughout the firm small businesses developed where specialized trading and investment skills and the ability to risk a certain amount of partnership capital gave the firm an edge.'[14] It's there again – that word 'edge' – although in the post-Spitzer era not many firms would have been quite so 'refreshingly candid' in their hours of interviews with Lisa Endlich.[15]

Proprietary trading went underground in 1998 at many firms: 'By the late 1990s, almost every investment bank on Wall Street had, to some degree, gotten into the game. Most had separate arbitrage desks, with traders specifically assigned to look for opportunities in every nook and cranny of the business.'[16] However, the Long-Term Capital Management crisis of that year persuaded many of the banks that specialist proprietary trading units were dangerous and they wound them down. Most dramatically, Citigroup's Sandy Weil, having just bought Salomon Brothers, kings of the trading jungle, ordered the closure of proprietary trading at the firm.

However, the closure of some arbitrage desks on Wall Street and ring fencing at others did not mean that proprietary trading went away: it is embedded into customer market-making by the very nature of the business. Whether in equities, bonds or commodities, derivatives or cash, proprietary and client trading are inextricably entwined.

Client trading depends on the bid–offer spread, the difference between the prices quoted to buyers and sellers. Where the price is $100 to a seller and $101 to a buyer the bid–offer spread is a dollar and market makers able to match up buyers and sellers would make a turn of one dollar. In reality life is rarely that simple. The bid–offer turn is usually much less than one per cent and in some markets, such as currency, there is often no turn at all. Market makers cannot rely on taking a turn out of matched customer orders and have to make their money by positioning their books long in a rising market and short in a falling market. But customers nearly always want to be the same way as the market, buying when things are going up and selling when they are falling. Therefore market makers have to get in position early, use derivatives to hedge their book or be so well informed and well capitalized that they can ride out the storm.

Any trader that can see the flow of customer business early has a great advantage. On the New York Stock Exchange, firms known as specialists – leading firms include Spear Leeds and Kellogg, owned by Goldman Sachs, and Bear Wagner, part owned by Bear Stearns – are responsible for ensuring smooth trading in shares. It is a controversial system of trading now being supplemented with electronic methods, and this may weaken the specialists' role. However they come from a position of strength as explained by Arthur Levitt, chairman of the SEC from 1993 to 2001: 'Specialists are in business for themselves and they often buy and sell shares for their own accounts. Unlike other types of auctioneers, the specialist is allowed to bid for shares while conducting the auction. If you think a specialist's ability to see incoming orders gives him a built-in advantage when trading for himself, you're right. It's like being in a card game in which only one of the players got to see everyone else's hand. Specialists exploit that advantage too: in late 2001, they were accounting for about 32 per cent of all the shares traded.'[17]

When market makers pre-position their books, the boundaries between customer facilitation, hedging and proprietary trading are fluid and difficult to define. At what point does loading up ahead of expected demand move from being client facilitation to taking a view on the firm's own account? When does leveraging up to play the yield curve because you know that's what your customers will do become a proprietary trade? No outsider, and perhaps no insider either, can really tell, making it very difficult to divide trading profits into customer and proprietary. A survey of a group of banks operating in London in 2003 found that several made no distinction in their management accounts between client and proprietary trading.[18] It was either an unimportant distinction or, more likely, it was just too difficult to separate out.

One side effect of the closure of the specialist arbitrage desks in the late nineties was to give shareholders the impression that proprietary trading had gone away. Investors like to hear this, for they regard it as a high risk and unreliable business. They would not give the investment banks a high share price if they thought that too much profit came from proprietary trading. The investment banks disclose that they do proprietary trading and admit that it is managed alongside client business, but they tuck such news away in quiet corners of the financial statements.

For example, Morgan Stanley admits that its 'institutional sales and trading activities are conducted through the integrated management of its client driven and proprietary transactions along with the hedging and financing of these positions. While sales and trading activities are generated by client order flow, the Company also takes proprietary positions based on expectations of future market movements'.[19] However, you have to look pretty hard to find this and other references to proprietary trading in Morgan Stanley's Form 10-K, a technical document that is heavy reading even for financial specialists. There was no explicit mention of proprietary trading in the glossy, more commonly used version of the annual report.[20] Morgan Stanley is not untypical. Every other large investment bank carries out proprietary trading, and every one gives a full disclosure, but rarely, if ever, in a prominent place in the financial reports.

Numbers are few and far between. The investment banks disclose value-at-risk data, which gives some clue as to the scale of activities; but everyone's model is slightly different and it is not possible to estimate what profits the stated value-at-risk might generate. The average daily value-at-risk of the large investment banks varied in 2003 from, for example, $15m at Bear Stearns to $58m at Goldman Sachs. As Goldman Sachs said, 'This means that there is a 1 in 20 chance that daily trading net revenues will fall below the expected daily trading net revenue by an amount at least as large as the reported value-at-risk.'[21] Even with annual trading revenues of over $10 billion, this is a far from negligible risk but there is some protection from shareholders' equity, which is several hundred times value-at-risk – and of course from the Edge, which substantially reduces the real risk.

In the absence of profit numbers, qualitative comments are made about proprietary trading and, like Lehman's in 2002, annual reports tend to play down the activity: 'Instead of using a high percentage of the firm's capital for proprietary trading, we held strong to our well-defined risk appetite and remained committed to our customer flow business model.'[22] Other firms liked to under-emphasize this business: 'To a lesser degree, Merrill Lynch also maintains proprietary trading inventory in seeking to profit from existing or projected market opportunities.'[23] Because most proprietary trading actually occurs as an integral part of customer trading, Goldman Sachs, believed to be the most aggressive proprietary traders amongst the large investment banks, is able to state truthfully that equities arbitrage 'is the only purely proprietary business we are in'.[24] However, a former member of the management committee at one of these firms told me: 'The investment banks have made a fortune from proprietary trading, especially in fixed income and mortgage-backed securities. A desk of about twenty-five people gave us 60 per cent of group profits one year.'[25]

The embedded nature of proprietary trading is illustrated by the fact that the top investment banks rarely have a designated head of proprietary trading. Within each product area proprietary and customer business are so mutually dependent that they are seamless and are often carried out by the same people. A good example of this is the career of Lloyd Blankfein, the president, chief operating officer and perhaps chief executive designate of Goldman Sachs: 'Mr

Blankfein grew up in one of the more carnivorous and anti-social corners of Wall Street. He makes money for clients but it is as a manager and proprietary trader betting the firm's own capital that Mr Blankfein really made his name.'[26]

Where specialist proprietary trading desks did still exist, mainly in fixed income, currency and commodity trading, proprietary and customer traders often sat together on dealing floors; they saw and heard all that went on. In some cases they might even have had access to the order routing systems that displayed the progress of client orders and they could speak to the firms' customer-facing staff, including researchers, facilitation traders and salespeople. In the post-Spitzer clean-up, many firms tackled the conflict of interest issues that arose from integrating customer-facing and proprietary trading staff by separating the two sides. In equities it is now rare for specialist proprietary traders to sit with market makers who are working for customers (although, as we have already discussed, market makers themselves carry out proprietary trading as part of their function).

Some banks have gone even further. Morgan Stanley, for example, ring-fenced its bond analysts from the rest of the trading floor and cut the link between their pay and the traders' results. It is a praiseworthy initiative, although clients of the firm might well wonder what Morgan Stanley's bond analysts had been up to under the old arrangements: working for them or helping the traders?[27]

An advertisement placed in the financial press in 2004 by an agency broker spelled out the kind of games that are possible: 'Not done. Proprietary trading/Front Running/Back Room Dealing/Whispers/ Smoke and Mirrors/ Preferential Treatment/Conflicted interests/ Secret handshakes/Ethical Shenanigans/Trading Against Our Clients' Order Flow'.[28] In a world inhabited by hundreds of thousands of investment bankers and securities professionals, inside trading and front running client orders are bound to occur occasionally, but there really is no need. For a skilled trader with adequate capital and good information technology, the Edge is enough to guarantee success.

Henry Kaufman had a good opportunity to understand trading businesses for himself during his great years at Salomon Brothers. The source of the profits in some areas remained a mystery: 'Is it from making markets for customers? Or is it from proprietary trading? No outsider really knows. According to the principal market makers in financial derivatives, they are in the business of helping their clients meet their perceived needs for risk management products. While admitting that much of their profitability stems from that function, they also concede that their traders take sizeable positions for the institution's own account – whether the institution is a bank, securities firm, insurance company or finance company. Few dealers have revealed precisely how much of their profits come from market making activities and how much from proprietary trading.'[29]

In the absence of disclosure we have to try to work it out for ourselves. There are some clues in our earlier discussion of margins. Equities, a product area thought to be under pressure, achieved margins of 60 per cent in 2000. These margins have to come from somewhere and with falling commissions and tightening spreads, straightforward customer business is unlikely to be the whole answer. That leaves IPOs, certainly a factor at the top of the cycle, and derivatives, including proprietary trading, a highly significant and profitable activity that forms an accepted and legal part of an investment bank's business.

It depends crucially on the Edge, that combination of power, knowledge and integration that gives the investment banks a huge advantage over other market participants. As one managing director at Morgan Stanley told me: 'There is nothing we know nothing about. We make very few mistakes.'[30] They have learned how to use that information profitably and – to the best of my knowledge and in most cases – legally, and it gives them a great advantage when they trade. Later chapters will reveal who is on the other side of those trades.

The Investment Bankers

Whilst the term was originally used in a trading context, the Edge crops up in other areas of the top investment banks. It is particularly powerful in corporate finance, where, despite the constraints of client confidentiality and insider trading laws, the familiar combination of market share (typically over 30 per cent in global mergers and acquisitions – the numbers add up to more than one hundred because of the use of multiple advisers), knowledge and integration give the big banks a great advantage.

The investment banks are party to dozens of intimate, private discussions every day and they are the only institutions in the world that are in this position. A corporation's lead-relationship bank knows what it is planning to do or contemplating long before it becomes public knowledge. Lead-investment banks become part of the client CEO's inner circle and are involved in strategic discussions about key issues such as acquisitions, disposals and funding. Multiplied two hundred times over to represent an investment bank's typical big company client list, there are very few sectors of the global economy, and very few parts of the developed world, where the leading investment banks do not have their finger on the corporate pulse.

They know what's for sale and who the buyers might be. They know corporates' funding needs and where assets are cheap or dear. The bankers get to learn very quickly how business is going on a day-to-day basis: retail sales, stock levels, demand for automobiles, semi-conductor inventories are all likely to be in the investment banks' knowledge base. It becomes very easy to build up a picture of the world economy very early with this kind of access.

Investment bankers at the big firms carry in their heads the actions – planned, possible and probable – of many clients. I asked one senior banker whether they used this information to join up the dots: 'In consolidated industries where clients are looking at similar strategies it is a business imperative. The top bankers in, say, telecommunication probably have six of the top eight telcos as clients. How can they possibly serve one and not let that affect their advice to the others? It is a human impossibility. The head of a global industry group like Autos does business with Daimler, Chrysler, Ford and countless others. The clients expect it. They pay you to be informed about what their competition is doing. How can you not join up the dots?'[31]

They know what products to pitch and where to pitch them. Client knowledge is shared amongst those employees who are 'the right side of the wall' and not involved in activities where knowing too much might make them guilty of inside trading. The aim is to ensure that the investment bank takes every opportunity to get revenue from the client. It might be structuring a complex derivative to solve a pension fund problem, arranging a trade sale for a client's unwanted small business in Asia or refinancing a property portfolio: nothing must be missed.

The Edge was taken a stage further in the nineties when legislative changes allowed the commercial banks into investment banking and lending products became tied up with the investment banking and broking bundle. Integration was now complete: investment banking and securities; commercial and investment banking; proprietary and customer trading, all joined together in one powerful machine.

Banks were able to make this count. In May 2001, according to reports, Salomon was co-lead manager with J. P. Morgan in a prestigious $12 billion bond offering for WorldCom, the third largest ever. WorldCom gave Salomon the co-lead role provided that Citigroup committed at least $800 million to a line of credit that WorldCom was trying to refinance. In another example, according to a court-appointed bankruptcy examiner, CSFB's close co-operation with Enron on investment banking matters gave it a better insight into Enron's true condition. The examiner said that CSFB knew that Enron carried about $4.5 billion of debt that was not shown on the balance sheet and that it needed cash. The bank also knew that many of Enron's overseas assets were worth less than advertised because it was actively trying to find a buyer for them. The report found that CSFB may have used its knowledge of Enron's poor financial condition to reduce its exposure at the expense of other investors. While its equity analyst on Enron continued to recommend the stock to clients, CSFB appeared to be following the advice of an internal note by its fixed income analyst and reduced its credit exposure to Enron from over $600 million to less than $200 million. CSFB objected to the examiner's findings.[32]

The dream scenario is the Triple Play where one bank provides private equity funding; advises on mergers and acquisitions; and arranges debt financing. This is why some investment banks pop up as private equity backers whenever there is a prospect of corporate action.[33]

Joining the Dots

The Edge sustains the investment banks' profits and enables them to regenerate. Because they are in the know they can think, look and act smarter than clients, trading counterparties and any competitors in a less privileged position. It is difficult to quantify the effects. In the same way that proprietary trading is inevitably embedded into customer market making, the integration of product areas is so much part of the investment banks' fabric that it is impossible to disentangle. A senior executive at a bulge-bracket firm told me that cross-selling, the explicit sale of one department's products by another department, accounted for about 20 per cent of investment banking revenues. But integration is about much more than cross-selling. As Josef Ackermann, chief of Deutsche Bank, remarked when appointing the heads of corporate finance and sales and trading to co-manage the firm's investment banking division, 'The alignment of complementary businesses and streamlining of the bank's management structure will unlock revenue and cost synergies.'[34] The revenues from integration flow thick and fast and the modern investment bank would not exist without them.

These benefits are achieved perfectly legally. Blatant insider trading and front running are not significant to the industry's profits and the large majority of investment banks and brokers respect client confidentiality and the law. But there is an awful lot of information flying around the integrated firms and news of what is going on seeps along the corridors of the tightest of organizations.

This helps to explain why share prices nearly always move in advance of significant corporate action. Between 1995 and 2002, the average run-up in a target's share price in the month before the announcement was 4.1 per cent in the UK, 10.1 per cent in Europe and 11.3 per cent in the USA.[35] Leaks could have come from a variety of sources: company executives in the know or any of the many professional advisers involved, whether investment banker, management consultant, lawyers, auditor or public relations experts. Some of these cases were coincidental, others were triggered by legitimate pre-bid market activity; but it is difficult to avoid the conclusion that someone, somewhere, was using the Edge.

8

Voodoo Management

At the end of 2002, in the depths of the Spitzer scandals, *The Economist* dubbed the investment banks 'among the worst managed institutions on the planet'. Surprisingly, this damning verdict was not reached because of their breaches of compliance laws and regulations but 'because they are built on a loose confederation of franchises and outsize egos'.[1]

It is certainly true that investment banks and investment banking people are difficult to manage. The industry has always attracted free spirited, independent minded individuals who think they know best. Managers have to know when to stand up to their stars and when to let them have their own way, when to back off and allow entrepreneurship its head, and when to turn every stone. When do you leave a Joseph Jett or a Nick Leeson to do their own thing because their results are great, and when do you dig up the drains because you smell a rat? Risk taking is an essential part of the business and managers have to create an environment where people take necessary risks without being reckless. It is an instinctive thing. A reason that firms such as GE, generally acclaimed as well managed in the other financial and industrial fields where they operate, had difficulties with investment banking is that it appears not to follow normal business rules. Management in any business is an art not a science; in investment banking it is voodoo art.

The task has been made harder by the expansion of the industry over the past thirty years. The end result of globalization, scale and new products was that a set of organizations moved from being straightforward agency businesses in 1975 into the most complex in the world to manage. Firms changed from stable partnerships in which all the principals knew each other into shifting sprawling corporations where the average stay was less than three years and where the managing directors might not even know each other's names.

As they expanded and became more global the investment banks had to take management more and more seriously. It became a highly valued discipline, not something that the top producers did in their spare time between seeing clients. Structure, delegation and co-ordination were required to cope with new products, new geographies and new people. In the nineties alone the number working in the securities industry doubled. People were no longer working in isolation; they became part of global teams that needed managing and organizing. Development programmes were set up to teach new skills and broaden out careers. Culture became a buzz word. Traditional value statements like J. P. Morgan's 'first class business in a first class way' were dusted off and revived, and firms without a history employed slick agencies and smart copywriters to create one.

Investment banking people remained difficult to handle and some firms never mastered the art. But during recent years the outsize egos referred to by *The Economist* have been brought under increased control. The super-bulge firms of Goldman Sachs, Merrill Lynch and Morgan Stanley, despite the odd blip, strengthened their corporate franchises by generally managing their star people on the organization's terms without stifling creativity. Others, for example Bear Stearns, found ways to carry partnership values over into a corporate world resisting the star culture and sticking stubbornly to their principles[2].

Creating a team ethos is often the key to success as Lehman Brothers, to name but one, has shown. Richard Fuld, the firm's chairman and CEO, explains: 'I want my people to be strong individuals as well as part of a team. And that's a rare balance.' He requires what he calls a 'come in at 6 o'clock in the morning and I will go home when I'm finished mentality'. Employee stock ownership has risen from 4 per cent when the firm went public in 1994 to 30 per cent, a high proportion that encourages people to act like owners. According to Fuld, it helps to foster an attitude that says 'Is there a place where I can do my business, are there people with whom I can interact during the day and call them friends? Is this a place where I can learn, is this a place where I can develop to the next level? Because if I am going to be spending 12 to 15 hours a day in this place, it's got to be more than just a pay check on Friday afternoon.'[3] What Lehman, Bear, Merrill, Morgan Stanley and Goldman learned, others have also discovered.

The investment banks might once have been the worst managed institutions on the planet, but not now, at least not in the way that *The Economist* meant. For many years they have been getting better and better at running their own business. Ethical values and standards often slipped but solid fundamental management in the areas of risk, product development and cost control were important factors in keeping the returns from investment banking so high.

Risk Management

Risk management skills simply had to improve as the stakes rose during the capital markets boom of the late twentieth century. Institutional investors drove the investment banks into using more and more risk capital. On the one hand they wanted to change their portfolios instantly, buying and selling huge blocks of stock, currency and bonds and demanding that the banks put up more and more capital to trade with them. On the other hand by cutting commission rates and squeezing market-making spreads they drove the investment banks to commit more and more capital to proprietary trading in order to keep up profits. This combination of increased customer demands and more own-account trading meant that the amount of capital tied up in the American securities business was more than twenty times bigger in 2003 than it had been in 1980 and totalled $157 billion stretching across numerous currencies and asset classes.

Managing this huge sum had to move off the back of the envelope as the investment banks discovered during a steep and painful learning curve. It was a continuous process but there were four key events: the equity market crash of 1987; the bond market slump of 1994; the emerging markets crisis of 1998 and the millennium crash.

The contrast between the first and last of these episodes shows how far the investment banks had come. If anything, business conditions were worse in the millennium crash than they had been in and around 1987. Share indices and market turnover fell further and capital markets activity – mergers and acquisitions and share offerings – remained depressed for longer; but by this time the investment banks had learned how to cut costs, manage risk and grow revenues in adversity, and it showed in the results. Whereas it was five years after the crash of 1987 before the industry's peak profits were next beaten, this time recovery was under way after two years.

The equity market crash of 1987 shocked those of us who were there, but looking back it now seems like a storm in a tea cup. It was triggered when US interest rates rose for the first time in three years and when equity prices were stretched after a five-year bull market. For a few months, equity investors were slow to realize that the interest rate cycle had turned, but then on 19 October panic set in. Wall Street and London fell by 20 per cent inside a day and stock markets throughout Continental Europe, Asia and Latin America plunged in sympathy.

It was the first crash in the modern age of investment banking. There was wave after wave of computer generated selling. Arbitrageurs were learning how to play the futures market, betting with futures that the market would go down and then selling shares to ensure that it did. There was chaos in New York: 'There were trading breakdowns in all markets related to stock. The volume of sellers was overwhelming . . . Telephone lights were flashing everywhere, with most seeming to go unanswered. Many of the young traders and salespeople were so awestruck by what was happening that they didn't know what to do. It was mostly the older and more experienced people who manned the phones in an attempt to relate information to clients and take orders, hoping that at least some of them would be executed. It was a tumultuous scene.'[4] London was little better: 'We lost the thread. The Monday was unreal, we had some awful options positions. I was told about them very early in the day and we then worked furiously trying to place stock to ease the situation. The whole day was a blur to me. It got worse on the Tuesday, settled down for a bit and then the real nasties started to emerge.'[5]

For most investors the panic lasted only a few days. Share prices and stock market turnover recovered quickly and although they wobbled again in 1990 ahead of the 1991 recession, for investors October 1987 looked like a correction not a crash.

Not so for the investment banks. The three years after the crash were the worst in modern investment banking history and 1990 was the only loss-making year for the American securities industry in the last thirty. UK Stock Exchange firms lost £570 million in the fifteen months after October 1987, bringing to an end many of the grand plans laid in Big Bang the previous year. In America and Britain it was evident that risk management had not kept up with the increased scale and complexity of the industry, and many doubted that it ever could. The commercial banks, in particular, concluded that the business was unmanageable and some, like Citibank, Security Pacific and Midland Bank, packed up their investment banking tents and left London. Four prominent American firms, L. F. Rothschild, Drexel Burnham Lambert, Thomas McKinnon and E. F. Hutton, disappeared from Wall Street, and others were kept alive only after parental support totalling $3½ billion.[6] The top investment banks, however, had no intention of quitting, but they went forward more cautiously now, expanding slowly overseas and being risk aware throughout their business.

As markets recovered in the early nineties, so did the investment banks' profits and confidence. The years 1991, 1992 and 1993 broke previous records for American securities firms' profits and the industry appeared to have recovered its poise. But there was a nasty surprise in store and the bond market crash of 1994 underlined the lessons of 1987–91. Again, it was a rise in interest rates that did the damage, this time in February 1994 when the Federal Reserve stunned markets by raising short term interest rates for the first time in five years. Bond markets took fright – US Government thirty-year Treasury bonds fell an incredible 16 per cent in three months – as investors worldwide assumed that interest rates were on the turn.

Markets fell more than the Federal Reserve and the investment banks had expected and the damage was widespread. Three large hedge funds – Omega Partners, Tiger Management and Steinhardt Partners – lost billions; the life insurance industry lost about $50 billion and property and casualty insurers lost $20 billion. The investment banks were also hit very hard, Bankers Trust recording its first ever loss and Salomon Brothers losing $371 million in the first half of 1994.[7] The major 'risk-taking' firms were in loss for the second year in five and this prompted a further reassessment of how risk should be managed.[8]

Now the message really got home. International markets were clearly more closely connected than ever before: 'implosions in seemingly unrelated markets were reverberating in the US Treasury bond market . . . Such disparate developments as a slide in European bonds, news of trading losses at Bankers Trust, the collapse of Askin Capital Management, a hedge fund that specialized in mortgage trades, and the assassination of Mexico's leading presidential contender all accentuated the slide in US Treasuries that had begun with Greenspan's modest adjustment.'[9]

Unless the investment banks got their risk management skills up to speed to cope with this new interlinked world they would surely die. Existing practices suddenly seemed archaic: 'Traders for the most part decided on their own when to close positions down. Management rarely intervened. Trading managers had sat on the desks for which they were responsible and were kept apprised of the thinking and actions of those who reported to them. Top management was kept informed through reports and informal channels of communication. It was a system that until now had worked well. The level of trust and comfort between staff and management was high and until 1994 there seemed to be little need for a more formal approach.'[10]

The top investment banks had moved increasingly towards formal risk monitoring as trading became a bigger part of their business, but events in 1994 brought another step change in their efforts. Independent risk departments reporting to central management rather than to business heads were beefed up. Risk awareness had increased after the equity market crisis of 1987 but before 1994 it was not yet engraved in the culture and risk management was still seen as a low status, bureaucratic and not very well paid occupation. After 1994, and particularly after the unsupervised activities of 'rogue trader' Nick Leeson brought down Barings, the venerable British investment bank, in 1995, it was taken more seriously. Risk departments increased in size, were staffed by better qualified and better paid people and became more influential.

The IT revolution of the nineties helped this new commitment. The internet permitted the real-time data downloads that were needed to feed the risk models. Better networking, more processing power at lower cost and sophisticated software opened up new possibilities. The effect was startling: 'At the push of a button, management can aggregate the firm's market and credit risks across the entire organization at any point during the day. Computers make all this possible; no longer is risk assessed with a series of phone calls and a quick tally on a scratch pad.'[11]

At the same time as risk management procedures became more structured, value-at-risk (VAR) was adopted as the industry's risk modelling tool. VAR is based on a paper called 'Portfolio Selection' published in the *Journal of Finance* in 1952 by Professor Harry Markowitz, which explored how investors could construct portfolios in order to optimize expected returns for a given level of risk. These techniques were taken up by asset managers, but it was not until 1993, when the Group of Thirty coined the term value-at-risk in a report on risk management for derivatives dealers, that they spread to investment banks. Then in 1994, the year the bond market crash pushed risk further up management's agenda, J. P. Morgan launched its free RiskMetrics service, which further promoted the use of VAR. The following year the Basle Committee on Banking Supervision based its market risk capital requirements for banks on VAR and over the next year or two VAR became the industry standard for risk management in financial institutions, corporate treasuries, commodities firms and energy traders.[12]

As we saw in the previous chapter, VAR is a statistical technique to measure market risk. It simulates how a portfolio will behave based on historical changes in market prices and risk sensitivities. The number that the model produces is the potential loss in a portfolio over a defined period of time with a specified confidence level. For example, an investment bank reporting 'Daily VAR of $20 million to 95 per cent confidence' is saying that its models predict a 5 per cent chance that daily trading revenues will fall below expected levels by at least $20 million. VAR is not foolproof but it did provide the investment banks with a number that managers could focus on. Around it they were able to put in place a structure of committees and teams of risk experts to monitor and manage risk. For the first time since 1987 the investment banks appeared to be in control of the risks that they were running.

This sense of security was shaken in September 1998, the month 'when genius failed' and Long-Term Capital Management, a high profile hedge fund, collapsed. The firm had about $5 billion of its own capital and borrowed getting on for $100 billion to leverage its trades. Under the leadership of John Meriwether, still then a legend for his time at Salomon Brothers, and with the expertise of a group of highly qualified arbitrageurs, professors and two Nobel Prize winners, the fund had a four-year winning streak of 40 per cent per annum and its models seemed infallible. However, the Russian financial default in the summer of 1998 set off a train of events that pushed market prices beyond what the firm's models had predicted. In August 1998 it was forced to close its positions, pushing prices even further out of line. VAR predictions were exceeded and the fund was insolvent. Such was Long-Term Capital Management's leverage – remember it had borrowed twenty times the firm's capital to invest in markets – that the Federal Reserve stepped in, believing that its failure would pose a systemic risk to the international financial system.

Most investment banks were exposed to LTCM but they managed to limit their direct losses by nifty footwork on the trading floor. The dislocation in markets that had triggered LTCM's problems hurt the investment banks too, but in most cases risk management worked well. Goldman Sachs, for example, managed to increase its revenues by $1 billion and maintain profits in 1998. Most securities firms and investment banks saw profits down by about a fifth in 1998 but some fared worse, including CSFB, which had gambled heavily on the Russian economy and other emerging markets and had to write off $1.3 billion.

The fate of CSFB and LTCM reminded the investment banks of the limitations of VAR. Models that tell you what happens if markets and stock prices behave as they have done in the past do not tell you what will happen if they behave in a different way in future. Many senior investment bankers had lost money personally in Long-Term Capital Management and they had been called into discussions with senior officials from the Federal Reserve and other government agencies to consider how to avert a meltdown in the capital markets. It was not surprising that they went back to their firms and focused even harder on risk management in their own businesses. This attention ensured that systems were in place to enable the investment banks to withstand the market turbulence of 2000–2002.

Product Development

Equal agility is required in product innovation in a business where products can change so quickly that firms need to 'shift, balance and turn on a dime'.[13] The lead time on a new product before competitors replicate it and squeeze the margins can be measured in days or weeks. A managing director at Goldman Sachs phrased the challenge as follows: 'It's not enough to be up with where the crowd is now. You have to work out what the clients will need in a month's time, a year's time and get ready to be there.'[14]

Anyone who doubts how fast the investment banking industry moves should take a look at any one of the standard books on the profession written a few years ago, such as *Investment Banking: A Tale of Three Cities* by Samuel L. Hayes and Philip M. Hubbard, published by Harvard Business School Press in 1990.[15] It is a very good book, both scholarly and readable, and is a complete account of the investment banking scene of that era. But to modern readers what is missing is nearly as interesting as what is there.

Aside from the fact 'the Golden Triangle of the investment banking industry: London, New York and Tokyo' now looks more like a Golden Apple after the demise of Tokyo and the swallowing-up of London's investment banks by the Americans, it is striking that so many of today's mainstream products scarcely merited a mention in 1990. The book's index contains no references to derivatives, portfolio or programme trading, structured finance, special purpose entities or options. Securitization features only five times; futures and swaps appear once, and there is neither sight nor sound of the term 'conflict of interest'. It is not that the book is wrong; these items were passed over because in 1990 they scarcely existed.

The investment banks are not always responsible for inventing the new products, but they are very quick to seize hold of and to adapt new ideas. Thus index futures opened up basket trading first as a defensive hedging tool, later as a source of arbitrage profit. Securitization spread from mortgages to anything you care to name: stadium receipts, music royalties, credit cards. Single-currency swaps led to structured notes linking many different currencies together, and then off balance sheet vehicles were created to hide them from prying eyes. Once the margin had gone from interest rate and currency swaps, the banks came up with credit swaps; no doubt the rocket scientists on Wall Street are already hard on the trail of the next hot product.

Within a space of twenty years whole new industries were invented, matured, and in some cases exited. Private equity first became a big business during the leveraged buy-out movement of the eighties. Firms such as Kohlberg Kravis & Roberts, Hicks Muse Tate and the Blackstone Group became major players on Wall Street. At the peak of the internet bubble in 2000 over $150 billion of private equity was raised and invested from institutional investors and state pension funds. In 2003 there were twenty-four private equity deals of over $1 billion in the USA, and six of the world's ten largest deals were in Europe. As the market recovered further into 2005, private equity firms and funds (in some cases owned by the investment banks) emerged as the driving force behind much corporate activity. Some of the independent private equity houses even encroached on the investment banks' territory, initiating IPOs, buy outs and mergers. But this threat was insignificant compared to the revenues private equity generated for the investment banks: Buy outs needed funding; revenues needed hedging and exit strategies needed implementing, all of which led to business for the investment banks.

For the moment at least, private equity is a hot area, but the banks are ruthless switchers of resources. They are committed to a product for only as long as it is profitable. Equity broking, the activity that helped make the nineties such a bonanza, offered less potential in the bear market and the investment banks stripped it down. A UK investment banker back from a fact finding trip on Wall Street in the summer of 2004 found that 'the big brokers are exiting the customer care business as fast as they can. Sure, they want the trading flow but spreads are so thin and IPOs so few and far between that they are cutting back on client service. They just don't think it's worth it any more.'[16] The head of equities at one bulge-bracket firm confirmed that 'it's all about cutting costs fast enough to stay in the game. It was all about getting volume; now it's all about margin, making sure there is one.'[17]

When equity revenues dried up the investment banks quickly switched to fixed income, which grew from being a third of profits in 2000 to two-thirds in 2002. They were helped by favourable market conditions. As interest rates fell to their lowest levels since the 1960s, corporate treasurers rushed to borrow money and to refinance debt at low interest rates. The investment banks were there in a flash, pitching new bond and bond derivatives issues and selling them to fund managers. The yield curve was steep and the proprietary trading departments were able to borrow short, invest long and pick up a huge interest carry. Fixed income people, out of the limelight during the equities bull market, suddenly found themselves the flavour of the month and gained in power, influence and compensation: 'Bond traders who not long ago were considered second class citizens by their colleagues in investment banking and equities were now back on top of the social pile.'[18]

The growth of the hedge fund industry also illustrates the investment banks' ability to latch on to new trends and work up a business around them. By 2003 hedge funds accounted for $21 billion of the investment banking industry's global revenues, 13 per cent of the total; ten years before, they were fringe players in the financial services industry and many brokers were wary of them.[19]

Fund managers in this new segment required a different kind of service from their brokers and in the twinkling of an eye special teams were created to pass on every price movement or news item that might be significant. Then there are special clearing and settling arrangements to be provided, especially securities custody, stock borrowing and lending. The investment banks are even prepared to provide financing if the hedge fund wants to borrow money to invest and to introduce new hedge funds to potential backers. The investment banks created a new industry, prime brokerage, to supply these needs, offering them a new profit centre and a new way of cementing the relationship with these commission-paying clients. Needless to say, the sector is dominated by the super bulge, especially in Europe, where Goldman Sachs and Morgan Stanley had over two-thirds of the market between them at the beginning of the century.

Equal flexibility is required to cope with swings in the balance of economic power. No sooner had they got used to the idea that China, not Japan, was the Asian honey pot than the Tiger markets collapsed in 1997. Companies that had spent years chasing a seat on the Tokyo Stock Exchange, and had then switched their attention to Shanghai, swiftly de-emphasized and then had to re-emphasize the entire region. Eastern Europe came and went like the Berlin Wall, and India's jewel in the crown remains an alluring prospect. Trying to steer a consistent business course between these constantly shifting sands requires concentration, agility and great management.

The regenerative and innovative qualities of the investment banks are the most admirable things about them. In 1975, in the last days of fixed commission on the New York Stock Exchange, they made their money from agency commissions, a bit of underwriting and, if anyone asked for help, from mergers and acquisitions advice. Thirty years on it is tooth and claw capitalism in which the investment banks do not merely facilitate capital markets activity, they frequently initiate it. Bond markets have moved from being a sleepy backwater into a casino; equity broking is merely a loss leader for trading and derivatives, and risk positions that are as big as the GDP of some countries are routinely put on. The investment banks have ridden every wave, quick to learn, quick to invent and quick to adapt to change. Whether you attribute it to market forces or rampant greed, to risk transformation or risk transfer, the effect is powerful and – even to a sceptic – rather impressive.

Cost Control

Learning how to manage their cost base has been a major factor in the investment banks' strong performance in recent years. Compensation is not just the biggest variable cost under management's control; it is the *only* significant variable cost. For the large investment banks, it forms 65 per cent of the total cost base, and even more at the top of the cycle when the pressure to retain staff is greater. Out of the remaining 35 per cent of costs, communications, IT, premises and execution charges are over 5 per cent each and are not truly variable. That leaves marketing, travel and entertainment as the soft targets and they are always first in the firing line: fly coach not business; take the subway not the limo; can the night at the opera and take the clients bowling; let the staff buy their own copies of the *Wall Street Journal* and *Financial Times*. Every firm does it when times get tough and, like Ace Greenberg's paper clips, it sends the right message. But there's no escaping the reality: people are not just the investment banks' greatest assets: they are their greatest costs too.

Most firms found themselves paying out more than they wanted during the internet bubble. Between 1997 and 2000 the top firms increased headcount by a third, yet compensation nearly doubled, outstripping even the growth in revenues.[20] This left them with the serious problem of too many people and not enough revenues when the markets collapsed. The dewy-eyed promises of career development and commitment for life that were made to new hires over the recruitment breakfast table were quickly forgotten and retrenchment was inevitable. Two firms stand out for the effectiveness of their cost cutting: Merrill Lynch and Credit Suisse First Boston.

Stan O'Neal became Merrill Lynch's CEO in December 2002. He had begun his career at General Motors but after he joined Merrill Lynch he ran Capital Markets, Global Markets and Investment Banking, and Private Clients and served as president, chief financial officer and chief operating officer. When he became CEO he knew exactly where to find the fat.

Pay and expenses were so out of control that the company had only made $200 million in profits from underwriting securities and advising on deals during 2000, the last year of the boom. O'Neal said: 'The costs were moving at such a rapid pace that they were going to overwhelm the speed at which the revenues were moving and the revenues were moving at a pace that we had never seen before. Unless you postulated that somehow the costs would come down or that revenues would continue to grow at that rate or accelerate, it wasn't hard to figure out that you had a problem – unless you wanted to sit around and hope that something would change and that's not part of my make-up.'

Although O'Neal distanced himself from press reports that made him look like 'some sort of Quasimodo, prowling around the dungeons of Merrill Lynch torturing costs out of the system', headcount was the crux of the problem and it had to be gripped. The number of employees was cut from 71,600 in 2000 to 50,900 in 2002, a decline of nearly 30 per cent. In contrast to the soft approach of earlier culls, when managers had met headcount quotas by firing junior employees, O'Neal went after Merrill Lynch's big earners. He figured that if he offered blanket redundancy terms that included honouring deferred compensation, shares and share option schemes, enough heavy earners would accept to make a real difference to the cost base. O'Neal was confident that the lack of viable alternative employment elsewhere in the beleaguered financial services industry would keep enough top people to protect revenues. He called it just right. Yesterday's stars like Henry Blodgett, the one-time internet king, were allowed to go, as were those in other bloated sectors such as telecommunications, but most of the top bankers and traders who the firm wanted to keep stayed on. Annual savings from the job cuts was $2.2 billion, almost half of which came from just 6 per cent of the jobs. Of 68 top executives in 2001 there were just 42 at the end of 2003.[21]

The firm took a $2.2 billion restructuring charge in 2001 and the compensation bill tumbled from nearly $14 billion in 2000 to $9 billion in 2002. Although O'Neal later made conciliatory noises – 'To be frank we probably de-emphasized the investment banking business more than I would have liked'[22] – the firm's revenue earning potential was scarcely affected by the 25 per cent cut in investment banking jobs. Merrill's CFO Ahmass Fakahany calculates that if no action had been taken, the company would have lost $3 billion in 2002 compared with its actual profits of $2.4 billion.

The second great cost-cutting story was that achieved by John Mack – Mack the Knife – at CSFB. Mack had been in charge of Morgan Stanley, had set up the merger with Dean Witter in 1997, and had been President and Chief Operating Officer of the merged firm for three years but then lost out in a power struggle and left in March 2001.

Three months later he joined CSFB, which had fallen from grace since the days in the mid eighties when it ranked alongside Morgan

Stanley as king of the investment banking hill. Losses, scandals, the Credit Suisse rescue and defections had taken their toll. There was a revival from the mid nineties as Allen Wheat, a former Bankers Trust derivatives chief, built the structured finance derivatives business, Credit Suisse Financial Products, that at times earned more than the rest of the Credit Suisse group combined. The profits were used to rebuild investment banking. Key hires included Frank Quattrone, America's most famous internet banker, and by 2000 the firm seemed to be riding high again with big profits and a claim to be the world's third largest debt and equity underwriter. In the middle of that year CSFB paid $12 billion for another large investment bank, Donaldson Lufkin & Jenrette. However, beneath the surface, all was not well. The culture reeked of greed and the Credit Suisse Group Chairman, Lukas Muhlemann, doubted the quality and sustainability of the business. He fired Wheat and brought in Mack.

Mack faced one of the toughest management challenges ever seen in bulge-bracket investment banking. By then the conflict of interest scandal was breaking and CSFB was in it up to the neck. Not only was it caught up in the general accusations of biased research but, along with Salomon Brothers, it was singled out by the SEC and in class actions for spinning hot IPOs to influential executives in return for promises of future business. Mack hired some of the best securities lawyers in the industry to deal with these and other regulatory cases and turned his attention to costs.

Like every other investment bank in 2001, CSFB had serious problems with a bull-market cost base and a bear-market revenue stream. It had further complications arising from the DLJ deal, having paid a top of the market price and then locking in large numbers of top employees on fancy packages. Not only did the firm now have too many people for a bear market, it was committed to paying them more than the business could stand.

What happened next was an impressive piece of management: 'Mack persuaded hundreds of CSFB executives to give up the most lavish packages on Wall Street. Meeting with executives one-on-one, Mack approached them with this pitch: "Look, we're not making money. We have a lot of young people here who aren't going to get bonuses unless you give up some money. It's about fairness and building a great firm. Trust me. I'll remember what you did."' The result was that 10,000 jobs were cut from a total headcount of 27,500 (the total had been just 5,000 in 1997). Mack managed to talk CSFB's investment bankers into giving up $421 million in guaranteed compensation and total costs were reduced by more than $3 billion. Even Frank Quattrone, whose high-technology investment banking team had apparently joined on a revenue sharing deal,was persuaded to tie his group's pay to the profitability of the entire firm.[23]

Later Quattrone resigned when he was indicted as part of the post-Spitzer clean up, and the future also contained some surprises for Mack, who left Credit Suisse in June 2004 after pushing a merger a little too strongly for the likes of his Swiss colleagues. The treatment of Mack and subsequent criticism of his management style and record seems harsh, for without his efforts during the previous three years there would have been nothing left to discuss.[24] Things evened out for him in 2005 when he returned to Morgan Stanley as Chairman and Chief Executive following the departure of Philip Purcell.

What O'Neal and Mack achieved at Merrill Lynch and CSFB was replicated at other firms on Wall Street in different ways depending on their individual situations. When in 2001 it was clear that the bear market was for real, jobs and compensation were rapidly chopped. During the next two years average compensation in the US securities industry fell by a total of 14 per cent and 35,000 securities jobs disappeared in New York City, 17 per cent of the total.

Morgan Stanley cut compensation for retained institutional securities staff by an average 20 per cent in 2002 and let others go. Goldman Sachs cut headcount by 13 per cent in 2002, Bear Stearns by 7 per cent in 2001 and even Lehman Brothers, which had continued to expand into 2001, trimmed by 6 per cent in 2002.

There was an element of 'needs must', but management's aggressive response probably saved the industry. The contrast with the late eighties, when costs stayed at peak levels for too long, is revealing. If costs had remained at the levels of 2000, industry-wide losses would have been $15 billion during 2001 and 2002. This would almost certainly have brought down at least one of the major firms, with potentially dire consequences for the global economy. Thanks to decisive and vigorous action, there was never any real danger of that.

It is clear that the investment banks' good results are no fluke. Basic control disciplines, sensitive people management and good judgement about when and where to invest have transformed the quality and quantity of earnings. A combination of good management and the structural advantages of the Edge have enabled the investment banks to shake off the tag of bad management and to become, if not the best managed institutions on the planet, at least not the worst.

9

The Big Squeeze

The ability of the leading firms to differentiate themselves from the rest over many years meant that there were barriers to entry that newcomers found hard to breach. There were three parts to the large investment banks' strategy.

- They developed a model that is expensive to replicate.
- They squeezed rivals out of the business using profits from the Edge, profits that only they had.
- They looked after big company CEOs whose support was pivotal.

Development of the Model

For the first fifty years after Glass Steagall waved through integration between investment and brokerage in 1934, there was little to integrate. New issues were few and far between and corporate advisory work was a low key, gentlemanly affair. As late as 1980 underwriting produced revenues of only just over a billion dollars for the entire American securities industry, and total fees on the fourteen public merger deals completed that year were probably less than $100 million.[1]

During these early years, brokers and investment bankers generally lived separate lives. Salespeople were occasionally called upon to distribute securities that the bank had underwritten, but there was no pressure or hard sell. IPOs were few and far between and analysts were hardly involved in them.

Equity research was something of a backwater. In 1981, when Judy

Bollinger, who went on to become a top-rated analyst and a head of research, graduated from Wharton with an MBA, it was not difficult for well-qualified people to become an analyst on Wall Street. She called the heads of research at Goldman Sachs and Sanford Bernstein and was put straight through. She says: 'At that time no one wanted to work in research. Luckily Goldman had decided that they wanted to hire two analysts that year and took me on.'[2] Bulge-bracket firms making only two research hires and heads of research taking cold calls from young MBAs? Six thousand people applied to Salomon Brothers in 1983, and in 1986 40 per cent of the 1,300 people graduating from Yale applied to First Boston alone.[3] But equities research in the early eighties had not yet become central to the investment banking model; it was where the boffins worked.

The analysts' job was to advise investors, particularly the institutions, who by then had enough money under management to pay a lot of commission. Any time that was left after desk research and visiting companies was spent talking to fund managers, not bankers. Judy Bollinger recalls: 'I would spend 150 days a year visiting investors. April for Florida, May for Minneapolis and so on; the clients knew when to expect me. I called the hell out of them. I never asked them for votes but one day a week I would do nothing but call the clients. I had them organized by time zone, east to west. I called people from payphones in airports, wherever and whenever I had a spare moment. Investment banking hardly figured in my plans at that time. Bankers had to get permission from the head of research before they could consult us. If it was a big stock they would be turned down because as insiders we would not be able to talk to investors.'

All of this changed very suddenly when the capital markets took off in the mid eighties. The value of deals announced and fees earned in 1984 exceeded the previous decade's total and for the first time corporate clients offered richer pickings than investing clients.[4] Quite suddenly and unexpectedly the balance of power between broking and investment banking had shifted.

In their new dominant role the investment bankers laid claim to the analysts. It occurred to them that as the analysts were out and about doing the research for their investment reports they were meeting companies and probably gathering useful information about them.

The bankers made arrangements to collect this from the analysts and began to use them as in-house consultants.

The new power of investment banking dawned on Judy Bollinger one day in the late eighties when she changed her recommendation from Buy to Hold on one of the biggest stocks she followed, Lockheed. It was not particularly dramatic or even unexpected, coming after a long period in which the share price had done well, but by this time she was one of *Institutional Investor* magazine's All-Star Analysts and Lockheed was an important client of Goldman Sachs' investment banking department. When they heard of the change in recommendation 'Lockheed was furious and so were our investment bankers. It hadn't occurred to me to tell the investment bankers in advance; we worked in different worlds. Investment banking were upset that they hadn't been given prior warning. They told me it was my fault and said that I had to leave the office right then, fly to California and repair the relationship. I said, "Wow, yes" and I did. I wasn't put under unfair pressure or abused but it was just obvious that the game had changed.'

Similar influences were at work in Britain when, in the mid eighties, the corporate financiers came calling. I was an analyst at that time and remember them working through the research department sector by sector asking us if we had learned anything interesting during company visits. Did we know of divisions that might be for sale? What kind of business was management interested in buying? We were encouraged to post notes of company meetings with the corporate finance people and 'contribution to the investment banking department' started to feature in our appraisals and objectives for the year. Rumours spread of analysts who had been rewarded with huge bonuses for initiating corporate finance deals. Within a couple of years we had all adjusted to new priorities: investors for the bread and butter, investment bankers for the jam.

The IPO wave of the early nineties further increased the analysts' profile. The number of American IPOs almost doubled and their value nearly quadrupled between the eighties and the nineties and the investment banks put all available resources into this lucrative area.

Winning an IPO and leading the distribution with the bank's own securities firm became the big game in town. The investment bankers realized that if they had a highly rated analyst they had a potent weapon. Analysts could use their knowledge to brief investment bankers on what questions to ask and what buttons to push with management. With few exceptions, issuing firms placed great importance on favourable analyst coverage. Top analysts carried a lot of clout with investors and their opinion on a stock could make a lot of difference to the price of a new issue, bringing more proceeds to the seller and bigger fees for the investment bank.

Before the 2003 settlement, analysts were involved in the IPO process from the soup course to the nuts. They appeared in the pitches, often centre stage presenting the investment banks' official view of the company; they wrote the research reports; they gave a view on pricing; and they embarked on massive, exhausting global road shows presenting the case for investing to institutions. They remained involved once the issue was safely launched, providing ongoing supportive research known as 'booster shots'.

One of Merrill Lynch's top analysts describes a typical nineties IPO: 'In the early pitches to the company we would send a team of about twelve. My role was to talk glowingly about the business. If we were appointed, the bankers then took over for a while, shaping the prospectus. As the company got ready for its investor road show I would listen to the rehearsal and critique it. I would visit investors myself in a three- or four-week global tour and then make follow-up calls talking up the story. Once the closed period was over we published our report after it had been reviewed by the company and the bankers. It became a juggernaut; you had to go along with it or get out of the way.'[5]

In the ten years from the time that Judy Bollinger had first realized its significance, investment banking had become irresistible and along the way the truth got lost. Another *Institutional Investor*-ranked analyst, Tom Brown, experienced this at Donaldson, Lufkin & Jenrette, the firm that was later sold to CSFB after being co-founded by the same William Donaldson who later headed the post-Spitzer clean-up as chairman of the SEC. Brown had joined in 1991: 'Over time, DLJ's push to become a bulge-bracket investment banking firm created obvious conflicts with its heritage as "The House that Research Built". I watched one analyst after another discover the financial attractiveness of pitching deals for the investment banking division rather than competing for institutional equity research commission dollars. In my opinion, I witnessed these analysts lie, exaggerate, and exclude key information as they made presentations to DLJ's sales force and its clients pitching deals. What they were doing wasn't new on Wall Street but it was new at DLJ.'[6]

Journalists at the *Wall Street Journal* were amongst the first to highlight the conflict of interest problem. In 1992, the paper ran an article about Morgan Stanley after several analysts and research managers had left the firm: 'Few investment banks have been as successful as Morgan Stanley Group Inc in snaring a big slice of corporate America's record flood of new securities offerings. But its success may have come partly at the expense of another side of its business: stock research. Morgan Stanley's powerful investment bankers often have run roughshod over the firm's research analysts, some current and former Morgan Stanley analysts say. These analysts say Morgan Stanley's bankers have repeatedly pressured them to alter negative research reports on the stocks of the firm's corporate clients – particularly those for which it did underwriting deals.' The *Wall Street Journal* quoted from a memo written in 1990 by the then head of equity capital markets that outlined a policy of no 'negative or controversial comments about our clients'. Morgan Stanley said that neither this nor a parallel memo suggesting that analysts' pay be linked to investment banking transactions were ever adopted or put in place.[7]

The use of analysts in investment banking deals had become standard practice on Wall Street, and to some extent in the City, by the early 1990s. The British like to believe that it was mainly an American phenomenon but the recollection of an analyst involved in his firm's pitch for the IPO of the UK telecommunications company mmO2 suggests that mismanaged conflict of interest was a transatlantic and probably global problem in which the interests of the investor regularly and routinely got trampled in the rush to please the issuer. The team was planning its pitch: 'I arrived a bit late and apologized to the investment bankers who were running the meeting. They told me not to worry. I had arrived in time for the important bit. They were on valuation. They asked me for my view. I said $25 billion. They weren't happy, said the big figure has got to be a three. I said, "Well, I can always flex the DCF model to a certain degree; $30 billion is OK with me." The person in charge said, "To be honest, if we went in with $40 billion that would really blow the competition away." They weren't interested in my clients or what happened afterwards, just doing enough to please their client and winning the deal at all costs."[8]

Mismanaged conflict of interest is generally seen as a client issue but it had competitive significance too. Once investment bankers found that they could effectively compete for deals by committing to have a highly regarded analyst cover a stock and issue recommendations, the top firms used the promise of future coverage to charge high fees and gain market share.[9] Inadvertently they had stumbled across a powerful competitive weapon, for if they had the top ranked analysts, then their rivals did not and were powerless to compete. What started out as an innocent redeployment of the firms' resources morphed into an irresistible force that kept competitors out and the bulge bracket in.

Squeezing Out the Competition

Issuers' desire for research coverage suited the bulge bracket very well for most of them were already the leading research firms when the IPO surge began. The top three firms in the1985 *Institutional Investor* survey were Merrill Lynch, First Boston, and Goldman Sachs.[10] Other leading investment banks soon built highly rated research departments once they saw which way the game was being played. Within five years Morgan Stanley and Salomon Brothers had joined the leading group; within a further ten years Lehman, Bear Stearns and J. P. Morgan were boasting of the number of *Institutional Investor*-ranked analysts that they had. By the beginning of the twenty-first century there was a complete convergence between the league tables for the top investment banks and for the top research houses.

The top investment banks realized that they could distance themselves from the rest if they could persuade their clients of the superiority of the integrated model. In their pitches to clients they sold their research capability and the other advantages of scale very hard: the amount of capital they could commit, the size of their market share in secondary trading, the rankings of their sales force in client surveys and of course the status of their analyst. Spinning the statistics for pitch books became an art in itself. An analyst I know lost his *Institutional Investor* ranking and I asked him how the investment bankers had explained that in the pitch books: 'They just used the old numbers,' he replied.

Selling the integrated banking and broking package to corporates had the effect of raising a formidable barrier to entry. It became expensive and complex for new firms to break in. It was no longer enough to have smart investment bankers with great CEO relationships. They needed top-ranked analysts and global securities distribution to support them. The cost of a full-service equity research department soared to over half a billion dollars a year, an expense that was far more than could be justified by trading and commission income.

Securities without investment banking, or investment banking without securities, were not sufficient for a seat at the top table. If you wanted a place, you had to have them all. While newcomers tried to muster the nerve, cash and skills to compete, the established players used the extraordinarily high returns they were making to raise the stakes.

Compensation, particularly analysts' compensation, was the pressure point. Having a top-ranked analyst became essential to client credibility. There were perhaps five men and women in each sector who were reckoned to have pulling power with issuers and they were courted by the ten established bulge-bracket banks and a handful of aspiring new entrants.

The big banks were making so much money that they could afford to bid up for each other's staff. Analysts' pay soared, particularly in IPO-active sectors such as technology, media and telecommunications. The bulge bracket quickly learned to lock in their stars using deferred compensation and stock packages, so ambitious firms had to look elsewhere.

Analysts at the smaller investment banks were particularly attractive to the bigger players. They hoped to discover unrecognized talent who could be developed into a ranked analyst. It became a familiar pattern. The big bank drops a huge offer on the table; the analyst does not want to leave, likes the culture and the people but is earning less than what's on offer and has no guaranteed bonuses in place. The analyst talks to the head of research, the head of research talks to the CEO. The small bank pays up and ruins its cost base or lets the analyst go, leaving a gap in their product range and a wobbly balancing act to be performed with clients and the other staff.

I saw this on Wall Street in the 1990s when I had a close-up view of what happened to medium sized securities firms. Wertheim was a solid top twenty securities firm that had been bought by the British investment bank Schroders a decade or so earlier. Its strengths were in institutional brokerage and small and mid-cap investment banking. Schroders planned to turn it into an integrated investment bank but the super bulge came calling before they got very far. Some analysts left, others were persuaded to stay for more money, the compensation bill ballooned and Wertheim's business model was wrecked.

It happened to numerous medium sized investment banks in the 1990s. Most of the fifty-four American investment banks and brokers sold between 1997 and 2001[11] were medium sized firms outside the top ten, the kind that were rarely involved in a senior position in big-ticket advisory and underwriting deals. They made a living from junior roles, smaller deals, derivatives, brokerage or some other area. Provided that they could keep the lid on staff costs this could be quite a good living, but, under siege from the big firms, compensation went haywire in the nineties. Bidding up for staff spread quickly from analysts to traders, derivatives people and investment bankers. The cost–income ratio was destroyed and the smaller firms threw in the towel, denied the means to compete because they lacked the investment banking revenues to cross-subsidize other business areas.

The same thing happened in London in the 1980s and 1990s when the American investment banks used the super-profits from home to mop up in the City.[12] The Americans were prepared to run their European businesses at a loss for as long as it took. Charles Stonehill was one of the first hundred or so people to join Morgan Stanley's London operation in 1984 and went on to run European Capital Markets. He recalls: 'We never knew whether Morgan Stanley Europe was profitable but we were making so much in the USA and Japan that it did not really matter. We could run Europe out of the profits we earned there.'[13]

To those firms trying to compete without a big Wall Street pot to raid, it was a struggle. In the early 1990s I was running global securities for the British bank NatWest. We recruited promising, up-and-coming people, put them alongside experienced staff and in time many of them achieved a good reputation with clients. Amongst the many analysts that came through this system, two who had been trained over several years achieved the goal of a top ranking, thanked NatWest for its support and promptly resigned to join Goldman Sachs. They did not wait for their year-end bonuses and refused to discuss the move, saying simply that it was out of NatWest's league. It was disappointing but in broking you live and die by the sword and we all moved on. I only found out what really happened ten years later when I interviewed the person who hired them: Judy Bollinger.

She had been head of European research at Goldman Sachs in London at that time and remembered the episode clearly: 'It was a difficult time for us. The secondary business was not profitable and the European IPO market was quiet. We knew we had to flow primary deals through the sales team to get our margins up but we didn't have the research rankings to impress clients. Investment banking insisted we go on a hiring spree. We were poaching at absurd prices. I said that we couldn't justify it, it would blow my budget, I had headcount restraints. Investment banking said they would pay. I had fifty analysts reporting to me and then these several others who were paid for by investment banking. That's how we got your two guys.'[14]

What the bulge bracket was doing in Britain was what they did in America: cross-subsidize broking out of the super-profits in investment banking and put the two together in a package that was expensive and difficult to replicate. They were quite open about it. Speaking in the early nineties, Charles McVeigh III, chairman of Salomon's London office, said: 'The ability to invest in the markets of tomorrow is infinitely easier with the level of profitability Salomon Brothers has. My Chairman in New York calls it the Big Squeeze. To compete with the top two or three firms in the global business, you have to incur the same cost base as they do. The top people are garnering more and more of a war chest of capital and profitability and have more to spend and so it's harder and harder for the competitors to catch up.

The acceleration of the close of the circle has been faster in the last five years.'[15]

A decade later research by the *Financial Times* going back ten years showed that Citigroup Global Markets and its predecessor Salomon Brothers International, part of the bank's UK-based operations, had accumulated losses of $1.75 billion.[16] Over this period Salomon, and later Citigroup, was a major factor in the market for investment banking staff, part of the movement that drove up bonuses and forced British firms to sell. In 2000, Citigroup Global Markets' parent company (which by this time had bought Salomon Brothers) acquired the UK investment bank Schroders in precisely the circumstances that McVeigh had described.

The American business model was used to drive out competition, and it all started with integration. The integrated investment bank was expensive to build but once in place created the Edge that generated the high returns that subsidized the predatory hiring. It was expensive to replicate but, once established as the norm, formed a high barrier to entry, especially once the conflict of interest in research got out of hand.

It was a virtuous circle for those at the top. The more the firms that had tried to enter the market were forced out, the stronger the hand of the large investment banks. To clients they looked more and more like the only safe bet, helping them win more business and make their prices stick. When top firms stuck to their guns on price, it was as though they were saying: 'You have no alternative. Sure, you can go to Money Center Inc. with its shiny new investment bank or Mid-Market & Co. with its specialist niche. But how can you be sure they will still be there in a year? We have been around for twenty years and we plan to be here for another twenty. If you want a cut-price deal go to them; if you want quality and consistency stick with us.' The success of the top firms became a self-fulfilling prophecy. Choosing one of the leading investment banks became the obvious move, according to one client: 'You know they will still be around in ten years' time. They benefit from the charisma that surrounds their firms, from the patina of success.'[17]

Looking After Number One

The grip of the large investment banks was strengthened by the pivotal role that big company CEOs played in investment banking. At many companies they were personally responsible for deciding where to place the high-profile, high-margin capital markets business that investment banks had to win if they were to be in the bulge bracket.

There were perhaps only two hundred companies in the world that had reasonable amounts of investment banking business to give out regularly. Adding to them the few hundred companies that came to capital markets from time to time, the entire global community of 'bankable' CEOs was probably less than a thousand.

Not surprisingly, the top investment banks used every means at their disposal to cement these vital relationships. They needed to be able to offer clients the full range of investment banking products and smart people to deliver them, and the top banks were able to provide both. They threw more and more at corporate clients, sometimes blurring the CEOs' personal and corporate identities.

Citigroup's support for Bernard J. Ebbers, founder, chairman and CEO of WorldCom, a telecommunications company that was a prodigious generator of investment banking fees, evidently straddled both areas. According to a report for the bankruptcy court, Citigroup 'gave extraordinary financial favours and assistance to Mr Ebbers which were intended to and did influence Mr Ebbers to award WorldCom investment banking business' to the bank. Between 1996 and 2000, the report said, Ebbers made $12 million on allocations of IPO stock that he got from Salomon and its successor companies. According to the report, in 1999 Citibank lent Ebbers $60 million to refinance his Canadian ranch and in 2000 Travelers' Insurance, another Citigroup company, lent Joshua Timberland, a company owned by Ebbers, $499 million to buy 460,000 acres of timber property.

Once they had secured a place on WorldCom's roster of advisers, Citigroup and Salomon Smith Barney were able to cash in by providing a wide range of financial services. The report said that between 1996 and 2002 Citigroup–Salomon Smith Barney earned $106 million in investment banking fees from WorldCom, and an internal e-mail in support of helping Ebbers stated: 'This individual is associated with the No 1 fee-generating client of the bank as well as institutional fixed income/equities. In addition, retail does have WorldCom's stock-option exercise program.'[18]

Doling out favours to influential CEOs appears to have been a matter of routine on Wall Street in the nineties. Federal prosecutors in the case of Frank Quattrone flagged up for the jury an e-mail exchange in July 2000 between Quattrone and Michael Dell, the founder and chief executive of Dell Computers. Dell requested 250,000 shares in Corvis, an optical networking company that CSFB was about to take public. The shares were expected to be in strong demand and Dell noted that the shares 'would certainly help' to build a relationship between his company and CSFB. Quattrone acknowledged the request, invited Dell to appear as a keynote speaker at CSFB's annual technology conference and sought his opinion about a new analyst they were thinking of hiring.[19]

Looking after the CEO started out as relationship building: nights at the opera, corporate golf days, lunches and dinners; but every firm could do them and the bulge bracket needed to do more to maintain competitive advantage. What the firms outside the bulge bracket could not match was the full range of products and services.[20]

Their established position enabled the investment banks to stoke up huge profits and to alter permanently the competitive landscape to their own advantage. The investment banking oligopoly came from the integrated business model. The combination of corporate services such as underwriting with investor services such as securities trading connected two fundamentally conflicting activities. Once own-account trading was thrown in the ingredients were in place for the great profitability that gave the leading firms the resources to see off competition. The rewards became so great that the temptation to ignore conflict of interest was often irresistible.

The idea of integrating broking and underwriting was flawed from the outset. It was inevitable that it would lead to problems and it happened not once but twice, in the twenties and the nineties. The same broker–banking connection that facilitated the favouritism that led Spitzer to accuse CSFB and Salomon of spinning to their best clients in the 1990s was also behind J. P. Morgan's practice seventy years before of rewarding its 'preferred list' of customers with the juiciest underwritings in the years before the Great Crash.

The history of investment banking is littered with examples of putting the firm's interests above those of the client. In the late twentieth century it became institutionalized. The laughter and cynicism on the Salomon trading floor in the eighties when the naive rookie Michael Lewis unwittingly sold overpriced AT&T bonds to a hapless investor from the firm's trading book;[21] the derivatives misselling that Frank Partnoy wrote about in the nineties – 'Foreign exchange bet? What the hell are you talking about? We didn't bet anything and we shouldn't have lost anything. We didn't make any foreign exchange bet. We're an insurance company for God's sake. We aren't even allowed to buy foreign exchange';[22] the relentless advice from investment bankers to do it now before the client changes their mind or the competition can sneak in to steal the mandate are all examples of a cynical culture.

There used to be a tradition on Wall Street and in the City of advising clients not to deal if the timing was wrong. Investment bankers were not too worried about losing out on a fee in the short term because they could be sure that, all things being equal, the relationship with the client would still be in place when the time was right. Think back to 1974 and the battle between International Nickel and Electric Storage Battery. The advisers to the companies were Morgan Stanley and Goldman Sachs and they nearly walked away because it was considered unethical to get involved in hostile bids. They were in the business for the long term and were prepared to wait for their clients to act; it was called relationship banking.

Twenty years later investment bankers ditched their clients at the drop of a hat. At one time, if an investment bank's client wanted to bid for another client, then the bank would stand down from both parties; now they are more likely to attempt to work for both. One CEO I spoke to in 2004 described how one of the top investment banks had been working with him planning a hostile takeover; he was surprised one day when the target announced an agreed deal with another competitor – advised by that same bulge-bracket bank. The bankers called him up and assured him that everything had been approved by their internal compliance committee and that they had advised both clients objectively throughout, but it left a sour taste. Investment banks even have a name for this kind of thing; they call it transaction banking, where the relationship lasts for the duration of the deal but no longer. Caveat emptor indeed.

Standards fell equally far in trading. Henry Kaufman describes how in the early 1970s a Salomon Brothers trader thought to have overcharged a client in a trade was made to return some of the profit and the partner in charge of the area had his year-end profit share docked.[23] Ten years later, when Michael Lewis expressed concern at the losses suffered by his client in the AT&T bond trade, he was scornfully asked: 'Who do you work for, this guy or Salomon Brothers?'[24] Kaufman's memoirs neatly summed up the changed standards: 'We now live in a financial world in which older virtues – like knowing your customers, minimising rather than merely managing risk and learning how to turn down a promising but dubious deal – have been eclipsed and are even ridiculed as hopelessly out of date.'[25]

Much though they like to describe themselves as 'professional', many investment bankers have no guiding ethical framework in the way that exists in other professions such as the law, medicine or even auditing. There are many honeyed words about putting the clients first: Goldman Sachs is very specific. The very first of its 'Business Principles' reads: 'Our clients' interests always come first. Our experience shows that if we serve our clients well, our own success will follow.'[26] Given what we learned from Michael Lewis, Frank Partnoy and Eliot Spitzer, decade by decade through the eighties, nineties and into this century, an alternative doctrine for others in the investment banking industry appeared to have become: 'Our own interests always come first. Our experience shows that if we serve ourselves well, our clients will surely follow.'

We should not be surprised by this. If you take a bunch of alpha (mainly) males, incentivize them to the eyeballs, deregulate them, tell them that anything is fine as long as it creates shareholder value and give them a business model where they can see all and do all, the outcome is as likely as night following day – rewards will rise and standards will fall.

PART 4

Whatever Happened to the Invisible Hand?

10

Does It Matter?

This book has attempted to throw light on some dark corners of recent investment banking history:

- The very high returns generated by the banks
- The variable quality of their advice
- The state of competition at the top of the industry

It has sought to explain them in terms of:

- Good management
- The Edge conferred by the integrated model
- A ruthless approach to customers, competitors and regulations

The final part of the book tackles three remaining questions:

- Does any of this matter?
- Why did people go along with it?
- What will happen next?

Free market economics would not have been so successful without the help of the modern investment banks, and the modern investment banks would not have grown so big or so profitable under a different economic system. But neither the system nor the institutions has an unblemished record.

Despite the strong macro-economic performance of the last quarter century, the benefits have by-passed a large part of the population, even in the United States where just 13,000 taxpayers receive more than 3 per cent of all income and the national poverty rate is one in eight.[1] For many in the working population, despite twenty years of rising stock prices and pay, a pension crisis seems inevitable.

Depending on your point of view, increased productivity in America and Britain is either an economic miracle that vindicates the system or a myth created by the spin doctors.[2]

Just as the market economy is a mixed bag, so too with the investment banks. Their importance is often exaggerated and their faults are obvious, but their vital role has enabled them to ride out the storms. The consensus appears to be that, despite a few warts, the investment banks' overall impact is positive and they deserve their rewards. How much one can agree with this generous interpretation requires an assessment of the consequences of their actions.

Direct Consequences of What the Investment Banks Did

The Bubble

Although Wall Street's behaviour *during* the bubble has been roundly criticized, its role in *causing* it is often played down. Market strategists prefer fundamental explanations for the bubble such as the information technology revolution, complacency amongst investors following the twenty-year bull market, confidence arising from the apparently permanent benign economic conditions and the surfeit of cash looking for places to invest. Behavioural finance experts favour psychological interpretations of the mass hysteria that at times threatened to overrun markets. Historians look for context to explain recent events, turning for parallels to previous examples of markets overshooting such as the seventeenth-century Dutch tulip mania, the South Sea Bubble in the eighteenth century and the Roaring Twenties.

Defenders of the free market have been quick to use these explanations to deflect criticism from the system and the institutions they believe in. Prominent figures such as Alan Greenspan have qualified their criticism of corporate excess by saying that the nineties saw no increase in human greed, just an increase in the opportunities to be greedy resulting from economic growth. According to this view, it wasn't the system that was at fault, merely the re-emergence of familiar human foibles.[3] Michael Lewis went so far as to write an article 'In Defense of the Boom' for the *New York Times* in 2002, the first words of which were 'Wall Street Didn't Do It'.[4]

'These things happen in markets' is perhaps the most common conclusion to discussions about the euphoria, the bubble and the errors of judgement that were made. Whilst this is perfectly true, it is only part of the answer and it is doubtful whether the bubble would have happened without the investment banks.

It started with the analysts. They created a wall of sound that kept the volume high throughout the late nineties. If you have hundreds of articulate and well-informed people churning out research reports telling you to buy, it is hard to ignore them. If you have dozens of them appearing on television morning, noon and night with plausible jargon, polished communications skills and facts at their fingertips to back up their case, it is hard not to be affected. Sound bites in the newspapers, updates on the internet and calls from your broker added to the clamour to buy. What happened when the modern media met the integrated investment bank was that conflict of interest moved out of the closet into Main Street. Ninety-nine out of every one hundred recommendations made by analysts were to buy stock; hardly anyone ever said 'Sell'. By the time the marketing machines got hold of them there was an incessant roar encouraging investors to buy. No wonder the market went up.

Once the bubble burst, hyperbole was cast aside and reality dawned. Business fundamentals reasserted themselves, stocks were revalued and the NASDAQ index fell four fifths. It had been 80 per cent hot air. Naive, foolish, cynical or greedy analysts had talked the market up at a time when cool, clear, conflict-free thinking might have prevented the excesses. If ever a group of professionals missed a chance to justify their existence and compensation, this was surely it.

The investment bankers must also bear some responsibility. They brought many companies to the market that lacked a track record or a viable business plan. Andy Kessler, who moved from Morgan Stanley's research department to the venture capital industry on the West Coast, believed that the investment bankers lowered their standards after the Netscape IPO of 1995: 'Investment bankers used to insist on two consecutive quarters of profits before taking a company public. Now suddenly, it was all about growth – How quickly can you grow your sales? If you are doubling, we'd be happy to take you public.'[5] It is extraordinary that none of them were able to see that so many of these companies lacked the infrastructure and management to flourish as listed entities. Yet every issue was supported by an investment bank and, rightly or wrongly, many investors took the imprimatur of a top investment bank on an IPO to be a seal of approval and put their own doubts aside.

Investment bankers encouraged the casino mentality that contributed to the bubble by making IPO shares the currency of greed. Allocating hot shares to influential executives or to hedge funds had the effect of legitimatizing and encouraging spinning. Hedge funds, Michael Dell, Bernie Ebbers or the other recipients of generous favours were not the kind of long term institutional investors that the investment banks promised to find during the pitch meetings. The short term speculators were in it to make a quick killing after which they would sell their shares, presumably to someone not in the know who might just have listened to a top analyst hyping them up on breakfast television or received a 'booster shot' in the mail from their broker.

This bubble was no historical accident and it contained some unique features (as well as some similarities) compared to previous bull episodes. It was the almost inevitable outcome of a flawed model operating in the communications age, and the bankers and analysts were in it together: the bankers needed the analysts to shift the product and the analysts needed the bankers for the product to shift. If you have an entire industry lined up to prepare something for market and then tell the world to buy it, don't be surprised when they do. That's how mass communications works. In this case investors were left holding worthless portfolios of over-hyped internet companies whilst the investment banks and their analysts sat safely on their profits and bonuses. Was that how the free market was meant to work?

Corporate Corruption

Corporate corruption was not far behind dot-com euphoria in contributing to the millennium bear market. It wasn't the investment banks that falsified the accounts, but they were very close to the people who did. Often party to the innermost thoughts of their clients, they had a privileged view of what was going on in boardrooms, attending meetings for strategic discussions, answering questions from the other directors on what the CEO was planning and helping the CEO to make the case. Jack Grubman's attendance at WorldCom board meetings attracted a lot of criticism after it was known but it was unusual because he was an analyst, not because a representative of WorldCom's bank was there.

The investment banks protested their innocence to, amongst others, the United States Government Accounting Office: 'The investment banks expressed the view that it is a client's senior management, audit committee and independent auditors who are in possession of the information and decision making authority necessary to exercise an effective gate keeping role.'[6]

But though they are not gatekeepers to business in the way that the auditors are, it is extraordinary – one might even say incredible – that some investment banker somewhere did not stumble across the corporate misgovernance that caused six hundred American listed companies to restate their accounts between 1998 and 2000. As with the analysts, it was a time when they could have made a difference. A real professional would have provided an objective view and lived up to the title 'trusted adviser' by telling some of the more adventurous CEOs and CFOs to come off it. Instead, driven by the prospect of booking big fees, they appear to have interpreted their role as being to find ways to carry out the CEO's wishes, coming up with ever more innovative financial 'solutions'.

It was not only a problem in America. In discussing Parmalat, the FSA, the financial services industry's regulator in the UK, warned 'that banks and other lenders need to be especially vigilant where their counterparties are making use of complex structured finance arrangements'.[7] In other words, responsibilities to investors are not eliminated by the standard health warnings, which state that banks have relied solely on information provided by management.

It was a very important distinction to make. Whilst it may not have been the direct responsibility of the investment banks that structured products were sometimes used to deceive the market, regulators, shareholders and trustees, by going along with what was being done, rather like the analysts and the bubble, they missed the opportunity to stand apart. In my opinion, investment bankers who are hired by companies to develop derivatives to swap costs into revenues, to sanction inter-company transfers, to construct arm's-length entities that meet the letter but not the spirit of the law, or to help fund managers circumvent restrictive investment policies, are not like innocent bystanders who happened to be at the scene. They are not witnesses; they are accomplices. They helped make it happen.

Failed Mergers

An active mechanism for changes in corporate control is an important and powerful stimulus to under-achieving managements; but to judge from the outcome of many of the mergers that took place in the eighties and nineties, it was overdone. Carrying out a successful merger requires careful analysis before moving in on the target and disciplined implementation after it has been bought. The disappointing results suggest that this process was often skimped. There was evidently an enormous variation in management's skills in putting businesses together, the prices paid were often too high and some of the mergers should never have been attempted.

The late twentieth-century merger wave was not the invention of the investment banks but they helped it along. The environment of deregulation, cheap finance and globalization encouraged consolidation. CEOs anxious to make their mark during their average of five years in office preferred transformational change rather than profit-sapping long term investment. They were encouraged by institutional investors who frequently positioned their questions along the lines of revolution not evolution, 'What are you going to buy?' being a more common question than 'What are you going to build?'

Investment bankers, of course, encouraged this, doing everything in their very considerable power to persuade companies to transact. They make nothing from a $1 billion research and development programme; they might make $10 million from a $1 billion acquisition. Some investment bankers continued to think like this, according to a senior analyst at a top investment bank. In the summer of 2004 the analyst was approached by a colleague who worked in corporate finance and was asked for his opinion about a certain Fortune 500 company's acquisition plans. The analyst believed that the company would be making only small infill deals. The investment banker was disappointed: 'We won't make any money out of those. Can't we get them to do something bigger?'[8]

The banks' powers of persuasion were enhanced by the profits that they made. They are able to hire the best people in such numbers that they can generate any number of ideas to put to CEOs. Their industry teams are like ideas laboratories for the sectors they follow, building up detailed knowledge of people, companies and products. There is a rigour to their client analysis that enables the best of them to pitch in exactly the right place at the right time. These are quick-witted, charming people backed up by huge resources. They are able to search out the soft spots and offer innovative financing deals to help put them right. As a result, CEOs were deluged with telephone calls and presentations from investment bankers with beautifully worked-up ideas.

And there was very little lined up against them for the circuit breakers in the system were ineffective. In the USA, despite the recent introduction of more stringent rules, the independence of boards of directors from executive management varies. The chairman and the CEO is frequently the same person and the other directors, although 'independent' in the regulatory definition of the word, are often non-executives drawn from the CEO's peer group. In the UK, executive boards are bigger and corporate governance gives non-executive directors more power and responsibility, but they too are usually drawn from a small group of connected people. Boardrooms in America and Britain are therefore full of people who in the corporate governance environment of the nineties were more likely to go along with the CEO's plan than to recommend alternative development strategies.

In the absence of restraint at board level, the shareholders were the obvious people to apply the brakes. Their support is needed in major deals, but they rarely voted against management. The average holding period for a stock fell from four years to less than a year in the last quarter of the twentieth century, and in this rent-a-stock environment shareholders did not act like long term owners. Few institutional shareholders worked in long term partnership with the executive management of the companies they owned. With some notable exceptions – such as Calpers, the California Public Employees Retirement System; the academics' pension fund, TIAA-CREF; Robert Monks's Lens Fund; and the British fund management company Hermes – for twenty-five years the majority of institutional investors went along meekly with management's wishes; if they didn't like them, they simply sold the shares.[9] That's what happens in the market economy.

Ironically, the most effective circuit breakers turned out to be refugees from the integrated investment banks. Advisory boutiques led by famous rainmakers such as Eric Gleacher and Bob Greenhill are sometimes hired by CEOs as a check on the advice they are getting from their lead investment banks. These firms work for a fixed fee, freeing them of the 'success fee' incentive that taints much advice, and they are being called on more and more. The need for clients to hire a second tier of trusted advisers to check up on the first shows how far the integrated investment banks fell during the late twentieth century.

Under-performing Funds

We have already noted that the average fund is bound to perform in line with the market because the market is the sum of everyone's decisions. But if the efficient-market theory is only about 90 per cent right, as it probably is, what happened to the other 10 per cent and why did so few funds consistently distinguish themselves from the pack?

One factor is excessive trading. The average fund turned over 15 per cent of its portfolio a year in the fifties; this had risen to 110 per cent in 2002, by which time, as discussed above, shares were changing hands every eleven months. The contrast with Warren Buffett's favourite holding period – 'for ever' – could not be greater.

Three things drove the trading. First, it became cheaper to deal, so funds could change their portfolios apparently for free. Second, trustees and plan sponsors got the markets religion, growing increasingly trigger happy and sacking managers if the funds performed badly. Fund managers knew they had to get results or get fired so they upped the turnover rate in a desperate effort to perform.

Third, the investment banks read these signs early and poured resources into servicing the fund managers, hiring more brokers and thus increasing the pressure to transact. There are so many people working in broking that it is one of the few industries in the world where the number of salespeople far outweighs the number of customers. Confronted with several hundred e-mails, a voice mail jammed full of messages and a diary full of broker presentations, the pressure on fund managers to deal was enormous – and they did.

The best hedge funds get it right by surfing the information wave with multiple short term decisions. But they have the resource, the incentives and the objectives that lend themselves to that kind of trading. The poor mutual fund manager got stuck somewhere in the middle ground between the hedge fund and Berkshire Hathaway's long term approach. Clients paid the price, suffering twenty years of mediocre performance.

Inefficient Allocation of Capital

The ultimate function of investment banks within the economy is to achieve an efficient allocation of capital, getting money to the most productive homes as quickly and as cheaply as possible. It is against this objective that the high returns and indifferent advice of the investment banks need to be measured.

The premium return on equity achieved by the American securities industry compared to the non-financial sector average between 1980 and 2000 enhanced its profits by an estimated $60 billion.

As we saw in Chapter 4, these amounts are only part of the story. Even higher returns were being concealed by the very high compensation that was being made by the investment banking community, reducing profits and keeping return on equity below the radar screens of clients and regulators. I calculated that over and above the standard rate of inflation, an extra $120 billion was taken out of the capital markets by employees in two decades. Added to the $60 billion I calculated for super-normal returns, a total of $180 billion was taken out of the capital markets over that period in the form of abnormally high profits and compensation. These are enormous sums that might have been used by new issuers to improve the productivity of their businesses or that might have stayed in the portfolios of investors.

If stock packages and stock options are taken into consideration – hidden benefits that were liberally spread around securities professionals – the disparity would have been even greater. Investment bankers and brokers took their share of the estimated $200 billion of wealth that was transferred from the shareholders of listed companies to employees through stock packages and option plans in 1999 and 2000 alone.[10]

The profits and compensation of the investment banks had to come from somewhere. This money was not created out of thin air by the magic of the investment banks; it was taken from someone else. For every dollar made there was a counterparty on the other side of the trade. Where did the $180 billion come from?

At first sight it appears to have come from two principal sources: companies that pay the bankers' fees and asset managers who use brokers' services. Closer inspection reveals that these sources are the same. Ordinary people, pooling their resources into mutual funds, pension funds and other investment vehicles pay the fund managers' fees and own the majority of shares in the companies that use the markets. That is where the $180 billion came from.

The public have been encouraged to use the markets to plan for old age and possible adversity and have entrusted their money to professional asset managers. They have faith in the industry and believe that they are paying those professionals to look after their interests. In many respects they do. Client funds are segregated and protected, investment guidelines are usually obeyed and the dividends and statements arrive on time.

But this comes at a price. When investors receive their quarterly statements and they see deductions for brokers' charges and fund management fees, they probably conclude that while it seems a bit rich it is within reason. They probably get more grumpy if they lose more through the bid–offer spread when buying in and selling out of their funds, but again they can live with it. But what they see on the statements is just a small part of what they really pay. If they knew the real cost, the mood of investors might be worse than grumpy.

Investors are on the wrong side of the Edge every time that they trade with an investment bank, and it shows up in the $180 billion deficit. Trading profits are how money gets siphoned from market users to the investment banks in millions of transactions every day in countless asset classes. The investment banks see more, hear more and know more and this helps them take advantage of those they trade with – most of whom see less, hear less and know less. Stocks, bonds, derivatives, mortgages, commodities, currencies, energy: anything and everything that is traded gets clipped on the way through, enabling insiders to beat outsiders every second of every day.

It is a long and torturous chain of responsibility. Accountability is difficult to pin down, transparency is rare and every twist and turn gives the professionals the chance to beat the public. And that is exactly what they did. For the $180 billion came from the public. It is a thudding great amount made up of such tiny pieces that no one noticed as the investment banks swept them up and put them in their pockets – like stealing bubble gum from a sweet shop, as one broker told me. But it all added up to a huge and significant sum. Not only could the money have gone for productive investment in other sectors, if invested properly it would have gone a long way towards wiping out the pension fund deficits of $300 billion in America and over $100 billion in the UK.[11]

Indirect Consequences of What the Investment Banks Did

A Mushroom Cloud

The integrated investment banking model made a mockery of the free market economy because as a result of the way it worked markets were not really free: the odds were loaded in favour of those in the know. Free market competition, the mantra much loved by the investment banks, appeared to apply to every industry except their own.

Market power enabled the leaders to make huge returns at the expense of their clients. In turn this enabled them to cross-subsidize ruthlessly, to raise substantial barriers to entry and to further reinforce their own position. As countless aspiring new entrants discovered, there is very little that is 'free' about joining the investment banking market, which appeared more like a closed circle than a level playing field. How absurd: a free market where every sector was wide open to competition except the one that was meant to make it all happen.

Whilst there is nothing illegal about how the investment banks made their money or what they did with it, the effect of imperfect competition easily spilled over. If you were a member of a profession that traditionally and legally used its market power to its own advantage at the expense of its customers in one area, it is easy to see how the practice could become extended into progressively less ethical practices.

The distortion at the very heart of the free market economy spread like a mushroom cloud. It is not fair to blame the investment banks entirely for the culture of corporate malpractice that occurred in America in the second half of the nineties, but if there is something rotten at the core we should not be surprised if the rottenness eventually spread to the outer reaches.

Without knowing why or how, everyone sensed that anything goes. The practices of trading for advantage off client business and being less than transparent created a culture that spread from the investment banks to the accountants and consultants and from them to corporations. In this free-for-all environment, senior executives might easily say to themselves: 'Well look, they are doing it – they are guardians at the gate, why shouldn't we?'

The American Way

Modern free market economics and shareholder value are American ideas that have swept aside competing creeds. It helped that the alternatives crumbled. In Continental Europe, Rhineland model debt-based companies struggled with Germany's economic problems and France's national champions do not look like real champions at all. The Japanese way that inspired the thought 'If Japan can, why can't we?'[12] in the eighties now serves only to prove that managing a team is not the same as managing a business, let alone the whole economy. The British system of equity finance – soft edged and paternal – was discredited in the complacency that shrouded industry after the Second World War.

What took over was the American way involving relentless pursuit of shareholder value to the exclusion of all other objectives. Anything goes; it is survival of the fittest. The model has many good things going for it: raising productivity, encouraging entrepreneurship and stimulating economic growth. But it comes with some heavy baggage: inequality, winner-takes-all mentality and an irresistibility that leads to standardization around American values everywhere.

The investment banks have acted as the standard bearers for the export of this model of capitalism across the world. Smart American investment bankers forced, charmed and bought their way into CEOs' offices wherever they smelled business. As soon as a nation or region showed signs of business life, the American investment banks arrived there in droves, pushing into Latin America in the eighties, emerging Europe and Asia Pacific in the nineties and now India and China. It was the same with companies and business sectors: whatever the fashion, the investment banks were up there with it. Conglomerates; break-ups; telecommunications; dot-coms and many more have all had their place in the investment banking sun during the last twenty years. If it is big and it trades, the American-style investment banks will be there.

What they offer CEOs is the full free-markets monty: 'advice' on mergers and acquisitions; structured finance 'solutions' to pension fund, tax, foreign exchange and interest rate problems; access to capital and capital markets – all backed up by the integrated services of commercial and investment banking and broking. The Americans are unstoppable when they hit town, redefining the way that business is done, subjecting companies and shareholders to the full force of the American way.

The first step is often to take control of the investment banking and securities industry. In Britain this happened in the eighties and nineties and it is already possible to see the American business model becoming the norm. British corporations have experienced enormous changes in the way they do business with their advisers. Relationship banking, where the advisers worked with companies on a long term basis and, as a result, felt under less pressure to push deals, was replaced with transaction banking, where the relationship lasts only as long as the deal and where 'Do it, and do it now' is the most common advice given. British companies appear to have been listening particularly hard. They made a third of all cross-border acquisitions in a recent ten year period, according to Professor Alan Gregory at Exeter University. But when it came to buying into the investment banks' own back yard, Professor Gregory found that the results were poor: 'The research shows on average that UK companies make disastrous acquisitions in the US.'[13]

The two most famous British companies, Marconi and ICI, that fell victim to the markets culture, unwisely listened to investment bankers and other advisers braying about the need to create shareholder value through buying and selling rather than investing in organic growth. They paid the price in the end with horrendous collapses in their share prices.[14]

Hector Sants, who worked for a full spectrum of British-, European- and American-owned investment banks before joining the FSA as Managing Director, points out that London's 'culture of separation in the wholesale area, harking back to the traditional divide between stock broking and merchant banking' spared London the worst of the investment banks' excesses. But not by much: 'Even in the UK there was evidence of systematic bias in analyst recommendations, poor management of conflicts of interest and a feeling that if it happened there it could happen here. I'm not sure the UK industry could put hand on heart and say in 2002 there was an inherently better conflict management culture in London than in New York.'[15]

It was clear that the City had to change, but did it have to swallow the American bait hook, line and sinker? I was surprised by a conversation with one British investment banker who became a divisional head at a bulge-bracket firm: 'It serves the clients right. They wanted the American model and they got it, complete with tainted advice and an incessant pressure to transact.'[16]

The British culture of separation is kept alive by the memories of a few people now in their forties and beyond who worked under the old system. As the investment bankers of Hector Sants' generation retire, the culture of separation will go with them. Clients will get full-blooded integration, New York style, with all that it brings.

The markets culture demands short term results and sees buying and selling as the way to get them. Enron is an extreme case, but its journey from being an energy supplier into an energy trader symbolizes the change in corporate values. It remains to be seen whether the markets culture can produce long term companies.

Whatever Happened to the Invisible Hand?

Adam Smith, the eighteenth-century father of modern economic theory, was not perturbed by the likelihood of collusion in free markets. He believed that the businessman is 'led by an invisible hand to promote an end which was no part of his intention . . . By pursuing his own interest he frequently promotes that of society.'[17]

Adam Smith's belief that conspiracy and contrivance would result in the public good is neatly summed up by another British economist called Smith, the journalist David Smith: 'The point was that the market did not let them get away with it, or at least not for long. Customers would abandon profiteers in favour of competitors offering lower prices. Attempts by groups of firms to fix prices by agreement – forming a cartel – would fail as long as it was possible for new firms to enter the market and undercut them. The invisible hand is the market, and through its operation the best possible or optimum outcome is achieved.'[18]

Adam Smith's theories are very popular with the investment banks. They support non-intervention and deregulation, the policies that create the best possible climate for them and justify their prices, profits and place in society. After all, if prices and profits were too high, the market would force them down and if output was poor, the market would drive it up. Supporters have been quick to claim victory for the invisible hand, arguing that the bear market had fundamentally weakened the investment bank's position.[19] This may yet prove to be so, but, given the investment banks' power and resourcefulness, it would be as well to keep an eye on how they fare compared to other market participants.

The fact that the regulators and the courts had to get involved in putting things right shows that the market mechanism did not work in late twentieth-century investment banking. Customers did not try, or were not able, to exert as much pressure on suppliers as markets theory expected. Effective competition, essential to the operation of the free market, was muted outside the bulge bracket. It was nearly impossible for new firms to enter the market except by buying established players. Better still for the incumbents, only some of their clients were sensitive to price levels. Price was not the top priority for corporate CEOs, and end investors were so far down the food chain that they could not see what was going on. In between, fund managers cut the prices that they could see, such as commissions and dealing spreads, but were not able to track what the investment banks were making on the other side of their trades.

The structure of the investment banking industry makes it very difficult for the end customers – the general public – to know what they are really paying, and the more complex the product the harder it is to tell. But somewhere between them and the investment banks who supply the services is a wide range of people with an interest in what goes on. Who are they, and what did they do?

11

The Greed Merchants

Did No One Care?

The investment banks are the shock troops of capitalism, an economic system that is devoted to wealth creation. We should not be surprised or critical if they reflect its characteristics, and provided that the invisible hand works it need not necessarily be a bad thing if they do.

But what if something gets in the way? According to market theory, customers should force existing suppliers to reduce prices and raise product quality by going to competitors. In late twentieth-century investment banking, that this happened in some areas but not in others was not entirely down to lack of choice. There were still three blue chip investment banks to choose from, three or four more close behind, and two or three more close behind them. Aggressive customers ought to have been able to play one off against the other to secure better and cheaper services whenever and wherever they wished.

Instead, investors continued to pay for and pay attention to the same old analysts whose recommendations often went wrong. Corporate treasurers and other officials allowed derivatives experts to make huge profits. Chief executive officers accepted advice that led to mergers that had a less than evens chance of creating value. Clients pressed the banks to cut prices in some areas but not in others. No one seemed concerned about the high returns being made by the investment banks and their employees. Why?

One reason is that the clients were committed to the market economy, trusted it to work and saw no need to intervene. Like Michael Douglas's Gordon Gekko, they believed that 'Greed, for want of a better word, is good. Greed is right. Greed works.'[1] Another reason is that they were also in the markets for their own greed, and as long as this was fed they would not disturb the system. They were using other people's money and were not too bothered about, to paraphrase J. K. Galbraith, 'the bezzle' – the amount of money siphoned out of the system.[2] Against this background, the investment banks slipped easily into the role of Greed Merchants, trading greed and taking their own turn on the way.

The general public who owned the money that the fund managers, the CEOs, and the investment banks played with, were like the victims of *The Sting*. They did not even know about the $180 billion hit, still less that they were its victims. In the bull market, they did not look too closely because it was taken from their winnings; and when the bear market focused attention on their losses, the bezzle was hidden away at the end of a very long chain of transactions.

The public perhaps took comfort from the existence of independent bodies such as boards of directors, pension fund trustees, central banks, regulators and governments that were meant to be looking after their interests. Such comfort was misplaced for supervisors faced familiar issues of integration, complexity and conflict of interest.

And the guardians were asleep at the gate. The auditors let their standards drop in the pursuit of consultancy fees. The lawyers were aligned with the investment banks, one admitting that 'It is difficult for the top eight or ten firms to bring a case against an investment bank. There is a group of players that lawyers feel unable to act against.'[3] Even the press for a time 'grew overly reliant on commentary from investment banks'.[4] Thus at nearly every level a mixture of misplaced confidence, self-interest and naivety contrived to keep the invisible hand at bay.

Corporations

CEOs

It takes a lot to become the chief executive of a large corporation. The people who get there are intelligent, determined, energetic and critical thinkers. They are not the kind of people to be talked into actions that are against their interests. It can be safely assumed that they only do something because they believe it to be in their own and their organization's interests.

They speak highly of their best advisers: 'Good investment bankers have an insight into markets and industries and also an independence of mind. They provide challenge to the beliefs and prejudices of senior management and this can be in short supply in the corporate environment. They are prepared to ask the questions that ultimately will be asked anyway.'[5]

The value they add can be substantial. Lord Stevenson, a senior British businessman who is chairman of the British bank HBOS, is broadly sceptical of the role played by the investment banks but admitted that on occasion they could add real value. He described the role a team from Morgan Stanley played in the refinancing of the aircraft leasing company GPA: 'They helped invent aircraft securitization, they really earned their pay. They put a huge team on the job, stood up to the big shareholders at crucial moments and helped us, in the end, return $5 billion to banks that they would never otherwise have got.'[6]

Another businessman, the COO of a large US company, described to me a situation in which Goldman Sachs was the investment bank: 'They fielded a very impressive lady. She knew all the companies and all the players. We showed her a list of companies we were interested in. She said "That's the one. It will be hard to get but they are very good people and the fit is right", and she ran through a list of reasons why.'[7]

But if the investment banks are so good, why did so many of the mergers that they arranged go wrong? One reason is that the quality of the bankers varies. In contrast to the excellent bankers he worked with at GPA, Lord Stevenson also recalled a team of investment bankers he worked with on another deal 'that added nothing to the transaction. They were just young men and women in suits, shirts and ties.'[8]

Yet the failure rate is not entirely about the bankers. It is partly to do with the CEOs being insufficiently sceptical about merger proposals. As fully paid and signed up members of the free markets club, CEOs grew up in a culture that valued buying and selling above organic growth. Organic growth is often slow to bear fruit and may actually reduce earnings per share in the short term. Thoughts turned to mergers, which under American and British accounting conventions offer a quick way of boosting earnings per share. Most CEOs knew that mergers were risky, but there were enough examples of successful mergers to encourage the optimists. After all, they might reason, if Sandy Weill can be a successful serial acquirer, why can't we?

The reward system encourages investment bankers to promote deals and senior management to transact. Bankers' bonuses simply reward them for getting the deal done, irrespective of whether they are successful for the client company in the long run. CEOs are ready to listen because they can expect tangible personal benefits from a successful acquisition. They get paid more for running bigger companies, are sometimes offered huge bonuses for pulling off deals, and it does not necessarily affect the CEO's personal financial position if the earnings growth runs out because the downside is not that great. If the deal goes wrong some CEOs are even protected by golden handshake contracts that are guaranteed to pay out whichever way the dice land.

Stock packages and options, which accounted for over 75 per cent of the average $40 million pay earned by the CEOs of America's top 100 companies in 1999, drove the CEOs to aggressive action.[9] As Joseph Stiglitz pointed out: 'Stock options meant that executive pay depended on stock prices in the short run, and in the short run, it was easier to improve the appearances of profits than to increase true profits.'[10]

Even though CEOs were committed to capital markets activity, their patsy approach to pricing still requires explanation. Some clients, mainly the very big issuers such as Ford and GM, have red-hot treasury departments that drive a hard bargain with the investment banks: 'We negotiate fees all the time. We nearly ended up in court because an investment bank tried to stick a fee on us that we felt had not been agreed. In the end the investment bank backed off.'[11] But a lot of companies were intimidated by Wall Street and meekly accepted what the investment banks proposed.

There are some legitimate reasons for not shopping around. One of the most famous rainmakers at a bulge-bracket firm fairly points out: 'One reason that price competition does not exist is that in many deals confidentiality is a factor and clients do not want too many firms knowing about their plans in case there is a leak. On disposals, where it is less important to keep things secret, there are more beauty competitions and more negotiation on fees.'[12]

Another banker points out: 'It's like going to the doctor. If you are sick and you can afford to pay, you will always go to the doctor that is best qualified and with the best record. You would not risk going to an inferior one just to save a few dollars. It's the same with M&A and IPOs.'[13]

In the context of the deal, price is not a top priority: 'The sums involved in the major deals are enormous and these are life changing events for the companies and the people involved. They value high class advice, they go for those who they think are the best possible people and they don't want to sour the relationship by quibbling about price. No one has found that price is an effective way of getting business.'

The lack of price sensitivity is also due to the accounting treatment of investment banking fees. The underwriting spread in capital markets issues is charged against the proceeds and merger fees are taken on the balance sheet, not the profit and loss account. Sir Peter Job believes that 'Charging investment banking fees to goodwill makes them invisible and so they are not challenged. It is a cost and should be taken up front.'[14] The bankers, by contrast, like the system just the way it is: 'There seemed to be two different kinds of money in circulation: free money that no one cared about and real money.'[15]

Because it is low down their priority list, CEOs often leave pricing discussions until the last minute. One CEO told me how his adviser threatened to walk away from a hostile bid at a very late stage over a disputed $1 million on the fees. He said: 'I had to decide what was in our shareholders' interests: dropping a deal that we really believed in or paying the extra $1 million that the bank wanted. We paid up. I guess we should have pressed them for an answer earlier.'[16]

He should indeed, but he was not alone in making such an expensive mistake. Who in the heat of battle, when decisions are being taken that can make or break careers and after a relationship has been built up with an investment banker they think they can trust, is going to quibble about price?

By the time the issue gets discussed, the company is too deeply committed to the bank and the banker to risk souring the relationship.

An investment banker used a familiar analogy to describe what happens: 'This is an incredibly sophisticated sale. The shape of the deal is moving all the time and the players only know its precise form, or even whether it is going to happen at all, very late in the day. Negotiating fees at that point would be like arguing with your heart surgeon in the middle of the operation.'[17]

With exhaustion setting in, nothing to lose personally and the expenses being tucked away in the balance sheet, not charged to earnings, it is very easy for company bosses to decide not to press for price cuts: 'There is a point where you become absolutely exhausted and where it is easy to say "What's another $5 million between friends?"'[18]

Outsiders are amazed by such anecdotes: 'Why on earth don't CEOs ask the question about price in the first meeting with the bankers? When we meet the architect who is going to oversee extending our home, or when we make any major decision involving professional advice, the question about price surely comes up very early on.' It does indeed, but not, it appears, when businesses were giving millions of dollars of other people's money to their trusted advisers.

Boards

Strong and independent boards might have stepped in to cross-examine the CEOs and their advisers but they were often hand in glove with executive management and the investment banks. Independent directors were frequently invited on to the board by the CEOs. Many independent directors are top corporate people themselves familiar with investment banks, in tune with their thinking and sometimes even sitting on their boards. Filings by J. P. Morgan Chase in 2003 revealed that thirteen of its directors were also directors of a further twenty-four prominent companies, including the New York Stock Exchange.[19]

Inviting influential business people onto the boards of banks can create unfortunate perceptions. Klaus Zumwinkel, chief executive of Deutsche Post, which listed its Postbank subsidiary in 2004 through an IPO, is also a director of Morgan Stanley, which co-led the issue. His appointment to Morgan Stanley took effect within two months of the selection of the issue's investment banks. All concerned deny that the appointment affected the decision.[20] But when a senior manager of a top corporate joins the board of a leading investment bank – and there are many similar examples – powerful connections are being made. With such overlapping circles, it is the perception of a conflict of interest or of an over-close relationship that can cause concern whatever safeguards are put in place.

The close connections between senior business people and their advisers mean that the investment bank is frequently selling into a receptive environment. A consequence was outlined to me by one of the world's top investment bankers: 'A true relationship comes when the CEO feels comfortable with one person and one bank. You are expected to deliver a reasonable price but it is not the be-all and end-all. Everyone feels comfortable and does not inquire about price. It is a rough and ready thing.'[21] A better description of crony capitalism I have yet to hear.

Issuers

One of the mysteries of the IPO process is why issuers were so forgiving of the investment banks, allowing them to persist with high fees and not objecting when the shares they had just sold very often rose to a premium. The difference between the price at which shares are issued and the price at which they open is known as 'money left on the table' by the issuer. As the academics Loughran and Ritter pointed out, 'The average IPO leaves $9.1 million on the table. This amount is approximately twice as large as the fees paid to investment bankers, and represents a substantial indirect cost to the issuing firm.'[22]

It is not as if the issuers are financially naive. Hard-bitten private equity firms have a hand in most IPOs and like other sellers, such as corporations spinning off divisions or governments privatizing companies, are regular users of the capital markets and should be able to use their experience and muscle to drive a hard bargain. But although a few in San Francisco's Sand Hill Road venture capital community grumbled during the bubble, on the whole issuers were as quiescent about the money left on the table as they were about the 7 per cent spread.

Academics use prospect theory to explain why vendors are prepared to accept underpricing. People and organizations on the point of selling something for tens, hundreds even thousands of million dollars appear reluctant to jeopardize the whole process by upsetting the advisers on price. Similarly, most of the money left on the table occurs when the offer price is raised during the book-building. Issuers are more tolerant of excessive underpricing if they simultaneously learn about a valuation that is higher than they were expecting.

There may also be a more fundamental reason why the sellers were prepared to accept lower prices. They instinctively knew what subsequent performance confirmed: the first-day premium is not to be trusted. IPOs are classic cases of 'insiders know best'. Stock market analysts have always studied the share transactions of insiders very carefully and avoid recommending shares where the directors or other insiders are selling. The inside track is always the fast track and so too, it appears, with IPOs. Buyers beware!

Governments

The investment banks depended on the support of the American and British governments for their success. From the time of President Reagan and Mrs Thatcher onwards, they gave that support through conviction and expediency.

Successive rulers in Washington and Westminster believed that businesses worked best if freed of regulation and the financial services industry seemed to be an obvious place to start. Rule after rule, sometimes law after law, were changed to make it easier for the world to do business with the financial services industry, and for the financial services industry to do business with the world. During the eighties and nineties nearly every change and every new interpretation of existing laws and regulations went in their favour, culminating in the Gramm-Leach-Bliley Act of 1999, which effectively repealed Glass Steagall. The results were acclaimed by economic liberals: 'Over the past two decades financial deregulation has brought huge benefits in the form of more competition, greater innovation and easier and cheaper access to capital.'[23]

Expediency followed conviction when the American and British governments found that they needed financial markets to survive. The ability of markets to fund the US budget deficits was crucial to Presidents Reagan, Bush, Clinton and George W. Bush. In Britain, privatization generated receipts of £60 billion, 1981–96, in many years baling out a budget deficit. It funded the tax cuts of the Thatcher years and the investment banks were the organizations that made it all possible. Britain was also very heavily dependent on the City's overseas earnings, which kept the trade account in reasonable balance.

This mutual dependence reminded governments how dangerous it would be to rock the boat. It explained the willingness of Washington to encourage the banks to bail out the failed American hedge fund manager Long-Term Capital Management when it got into trouble in 1998. The failure of an institution of that size would have jeopardized the financial services sector. It simply could not be allowed to occur. Washington and Westminster had so much riding on Wall Street and the City that they could not and cannot afford to upset them.

Mutual dependence was cemented by close political connections between government and the investment banks. As ever when Wall Street was involved, money played a big part. In the 2004 election cycle, the securities and investment industry was the fourth largest political contributor, 52 per cent going to the Republican Party and 48 per cent to the Democrats.[24] Midway through the elections, Goldman Sachs staff had reportedly given more to each party than any other donor gave to both parties combined, whilst Morgan Stanley was reportedly the second biggest political backer in America.[25] According to the securities law expert Professor John Coffee of Columbia University, the financial support of the Business Roundtable, the trade association representing the most powerful group of CEOs, was 'crucial to funding' President Bush's 2004 campaign for re-election.[26]

Frank Partnoy described how politicians encouraged the financial services industry with some fairly obvious messages: 'When Republicans decided to hold this year's [2004] presidential convention in New York they aimed to capitalise on more than memories of September 11

2001. They also wanted money from Wall Street. Likewise Democrats chose Boston not only for its history and charm but because it is the headquarters of many embattled mutual funds eager to avoid the regulatory spot light. These financial firms were hungry for ways to influence and reward their preferred legislators.'[27]

Financial support was reinforced by close personal relationships. There is a regular traffic between Wall Street and Washington often involving senior people from the investment banks. For example, in the early nineties Robert Rubin and Stephen Friedman were co-chairmen of Goldman Sachs until Rubin left for Washington, eventually becoming Treasury Secretary under President Clinton. Rubin went back to Wall Street with Citigroup in 1999 and then Friedman became President Bush's chief economic adviser in 2002. In common with many senior investment bankers, Goldman Sachs' partners were so wealthy, especially after the IPO in 1998, that they were able to take a not-for-profit approach to later life. Jon Corzine spent an estimated $60 million on the road to becoming Senator for New Jersey in 2000. Reuben Jeffrey became a special adviser to President Bush after eighteen years as a partner, and another former partner, Andrew Alper, took charge of New York City's Economic Development Corporation after being approached by the city's Mayor Michael Bloomberg. Bloomberg himself had made his fortune out of serving financial markets through his media and information technology network.[28]

A problem with involving investment bankers in government business is that their motives can be misinterpreted. When at the height of the Enron crisis Robert Rubin, by this time a top executive of Citigroup, called Peter Fisher, a senior official at the Treasury Department, to see if he thought it was sensible for him or someone else at the Treasury to call the ratings agencies and defer downgrading Enron's debt, Rubin's intervention was much discussed. He had begun the conversation by saying this is 'probably a bad idea'. Joseph Stiglitz wrote that: 'at the time many did not know the extent to which Citibank was exposed, how much it had helped Enron to engage in its duplicitous practices and how much money it had loaned to Enron, money which would likely not be fully repaid if Enron went bankrupt.'[29] Rubin fairly commented: 'I can see why that call might be questioned, but I would make it again under those circumstances and knowing what I knew at the time. There was an important public policy concern about the energy markets – not just a parochial concern about Citigroup's exposure.'[30]

The Gramms are another case in point. Texas Senator Phil Gramm played a leading role in banking deregulation and later joined UBS Warburg as a vice-chairman after he left Congress at the end of 2002. His wife Wendy had joined the board of Enron in 1993 after serving as chairperson of the Federal Commodity Futures Trading Commission. Both Mr and Mrs Gramm played a role in keeping the complex energy derivatives trading engaged in by Enron free from regulation.[31] Doubtless altruistic support for a company with headquarters in Senator Gramm's state was the motive. But how much clearer everything would have been if they had both kept out of the energy and financial services industries after leaving public life.

Just in case legislators were not sufficiently swayed by conviction, expediency or cash, the investment banking trade associations kept up incessant lobbying. A former SEC Chairman described how the Securities Industry Association's Washington office employed about thirty people, of whom over half were involved in lobbying, and also hired outside lobbyists on special issues.[32] The International Swaps Dealers Association was particularly effective at keeping derivatives out of regulation. The large banks ran a successful campaign against Glass Steagall to allow the money centre banks into investment banking. One of the few occasions when lobbying failed was when SEC chairman Arthur Levitt introduced Fair Disclosure, a rule that required corporate executives to make public any information that they passed on to analysts, but even then 'When Levitt announced his fair disclosure plan, the Wall Street firms and their corporate clients raised a huge, self-serving ruckus.'[33]

Lobbying is of course the American way: every interest group lobbies Washington and the financial services industry's is a particularly effective lobby. Inevitably, after the takeover of the City of London by Wall Street's banks, a similar process is now under way in Britain. The Labour Government was initially uncomfortable with the City but sensed that it needed it and built relations with the investment banks. Prime Minister Tony Blair spoke at a meeting for business people organized by Goldman Sachs[34] and, as if to confirm that top politicians would appear at investment banks, shortly afterwards, in April 2004, Gordon Brown opened the new London offices of Lehman Brothers. Europe's banks have followed the Americans' example in taking lobbying seriously. London's Securities Institute appointed Simon Culhane as chief executive in 2004 straight from Deutsche Bank, where he was deputy head of UK government relations, having previously worked in the Prime Minister's efficiency unit.[35]

Just as in America, former investment bankers are turning up in government, and ex-government servants are turning up in investment banking. In 2002, James Sassoon, a former banker, took office as managing director of finance and regulation at the Treasury, becoming its most senior outside recruit in decades. At about the same time, Arnab Banerji, a former broker and fund manager, was appointed to be the Prime Minister's City adviser. The Prime Minister's principal private secretary Jeremy Heywood left in 2003 to join Morgan Stanley as a managing director. Heywood had previously held a number of positions at the Treasury, including time as personal private secretary to the Chancellor of the Exchequer, Gordon Brown, and head of the Treasury team that oversees the regulation of financial markets.[36] It is easy to see the road from Whitehall to the City becoming as well worn as that between Wall Street and Washington.

The involvement of former investment bankers in government is essential yet it is also a mixed blessing. It ensures that government is expertly briefed on the financial services industry, but the risk to the public interest is if it gets to hear too much of the industry's viewpoint. The recruitment of former public servants by the investment banks also raises public interest issues. Talented people have every right to work in interesting, well-paid occupations and it is understandable that the investment banks should want to hire them. The public interest, however, should surely require that the knowledge and contacts developed while in public office should not be used unfairly. It is very difficult to determine how far this principle is met by existing safeguards.

Regulators

In a laissez-faire economy, in which government is determined as a matter of principle to let the markets have a free reign, the role of the regulator becomes crucial. Not only do they have to ensure that market participants stick to the rules, they also have to be especially vigilant in keeping a level playing field for competitors and in protecting customers. If they fail and deregulation becomes unregulation, financial markets degenerate into jungle life. This is what happened in the last quarter of the twentieth century, when survival of the fittest broke out in the space left by the regulators. The fight to make more money and gain competitive ground cut across all other considerations, to the detriment of clients and new entrants.

Regulation of the American investment banks is a convoluted affair involving the SEC, the Federal Reserve Board and the Federal Deposit Insurance Corporation and others, depending on the main business of the parent company. Self-regulatory organizations, notably the New York Stock Exchange and the National Association of Securities Dealers, also have significant responsibilities over areas of the industry. With so many overlapping and at times competing agencies, there is room for financial services firms to exploit the gaps between the agencies, a practice known as regulatory arbitrage.

Even allowing for a confused structure and the 'hands off' messages that came out of government, it is hard to escape the conclusion that the US regulators should have seen the problems of the eighties and nineties coming and done more to prevent them. It was obvious that when negotiated commissions were introduced in 1975 and the advisory and underwriting businesses took off in the eighties, the potential conflict of interest that had always existed in the integrated investment banking model would come alive. This message was reinforced during the late eighties when the Boesky and other scandals reminded everyone of the free market's tendency to degenerate into market abuse.

At that stage a strong regulator* should have been on the alert. It

* Although the American investment banks had several regulators, the SEC was to all intents and purposes the lead regulator for client protection.

should have been obvious that the symmetry of the integrated model changed after about 1980. Aside from the fact that the SEC had access to the detailed accounts of the large investment banks, visited them regularly and should have had a clear view of what was happening, the change in the balance of the business was there for anyone to see in the statistics published by the SIA. Securities firms' trading profits overtook commission for the first time in 1984, at which point someone at the SEC should have asked whether the conflict of interest this raised was being managed properly. Underwriting started to become a significant factor from the early eighties and then soared in the second half of the nineties. Everyone in and around the securities business knew what analysts were doing. Someone should have asked themselves, and the banks they were supervising, whether the investors' interests were being looked after.

It did not help that the SEC's workload increased much more than its budget, rising by more than 70 per cent between 1992 and 2000, whilst its staff years rose by only 20 per cent. These were meant to be the years of America's productivity miracle but such an expected increase in regulatory productivity was ridiculous. According to a US General Accounting Office report from 2002 it meant that the 'SEC faces increasing pressure in managing its mounting workload and staffing imbalances that resulted from its workload growing much faster than its staff'.[37]

With staff under such pressure from increases in the number of firms, individuals and new products that they were meant to be watching, it was impossible to provide close supervision. But it is doubtful whether doubling the SEC's budget, as happened at the beginning of this century, or unifying the structure down to a single regulator, as happened in Britain, would on their own have been sufficient to have prevented the crisis. The problem with regulation of the American financial services industry is that it was regulated by the people for the people – but too often 'the people' were insiders rather than the American public at large.

There are many thousands of diligent, public-spirited people working in financial services regulation. Arthur Levitt, chairman of the SEC from 1993–2000, was one, and his memoirs provide a telling account of inadequate resources, inside influence and business-inspired political pressure. Time after time his attempts to stiffen the rules on key issues such as accounting for options and conflict of interest were stalled by influential obstructionism from business and its funded political allies.

The background of the regulators worked to the advantage of the existing structure and against radical change. Even Levitt, who is regarded as having been a crusading chairman of the SEC, emerges from his book as a member of the financial services establishment (he had spent sixteen years working for a broker and twelve years at the American Stock Exchange), as someone who believes in the system as devised and that it can be put right without structural change. After Levitt, the chairmanship of Harvey Pitt, described at the time of his appointment by *The Economist* as a 'lawyer who built his career by getting the most powerful Wall Street firms and individuals out of some nasty scrapes – and most notably out of distressing investigations by the SEC', was another example of inside breeding.[38] And when Pitt left after little more than a year, where did they turn to for help? Why, Wall Street, of course. However, as SEC Chairman, William Donaldson turned out to be a vigorous and tough proposition, to the disappointment of those who expected sympathy from the founding father of the bulge-bracket investment bank Donaldson Lufkin & Jenrette, now part of CSFB.

Events at another key institution, the New York Stock Exchange, illustrated the entwining of regulators and practitioners in a slightly different way. The NYSE is a self-regulatory organization and until governance reforms were announced in 2003 conflict of interest concerns surrounded the way it combined supervision of its members' trading activities with looking after their interests.

Earlier, under the leadership of Richard Grasso, the exchange had looked like an insiders' club as a result of the proliferation of investment banking and brokering bosses on the board. A furore broke out in the media in 2003 when it emerged that Grasso had been awarded rolled-up compensation of $187 million. The NYSE compensation committee, the body that approved Grasso's package, included current and former heads of Bear Stearns, Merrill Lynch, Goldman Sachs, Lehman Brothers and Morgan Stanley.[39] The conflict of interest this created was highlighted by Eliot Spitzer, who pointed out that when they were approving

Grasso's pay they were also discussing with him how to resolve conflict of interest in equity research without regulatory action.[40]

When Grasso was ousted the next permanent CEO was another Wall Streeter, John Thain, who resigned as chief operating officer of Goldman Sachs to take up the position. Thain knew the NYSE well before he arrived. Not only are Goldman's shares listed there but it owns the second largest specialist on the floor, Spear, Leeds and Kellogg. As the former Goldman Sachs chairman, Jon Corzine, said: 'It will be imperative that John Thain separates himself from Goldman Sachs and their interests.'[41] Thain has an outstanding reputation as an able and clear thinking manager, a reputation that was not tainted by controversy over the extensive role played in 2005 by Goldman Sachs in the planned merger of the NYSE and the electronic exchange Archipelago.

The National Association of Securities Dealers (NASD) is another self-regulatory organization that had to face two ways but that for a long time appeared to be better at protecting its members than regulating them. During the early and mid nineties it failed to grip price fixing and during the late nineties was slow to address the conflict of interest issue, despite being responsible for setting the securities industry's code of conduct. In the year 2000 it separated market regulation and operation by deciding to sell the NASDAQ market but criticism lingered on. Arthur Levitt recalled his frustration in a phone call to Mary Schapiro, president of the regulatory arm of the NASD, in December 2000: 'I said that she and NASD chairman Frank Zarb were letting their group revert to the old NASD – one that Wall Street's entrenched interests led around by the nose, to the detriment of the investing public – and that they had to regulate.'[42] The market that the NASD had owned, NASDAQ, was 'blindsided by a series of conflict of interest issues and other questionable practices', according to the *Washington Post*, and 'declined to raise its listing standards to stem the flood of shaky dot-com stocks'.[43]

The two-way street that ran between Wall Street and Washington worked in regulation as well as it did in government. Just as the regulators made top appointments from the ranks of senior bankers, so the bankers increasingly hired senior regulators. After the conflict of interest scandal broke in 2001 many former SEC employees found a demand for their services in new jobs in compliance on Wall Street.[44]

In the most high profile of these moves, Eric Dinallo, who had been chief of the investor protection bureau for Eliot Spitzer, became Morgan Stanley's head of regulatory matters in 2004.[45]

Financial regulation in Britain, which lagged behind that in America in the years after Big Bang, is now generally agreed to have taken the lead. John Reed, formerly boss of Citigroup and interim chief of the NYSE, said: 'I like the British regulation; it works and I can tell you that when I was at Citibank [in London] you certainly knew you were being regulated.' But already the two-way street is opening up in London. The FSA recruited Hector Sants from CSFB in March 2004 to oversee regulation of wholesale and institutional markets.[46] Regulators have to get their staff from somewhere and Sants has a reputation as a fair-minded individual, but it is important to ensure there are plenty of able and experienced career-regulators to work alongside the recruits from investment banking.

Going in the other direction was Sir Howard Davies, the highly effective former chairman of the FSA, who was nominated to the Morgan Stanley board three months after stepping down from his regulatory position.[47] It says a great deal about how well the investment banks have smoothed their profile that students at the London School of Economics, of which Davies is Director, chose to protest not at his board appointment at Morgan Stanley, but at the proposed appointment to the board of Total. The French oil company's links to Myanmar, where the ruling junta was accused of human rights abuses, attracted student ire; Morgan Stanley's alleged role in the mutual fund and other scandals appears not to have offended the budding economists at the LSE. Davies abandoned his plans to join Total but remained on the board of Morgan Stanley.[48]

The widespread practice of hiring former regulators smacks of expediency.[49] Why does an investment bank hire former top regulators such as Davies and Dinallo? The explanation is that Dinallo will help 'each of the business units in their continuing efforts to identify practices or perceptions that may be in conflict with the spirit of the regulatory law and address potential issues before they become problems'[50] and that Davies's 'public policy DNA will add an important new dimension to Morgan Stanley governance'.[51] Both men are very well respected and by reputation independent minded, but the investment banks' decision to appoint them recalls a visit to the health club after the year-end holiday binge. It makes you look good, feel good and helps you follow a better lifestyle, but does it last? Ask any health-club owner what happens to business after the New Year resolutions have worn off. Unless the culture changes, Dinallo and the many others who have moved out of regulation into the industry will have a tough job standing up to the bankers if the competitive pace quickens and the pressure grows to sanction practices that get deals done 'because everyone else is doing it'. We have, of course, heard that before.

Fund Managers

Institutional investors have been kind to the investment banks and brokers. Whereas private investors piled on the law suits in class actions, asset management organizations took what might be called a grown-up attitude. They accepted biased advice, saying that it is their job to pick the stocks; the broker's job is merely to give an opinion. If that is the case, the fund managers, to judge from their results, did a remarkably poor job.

Indeed, one reason for their reticence to take action against brokers is that many fund managers were in no position to have a debate about poor performance. Because so many mutual fund shareholders started to invest close to the top of the market, the average shareholder's annual return between 1984 and 2002, according to one estimate, was a miserable 2.6 per cent – far short of the S&P 500's 12 per cent annual return over the same period.[52]

Fund managers might not have wanted to draw attention to their own poor performance by seeking recovery from brokers, but they should have pushed the point: conflict of interest contributed to the collective failure to see the bubble for what it was. At just the moment when the fund managers needed help, the brokers were deficient. They should have been shouting from the rooftops what they were saying to colleagues in private: sell, sell, and sell. A consequence was that millions got sucked in at the top and no one told them to get out.

Vested interest and influence also kept fund managers on the sidelines, for institutional investors and mutual funds, in particular, were connected to the brokers in all sorts of ways. The fund managers were not in a position to get very upset about laddering and spinning because all too often they were the recipients of the brokers' favours. They relied on them for generous allocations of hot new issues to keep their performance up with the pack and in return were prepared to generate lots of commission.[53]

Mutual funds habitually gave brokers extra trading business for pushing their funds through the brokers' distribution network. Paul Roye, when director of the SEC's investment management division, estimated that directed brokerage accounted for about a fifth of all commissions paid by mutual funds to brokers.[54] In addition to these informal connections, there was also the question of ownership. Eight of the world's top twenty largest institutional investors belonged to organizations that also owned investment banks; they were hardly likely to sue each other.

A further factor in keeping the mutual funds on the sidelines when it came to litigation is that they were involved in their own market timing scandal, a scheme which gave favoured insiders better prices and information than ordinary retail investors by allowing them to buy and sell mutual fund shares at prices established earlier when circumstances were different. It is estimated that this cost a shareholder in the average international mutual fund 1.15 per cent of assets in 2001.[55]

In the absence of action by the fund managers, the directors and trustees who were meant to be looking after the interests of mutual and pension fund members could have stepped in. But virtually all of these worked part time and many were not investment experts: 62 per cent of British pension-fund trustees had no professional qualifications in finance or investment according to a UK Treasury report in 2001.[56] They were advised by consultants who gave tough advice on the asset managers' performance, but they had invented and depended on the whole relative performance game and were hardly likely to question the system. The part-time directors and pension fund trustees were so hindered by myriad responsibilities that it was virtually impossible for them to do more than the bare minimum given the time and expertise that they had available.

Fund managers were more aggressive towards the brokers on price and the commitment of capital. They have successfully driven commissions down to zero in bonds and currencies, and in equities rates have been falling and the proportion of non-commission-bearing net trades has been increasing. The powerful trading desks on the buy side are one of the few points of confrontation in the broker–fund manager relationship. They drive a hard bargain not just on commissions but also on capital commitment, forcing the brokers to put up more and more capital to facilitate their trades. These dealing desks have kept a close watch on the visible costs of trading. The total commission paid is kept under pressure and every trade is closely monitored to check that it is done at the best available price.

However, despite focusing on visible execution costs, institutional investors have been more forgiving of what goes on behind the scenes. A leading broker admits: 'The institutions have cut commissions but commission is only a fraction of the real cost. Market impact is the bigger cost, but they just cut the bit that their customers can see.'[57] Institutions do their best to track market impact but it is a difficult job and they rarely object to proprietary trading by brokers, which is an important but deeply hidden charge on the cost of transacting.

Brokers staunchly defend proprietary trading, arguing that it is an important source of liquidity. Clients and fund managers value the depth of markets above all else when it comes to execution so are reluctant to prompt changes in a system that is very liquid. They back off challenging proprietary trading and are reassured that competition is working by the sight of falling commissions and spreads; in changing the system, they see only risk. One wonders whether their satisfaction would persist if they knew how much the brokers were making from trading with them. A rare public example of displeasure occurred at the end of 2003 when the California Employees Public Retirement System filed a lawsuit against the NYSE and its specialist firms seeking to recoup more than $150 million it said it lost through improper trading.[58]

Generally, clients do not have enough information to see where the investment banks make their money because the results of integration are never split up. Finding the profitable areas in investment banks is like chasing the soap in the bath tub: it is slippery, elusive and always pops up where you are not looking. I have been told by reputable sources at different times that equities, fixed income, derivatives and even advisory work are 'not much better than break even after a full capital allocation'. It all sounds very plausible until you add up the numbers and realize that all those profits must be coming from somewhere. Such lack of transparency makes it impossible for clients to tell who is making what and from whom.

Market users have not helped themselves by accepting bundling, the term given to the investment banks' practice of charging trading commissions without breaking down exactly what the money pays for. By mixing up the costs of trade execution, stock research and various other services, brokers have been able to hide all sorts of inefficiencies and asset managers have been able to pass on part of their own costs to clients because commission charges are deducted directly from their portfolios. The practice came under pressure first in Britain, in a Treasury-sponsored report written by a former top fund manager, Paul Myners.[59]

The asset management industry resisted pressure to abandon bundling for they are able to use it to pass on to their clients costs that they would otherwise have to bear themselves.[60] Brokers' charges are deducted from client portfolios and asset managers have managed to sweep up all sorts of services, including the provision of computers and data, into bundled charges. The big mutual fund Fidelity is in a minority in supporting change,[61] and many asset managers in America and Britain lobbied against unbundling. Unbundling is also unpopular with many brokers, who fear that if the charges are broken down the fund management companies will argue that they are overpaying for research.[62] New rules in Britain in 2006 limit investment managers' use of dealing commission to the purchase of execution and research services and require them to tell customers how commissions have been spent. At the time of writing, the SEC is considering the position in the US in respect of unbundling and soft commission. This is a major issue for the regulators to tackle, for US and UK fund managers pay out over $10 billion annually in equity trading commissions.

In addition to paying investment banks directly through trading with their brokers, institutional shareholders also pay them indirectly. Every M&A fee, every structured finance premium, every IPO spread in the end comes out of shareholders' funds. Individual shareholders try hard to influence company boards, but they lack clout. The asset managers who are looking after other shareholders' interests in pooled funds have the clout but not many make the effort to challenge management. Many fund managers appeared not to make the connection between their own lack of interest in the companies in which they owned shares and mismanagement. A report called *Restoring Trust: Investment in the Twenty-First Century* by the British think-tank Tomorrow's Company, chaired by Sir Richard Sykes, the former chairman of Glaxo-Smith Kline, made such a connection, but it was not well received by sections of the asset management industry. Lindsay Tomlinson, chairman of the Investment Management Association, said he was 'disappointed that all the recommendations were directed at fund managers'. He added: 'We weren't responsible for Enron, WorldCom and conflicts of interest at investment banks.'[63]

Maybe not directly; but by not voting against under-performing boards, excessive compensation or dangerous mergers, and by acquiescing in and sometimes investing in off balance sheet special purpose entities, the investors contributed to the misgovernance. Their inactivity needs explaining. It resulted partly from their belief in the markets culture: they preferred to sell shares they did not like rather than getting involved in sorting out the problem, but they also had vested interests to protect. Managers could derive a large fee income from selling 401(K) personal pension plans via lucrative contracts negotiated with the employing companies. They almost always held shares in these companies somewhere in their portfolios and were reluctant to vote against board motions for fear of damaging these relationships. The American Federation of Labor–Congress for Industrial Organization observed: 'While mutual funds have legal duty to cast these votes in the best interests of these investors, mutual fund firms can have an economic interest in voting with management.'[64] Company pension fund managers faced similar pressures. Some hedge funds use shareholder activism as an investing tool but others are in and out of the shares before they can blink, let alone vote. In many cases, there was a vacuum at the shareholder level that allowed the investment bankers and their CEO friends to do as they wished.

As Professors Roy Smith and Ingo Walter have said: 'The behaviour of institutional investors acting on behalf of the ultimate owners of companies has played a critical part. In the US they control more than 60% of all traded stocks and account for about 80% of total trading volume. In 1998–2000, when the markets peaked, more than 600 companies restated their certified financial results, more than four times as many as in the preceding three year period. Yet these institutions failed to use their muscle to protect clients from the companies responsible for some of the worst acts of financial misinformation.'[65]

What emerges is that the asset managers, investment banks and CEOs were all in on the free markets ball, enjoying generous returns themselves and unwilling to do anything that spoiled the party.

'Core Values Start at the Top'

An article in the *Financial Times* in July 2002 under this headline written by Sanford Weill, then Citigroup's Chairman and CEO, is a patriotic call to arms in the cause of corporate governance: 'America has long had a financial system to be proud of and it is therefore critical – particularly at a time of danger and uncertainty – that both industry and government enact changes to address the recent corporate governance scandals.' Weill had no doubt where the responsibility lay: 'The current crisis is an opportunity to recapture core values. But this will only be possible if CEOs accept the responsibility that comes with their rank. It is up to us to lead the way.'[66]

It is stirring stuff – until you remember that at the time Sandy Weill was one of the world's top bankers who had put together Citigroup's investment bank Salomon Smith Barney. Not only did he then preside over an institution that was at the forefront of the Spitzer scandals; it later emerged that he was linked to some of the most controversial issues, asking the firm's telecommunications analyst Jack Grubman to 'take a fresh look' at AT&T and helping Grubman's children into a prestigious nursery school. As a former broker, Weill was aware of the different roles and responsibilities of the different parts of an investment bank and denied any improper motive. Once the scandal broke he moved aside his head of investment banking and made other senior management changes.

Analysts speak of the intolerable pressure that they were put under as investment bankers moved further and further over to the electric fence that marked the boundary between fair means and foul: 'I fought very hard against the internal pressures to promote the IPOs. You had to be very strong to withstand the bullying, the pressurizing, and the belittling. My attempts to call stocks a sell led to the most torturous, stressful time that you can imagine, including conference calls with the head of research, teams of bankers who tried to destroy my argument and me. They did everything in their power to get me to change my mind, including going to the main board. At a managing directors' meeting I was introduced to the chairman and CEO. "Oh I know all about you," he said, and "playfully" punched me in the stomach.'[67]

Internal politics were decided by the size of wallet, and investment banking had the biggest. At most firms they paid half of the research department's budget and they called the shots: 'Research had a weak position internally and all the terms were dictated to us. We were put under great pressure to cheerlead. The heads of research just went along with it.'[68] Another analyst told me that a link with compensation reinforced the investment bankers' influence: 'At appraisal time we get our peer reviews, thirty or so people giving grades on how you had worked with them during the year. The comments were anonymous but it was obvious that a lot came from investment banking. Comments like "not helpful" or "obstructive" would follow if ever we tried to call the stocks the way we wanted to.'[69]

The senior managers at the top of the investment banks were in a position to know what was going on and they encouraged it, frequently appearing at pitches themselves and encouraging the analysts to cheer even louder. In the opinion of one analyst who was close to the heart of the IPO action: 'They got the wrong guys in Blodgett and Grubman; they should have got the investment bankers and their bosses. You were given no choice: go along with it or resign.'[70]

It is an unimpressive episode. Whilst simultaneously proclaiming the values of the Trusted Adviser, claiming to put clients first, to deal with one client at a time and professing loyalty to the integrity of the market, in reality they gave approval to practices that put the interests of their most valuable clients above the smaller fry and that put their own interests first. It boiled over during the internet bubble, but it had been going on for years. What blinded them to the obvious was a mixture of creed, greed and narcissism.

Creed came from a strong belief in capitalism, the market economy and the virtues of shareholder value: 'a commitment to pursuing market driven reforms', in the words of Henry Paulson, current chairman and chief executive of Goldman Sachs.[71] The unequal distribution of wealth and the flip side of survival of the fittest are not, to people at the top of investment banks, faults in the system at all, rather the reverse. By incentivizing success and motivating the weak to help themselves, many people in investment banking see these attributes as strengths, not weaknesses.

But whatever you think of these beliefs, once they were fed by greed for money and success they became dynamic forces. The industry attracts competitive type A people who are driven to prove themselves King and Queen Rat. With the prospect of making life-changing sums through the annual bonus and share options, the determination to win became all-consuming. The problem was that there was nowhere for all that energy to go. In many businesses it would have spurred firms to make a better product or to win more business by cutting prices. But investment banking is different. Better product is a matter of inspiration, not perspiration, and in many areas – such as investment advice and advisory work – trying harder does not necessarily make it better. The other possible strategy, cutting prices, was considered more likely to be taken to be a sign of weakness than to persuade customers to buy.

If making a better product is hard and cutting prices is counterproductive, management had only three choices. The first was to accept lower profits and profile, neither of which appealed to shareholder-value-wielding Type As playing the free markets game. The second was to cut costs, of which compensation was the only significant variable item. This would have alienated staff and opened the door to competition, especially new entrants, so was always seen as a last resort. The third was to bend the rules, which in many cases were open to interpretation and were increasingly less well supervised by under-pressure regulators. Thus began the creep towards the electric fence. It is easy to see how management got sucked in. Top management appeared to think to themselves: 'The competitors are doing it, the customers do not respond to conventional tools like price cuts and the authorities aren't looking. If we play by the rules no one else is and our firm will lose out. What else are we supposed to do?'

These feelings were encouraged by organizational narcissism. Grounded in Freudian psychoanalytic ideas and characterized by 'a kind of unconscious imperialism' in which 'the organization deludes itself into believing it has powers with no limits',[72] narcissism helps to explain the investment banks' behaviour. Many of their comments and attitudes exemplified hubris. Merrill Lynch boasted that its 'brand, represented by one of the world's most recognizable corporate icons – the bull – builds an enduring emotional attachment and symbolizes who we are'.[73] Morgan Stanley professed to 'see possibilities where others see confusion and risk. We see opportunities in places that others haven't looked.'[74] Goldman Sachs promised to succeed 'by virtue of the firm's global presence, unparalleled reputation and extraordinary people'.[75]

They were a self-confident bunch and they believed their own hype. They had the wealth, the connections and all the trappings of power, and they believed they could do as they wished with clients and the rules. It helped that they could resort to free market theory to justify what they were doing. They were driven further and further to extremes by their competitive streak and the feeling that anything goes in the survival of the fittest. But why didn't a Hank Paulson, a Phillip Purcell, a Sanford Weill (or even a relatively lowly Philip Augar) say: 'Stop. We are not practising what we preach. We talk about client interest and do the opposite. This has to be wrong.'?

The answer is that power leads to hubris and hubris leads easily to sleaze, and so to nemesis.[76] The images of 'fairness', 'trust' and 'openness' promoted by the investment banks in their marketing literature were undermined by the power that they have. Normally clear thinking and hard headed, management became so besotted with their success that they were unable to see their own flaws, promising to put the client first while often putting their own organizations above everyone and everything.

12

Here's to the Next Time

Has the Problem Gone Away?

The argument of this book has been that the integrated model of investment banking enabled a few corporations and individuals to exert great influence over business and government and to garner great wealth along the way. The consequences are not trivial, and are not confined to a few lucky winners and a few unlucky losers. The existence of such a powerful group at its heart distorted the operation of the free market economy. A substantial amount of money went from issuers and investors to the investment banks. It seems very likely that this represents an inefficient allocation of capital, one that weakened economic performance not just in the United States but globally, for the American investment banks spread the market gospel far and wide. It is not only the economies that have been affected: the export of US-style capitalism has changed social values and attitudes from Britain to Beijing.

Modern investment banks grew out of regulation and grew up under deregulation. The seeds were sown in the New Deal, the interventionist era during the 1930s when the US government ring-fenced the investment banks to prevent savers from getting mixed up with them. After fifty years as a protected species, the investment banks put down deep roots and were in a strong position to exploit the opportunities that came along with deregulation in the late twentieth century. The environment for investment banking was perfect as free market economics took hold and capital markets activity reached levels that were previously unimaginable.

By the late 1980s the established investment banks had an edge that enabled them to generate super-profits that they then used to squeeze competitors. This led to frequent churns in the ranks of the aspiring investment banks as their shareholders and management grew weary of an unequal struggle. There was a corresponding increase in the reputation of the top firms because customers perceived them to be the only 'committed' players in the market. They used this reputation to resist pricing pressure, to push clients into transacting and to consolidate their market position. In turn this created more knowledge, more profit and more barriers to entry.

The investment banks' clients acquiesced in the process through conviction, ignorance and vested interest. Regulators and governments stood back, thinking (if they thought about it at all) that the invisible hand of the market would sort out any mess. Only belatedly, when Eliot Spitzer exposed scandalous behaviour on Wall Street, did they toughen up controls. By then, rottenness on Wall Street had spread to other professions, notably auditing, and to boardrooms across America. The real losers are the ordinary people who through their mutual and pension funds were the shareholders in the companies that paid Wall Street's bills.

Is it History or Current Affairs?

As the Spitzer revelations and corporate scandal mounted, the public and the media demanded action. A combination of litigation and regulation produced a change in the corporate governance environment in America. Even the deregulation-inclined Bush administration was forced into action, publishing more pages of rules and regulations in 2002 than any previous administration in any previous year, much of it to do with the Sarbanes-Oxley Act passed by Congress in July that year.[1]

Change focused on two key areas: auditing and corporate governance. The establishment of the Public Company Accounting Oversight Board and more stringent regulation have helped to re-establish auditing as a 'guardian at the gate' profession.[2] The role and responsibilities of boards have also been redefined, with the intention of improving corporate governance. Gene O'Kelly, chairman and CEO of KPMG LLP, believes that as a result of Sarbanes-Oxley, directors are taking their responsibilities more seriously while 'The law's effect on management behaviour is equally striking. Certifying financial statements on penalty of prison time tends to focus a chief executive's mind and chief executives are taking a deeper interest in their organisations' financial reporting. Managements are reinvigorating their ethics policies and procedures.'[3] A study of corporate governance standards at more than 2,500 international companies carried out in 2004 found that American companies had risen to the top of the table for the first time.[4]

In 2006 new rules in accounting for options, the 'free' money that encouraged reckless management will require US companies to deduct the cost of employee stock options from profits.[5] The 'get rich quick' mentality that permeated boardrooms, and which created such fertile conditions for the investment banks to do business, is therefore being tempered.

Not only has the environment in which the investment banks ply their trade changed, so have the regulations under which they work. The Sarbanes-Oxley Act contained a separate section, Title V, on 'Analyst Conflicts of Interest', which set out a broad framework for how this was to be managed. The SEC was required to come up with detailed rules inside a year. The self-regulatory organizations, NASD and the NYSE, were stung into action and produced new rules in 2002. The 'global settlement' of 2003 between the coalition of regulators and the ten investment banks imposed yet more rules and the SROs had another bite at the cherry in 2003.

The upshot of all this was to separate research and investment banking physically, in reporting lines and in terms of compensation; to keep analysts out of investment banking pitches and road shows; and to make the analysts more accountable for the accuracy of their research. The banks have to publish charts that include analysts' names, performance, ratings, price targets and earnings forecasts at least every quarter.[6] The banks involved agreed to pay $432 million to provide investors with independent research for five years. Regulators across the world followed – including Britain, where the FSA additionally wants the companies it regulates to publish statements explaining to clients how they manage conflicts of interest.[7]

American regulators were determined to stamp out the sins of the past, whenever they could identify them. The new-issue market was an obvious target and new rules were devised for share allocation. As part of the 2003 settlement, all of the banks agreed to stop giving clients shares in IPOs with the aim of winning business and not to involve investment bankers in decisions to award shares to individuals. Before being given an IPO mandate a bank must notify the company if it has awarded company officials hot IPO shares in the past. In the current sensitive environment, in which the banks are falling over themselves in a rush to comply with everything and everyone, these guidelines should be sufficient to change behaviour, even though many of the people involved remain the same and stock allocation remains a largely discretionary activity.

Opinion on these measures varies. Wall Street complains that the rules have gone too far. Banning analysts and investment bankers from discussing certain subjects unless there is a lawyer present has been ridiculed as being unnecessary, expensive and cumbersome to operate. Consultants fear that 'the increased regulation in research will impinge on their value-added'. One head of research has been quoted as saying that 'The reforms are driving many good analysts out of the business, reducing the amount of research available and increasing the cost of servicing small investors.'[8] But generally the consensus is favourable. Kei Kianpoor, chief executive of Investars, which evaluates the performance of analysts, stated that the changes have 'done wonders for the performance of sell-side research'.[9]

The reins are also being drawn in on structured finance. Proposals jointly issued by the SEC, the Federal Reserve Board, the FDIC, the Office of the Comptroller of the Currency and the Office of Thrift Supervision were issued in May 2004 and at the time of writing are being discussed with the banks. The proposals would force investment banks to exercise greater oversight of complex derivatives and would make it more difficult for them to claim that they were unaware of what they were being used for in the event of problems. Senator Carl Levin, chairman of the Senate Committee that requested the report after examining the Enron scandal in 2003, believed that 'It essentially tells US banks and securities firms to get out of the business of making money off complex deals that aid or abet deceptive accounting or tax evasion.' The proposals called on banks to create independent committees to review and sign off on such transactions; supply regular reports about them to boards of directors; open themselves to outside review, and retain all documents associated with such deals.[10]

There are some signs that the new rules are being strengthened by market-led reforms, but these are tentative. Investment bankers report a reduction in IPO fees but this has yet to be confirmed by academic analysis. The Google IPO had the potential to break the IPO system, the price and the allocation of shares being decided by an online auction rather than by the investment banks, and the advisers' fees were trimmed; but previous evidence of 'groundbreaking' new issues is not encouraging. The European privatizing governments of the 1990s secured cut prices but had little impact on the industry norm and the influence of the Google IPO may be similarly restricted. In terms of achieving lasting structural change, one senior Wall Street figure goes so far as to say: 'The Google IPO is widely considered to have been a major failure. The venture capitalists in Silicon Valley tried to change the system and flopped big time.'[11]

One area of perceptible market-led change is in shareholder activism. Following the scandals, company managements are feeling increasing pressure from shareholders, whose hand has been strengthened by a requirement for all US-listed companies to have majorities of independent directors.[12] Traditionally active funds such as Calpers, TIAA-Cref and others have forced senior management change at organizations such as the NYSE (Richard Grasso was forced to quit) and Disney (chief executive Michael Eisner was forced to step down as chairman). Shareholder activism also hotted up in Britain after the bull market ended, focusing on the chairmen of under-performing companies. In 2003–4, Sir Peter Davis of J. Sainsbury, Luc Vandevelde of Marks & Spencer, Sir Clive Thompson of Rentokil, Sir Philip Watts of Royal Dutch/Shell and ITV's Michael Green all fell victim to shareholder power. In 2005, hedge funds and other activists used their influence to demand radical change in an increasing number of corporate situations. High profile examples include shareholders forcing Deutsche Bourse to withdraw its aproach for the London Stock Exchange and getting the Dutch business information group VNU to scrap a planned $7 billion acquisition in the US.

Shareholder activists in America, Britain and Europe have set up the International Forum for Active Shareowners, an informal network committed to co-ordinate global shareholder activism. The group lobbied the SEC to reform director nomination rules to make it easier for shareholders to change board members and targeted companies where the chairman and chief executive roles were combined. In November 2003, Calpers and the British Universities Staff Superannuation Fund came together to vote against the appointment of James Murdoch as BSkyB chief executive at the annual meeting. Organizations such as Institutional Shareholder Services and Glass-Lewis, which advise shareholders on how to cast their proxy votes, have also been increasing the pressure on managements.

Fund managers themselves are beginning to change. Many of the objectives and methods of the twentieth century that led a lot of active funds up a blind alley in pursuit of relative performance are being dropped. There is growing interest in absolute rather than relative performance; in liability driven investment; in alternative investments such as hedge funds, and in quantitative techniques topped up by active management. Asset management firms appear to be growing less reliant on brokers. The average number of in-house analysts at US institutions jumped from nine in 2002 and 2003 to eleven in 2004.[13] In doing so they are following the model of Capital Group, which has outshone other US fund managers over a long period by using its own research rather than relying on brokers.[14]

The cosy link between brokers and mutual funds is under fire from the SEC. Directed brokerage, whereby mutual funds directed commissions on trading shares in their portfolios to broker-dealers to compensate them for distributing fund shares was banned at the end of 2004.[15]

Faced with reviews from the regulators, fund managers are scaling down soft-dollar payments by which brokers provide fund managers with third-party services in return for enhanced commission. So too with recapture programmes, in which funds trade with brokers at full commission rates and the broker rebates a certain amount of the cost to the fund in a 'recapture check'.[16]

All three players in the market – the investment banks, the fund managers and the corporates – are facing a much more aggressive line from the regulators in the early twenty-first century. Having been wrong-footed by Eliot Spitzer, the SEC has made a determined play to recapture the high ground. As Chairman, William Donaldson was scathing about the financial services industry, notably at the SIA conference in Boca Raton in November 2003. Sounding more like Eliot Spitzer than any stereotyped SEC chairman, he condemned the malpractices in the investment banking and broking industries: 'These occurrences represent a fundamental betrayal of our nation's investors and are symptomatic of a disease that has afflicted far too many in our industry.' He urged the industry to pull together and live up to a higher ethical standard, warning them that: 'You can be sure that if you don't – those of us in government will.'[17]

To some extent the words have been backed by action. Its increased budget has enabled the SEC to bring in more resources and the agency has been reorganized and invigorated. Sarbanes-Oxley left the detailed corporate governance and audit reforms to the SEC and its rules and proposals in respect of hedge fund registration, director elections, mutual funds governance and market structure show that the SEC has taken up the running from Congress. The SEC also appears to have become more decisive in enforcement. A new Office of Risk Assessment has been formed to spot new problems early and, according to its first ever chief, Peter Derby, to change old attitudes: 'There has been a feeling that either certain things are not illegal or there really isn't a problem yet. We're taking a position of being proactive.'[18]

The NYSE has also responded to its crisis, improving its corporate governance structure by separating regulation and market operation and replacing the old insiders' club with a streamlined board of eight independent directors. The important change was the introduction of a more rigorous structure 'to ensure that NYSE Regulations is insulated from influence from NYSE members' in December 2003.[19] The much criticized specialist system of traders working on the floor of the exchange has been shaken by the board's introduction of some electronic trading alongside the traditional arrangements.

The voluntary actions of a few investment banks that have gone further than minimum regulatory standards also suggest that the message has got home. Morgan Stanley was especially high profile in the changes it made. When chairman Philip Purcell outlined the rigorous steps the firm had taken to deal with conflicts of interest, 'fully acknowledging them, disclosing them and forthrightly addressing them'.[20] Other firms followed a similar line in voluntarily extending conflict of interest controls into areas that deal with trading. They moved their proprietary trading desks away from the customer trading business, cut the electronic links between them and stopped proprietary traders from speaking to the firm's analysts, market makers and traders.

Proprietary trading by customer market makers remains, of course, embedded in the trading floors, but even sceptics are impressed by how far the investment banks have gone. One said: 'The investment banks have done a brilliant job at reinventing themselves. There is more transparency, more integrity and more efficiency than ever before.'[21]

Top management such as Hank Paulson, whilst choosing their words carefully, beat their breasts in public: 'For an integrated investment bank such as Goldman Sachs, conflict management has always been a core competency because it is critical to our reputation and a key to our success ... Generally we meet these challenges. But, unfortunately, particularly in the context of the technology and telecom bubble of the late 1990s, we have not done as good a job as we might have in preserving and protecting the perception of the independence of our research analysts who play a vital role in the investing and capital allocation process.'[22]

This may be the beginning of a new and decisive movement that will lead to a permanent clean-up, or it may be merely 'morning-after' good intentions that will fade once the hangover goes. It is extremely difficult to tell. The investment bankers' most practised art is presentation. They look so sincere, they sound so sincere and they can devote mountains of financial and intellectual capital to making things appear the way they are not. They may actually truly intend to do what they say they are going to do. But when the *Financial Times* refers to 'Honest effort to clean up research' it is as well to remember some of the other things the investment banks have said and done before joining in the applause.[23]

Take Morgan Stanley, for example. Purcell's comments at the SIA sounded good and the actions taken seemed concrete, but then so did the slogans 'First class business in a first class way' and 'One client at a time' and a recent annual report which said: 'A major accomplishment in 2001 was the continued move closer to true client centricity in every business. Each business has restructured to focus on and better serve our clients.' But in November 2003, without admitting or denying the allegations, Morgan Stanley agreed to pay $50 million to its customers who had bought certain mutual fund shares since 1 January 2000 after the SEC said that 'a select group of mutual fund complexes paid Morgan Stanley substantial fees for preferred marketing of their funds. To incentivize its sales force to recommend the purchase of shares in these preferred funds Morgan Stanley paid increased compensation to individual registered representatives and branch managers on sales of those funds.'[24] The SEC alleged that Morgan Stanley did not adequately disclose these arrangements to its retail customers. Presumably, some of these clients bought them believing that they were being sold 'first class business in a first class way' or enjoying the benefits of 'true client centricity'.

If the SEC allegations are to be believed, even a bank such as Morgan Stanley, which over any reasonable period emerges as an example of a well-managed intricate business, talks a cleaner game than it plays, and there are similar examples to be found at all of the leading investment banks. Merrill Lynch's annual report for 2002 stated that: 'Merrill Lynch was built on an inviolable set of Principles: Client focus, Respect for the Individual, Teamwork, Responsible Citizenship and Integrity. These values form the basis of our culture. They are a covenant amongst our employees, clients and shareholders.' Yet the SEC alleged that 'from at least July 1999 through June 2001, research analysts at Merrill Lynch were subject to inappropriate influence by investment banking at the firm' resulting in the publication of 'false or misleading research' and 'exaggerated or unwarranted research or research that lacked a reasonable basis'.[25]

Readers of Citigroup's annual report published early in 2004 must have been impressed by the pursuit of 'best practices in a given area' and by the acknowledgement that 'because of our size and scope, because of the benefits of our position of business leadership, we are held to a higher standard. We accept this responsibility.' Yet in August 2004 a Citigroup trader sold €11 billion of Euro-zone government bonds in just two minutes and bought them back lower down, having spooked other traders and crashed the trading system. The *Financial Times* journalist John Plender described these as 'worst practice actions' and challenged management to take disciplinary action or 'be seen as a bunch of hypocrites presiding over a thoroughly rotten culture'.[26] In September 2004 the firm sent a memo to all investment banking staff stating that it regretted the trade, which it described as an 'innovative transaction' but one that 'did not meet our high standards'.[27] Decisive management action followed, but it was not a good month for Citigroup for Japan's Financial Services Agency ordered it to close its private banking offices in Japan, accusing it of selling securities and derivatives at unfair prices without explaining the risks. The FSA said Citigroup had developed 'a law evading sales system that disregards the laws and regulations of Japan' and commented on 'a management environment in which profits are given undue importance by the bank headquarters'.[28]

It has been so long since the gulf between the investment banks' public statements and what was really going on emerged that it has ceased to be shocking. But it is important to remember what occurred and to be wary of accepting reform at face value. Not only do the investment banks have a history of saying one thing and doing another, they are amongst the most ingenious organizations known to mankind. They constantly adapt to new circumstances and evolve into new money-making machines. One investment banker recalls a conversation at Harvard in 1982: 'I was just coming up to graduation and I was set on a career in investment banking. But rule 415 had just been introduced simplifying share issues and the papers were saying that it meant the end for investment banking. Meantime Michael Porter and others were showing us graphs pointing downwards and saying the industry was headed for commoditization. But I went to see another professor and asked him whether he thought the game was over for the investment banks. "No," he said. "Investment bankers are the smartest people around. If new rules come in at 9 a.m. by 5 p.m. they are sitting down trying to find profit opportunities in and around the new rules. They will survive." '[29]

What they had been doing for half a century in 1982 held good for another twenty years, and their ingenuity will surely last for at least another twenty. They will doubtless find ways to live with new rules and to develop new products not covered by them. They are already hard at work at it, for example finding a way round the soft money ban on political contributions imposed by the McCain–Feingold 2002 electoral reforms by spending up to $5 million each on lavish meals and parties during the 2004 political conventions. It was neatly summed up by Frank Partnoy: 'The donations reinforce a prevailing ethos on Wall Street and in Washington that rules are made to be broken.'[30]

Lobbying is also likely to weaken the intentions of regulators and legislators. It seems likely to remain a feature of political and business life despite new attempts in Congress to control it.[31]

In the UK, hard-hitting Financial Services Authority proposals for brokers to be more transparent about their charges to fund managers were delayed and watered down in 2004 after a campaign led by the Investment Management Association and the investment banks and brokers. The lobbying was strong because the proposal threatened the ability of brokers and fund managers to sneak charges past the end users. Paul Myners, the author of the Treasury review that had first suggested the reform, commented: 'Delays over the reform of bundling reflect the power of the industry lobby and the relative impotence of the ultimate customer.'[32] One thing is certain: on a really important issue, the investment banking lobby rarely loses.

The passage of time is likely to diminish public interest in investment banking and to weaken the resolve to reform. It is already happening: within two years of the act being passed it was generally accepted that 'attitudes towards the Sarbanes-Oxley Act have changed. Business leaders and their lobbyists – including John Thain, chief executive of the New York Stock Exchange – warn that the pendulum of reform is in danger of swinging too far.'[33] In 2004 the US Chamber of Commerce launched a legal action against a new SEC rule requiring mutual funds to have independent chairmen, and widespread opposition to an SEC proposal that hedge funds should register with them got the support of Alan Greenspan.[34]

The outlook for investment banks' profits contains dangers of many kinds. Real annual returns from markets during the next decade are forecast to be closer to the 100-year average of 5 per cent for earnings, only a third of the level seen in the period 1982–2000.[35] Under these circumstances, the investment banks' returns, along with those of other financial services firms, are almost bound to fall.

Falling returns from the investment banks might be taken as a sign that market forces have prevailed and that abnormal profits and therefore malpractice have been outed. But it will be as well to keep an eye on what is happening elsewhere in the economy, for if corporate earnings growth, inflation and interest rates turn out to be as low as expected, the investment banks' relative returns might not look so bad after all. And although the bezzle might fall in absolute terms, its impact on investors' portfolios could be devastating given the low returns they are likely to be making in such an environment.

Falling returns for the investment banks would bring other dangers too. Unless the banks radically reduce their expectations – for example, Morgan Stanley's target ROE was stated to be 18–20 per cent in the 2002 Annual Report and Deutsche Bank has a 25 per cent target – the pressure on management and producers will be intense. This will mean more risk, more volatility and more pressure to cut corners as they try every measure to avoid permanently rebasing profits, returns and compensation.

Herein lies the danger in the post-Spitzer approach to reform. Nothing was done to remove conflict of interest, only to manage and regulate it better. History suggests that the combination of conflict of interest, high expectations and an incentive-based environment will always create huge temptations. History also suggests that the investment banks are prone to lapses; that regulators fall all too easily under their influence; and that institutional investors find it difficult to sustain interest in corporate governance. Simply tightening the rules may not be effective in the medium term, let alone the long term.

As Judge Brenda Murray noted in a judgment handed down against the auditing firm Ernst & Young, independence from conflict of interest is 'a state of mind, a subjective condition not easily demonstrated'.[36] The state of mind that needs to change in financial services was described by Sir Richard Sykes: 'It's all about making sales and getting commission, instead of providing products to meet long-term needs.'[37] For that to change, there needs to be a massive shift in culture, reinforced by new compensation practices, which are at present heavily weighted to performance-related bonuses.

Market economists have faith in reform through fuller disclosure: 'It would be more sensible to respond to past excesses by putting the emphasis on fuller disclosure. That would leave market forces to determine what kinds of intermediary are appropriate, how they should be structured and what they should earn. Indeed, the markets have already savaged the investment banks, which are fast slimming down and restructuring in response.'[38] The problem with this is that market forces are imprecise in application and give too much power to the established players. An alternative solution is the one that the investment banks have sought to avoid by clever arguments and intensive lobbying whenever it is threatened: structural reform.

Separation of Advice and Execution

Trading in the integrated model poses two problems. First, there is a conflict of interest between advising the client and making a proprietary profit that may be irreconcilable. Second, the combination of execution and advice creates so much market power that it is difficult for the market to operate fairly.

It is not possible to solve the first problem merely by separating proprietary and customer trading. Putting proprietary traders in ring-fenced areas and denying them access to non-public trading information systems addresses only the smaller part of the issue. Most own-account trading goes on in market making and it is there that client and proprietary interests most commonly collide. Allowing market makers to be owned by brokers who advise clients and operating them in close co-ordination is what creates the major conflict of interest in trading.

The investment banks argue that this conflict of interest can be managed. But it is virtually impossible to separate their own interests from those of their customers when it comes to trading. Through influence, relationships, informal pressure, nods and winks, salespeople will always tend to favour the in-house book and traders will always seek to benefit from advance knowledge of in-house order flow. Traders would need to be in separate legal entities and to have different reporting lines to customer advisory business for this conflict to be managed properly.

The investment banks defend the current system by referring to the extra liquidity provided by proprietary positions. Aside from the fact that it is questionable whether extra liquidity is advantageous to the end clients, leading as it can to portfolio churn, this is nothing more than self-justifying marketing babble: to argue that proprietary trading is there to help the client insults everyone's intelligence.

The strengthening of independent specialist trading and jobbing firms, such as exist in the New York Stock Exchange and formerly existed on the floor of the London Stock Exchange, and their enforced separation from the investment banks and brokers would stop the conflict of interest between trading and advising. Such firms would be able to transact on-exchange or off-exchange and be able to carry out proprietary trading. They would not be allowed to advise investors or to be owned by firms that advise investors. They would not be able to deal directly with investors, only with brokers acting on behalf of investors. Brokers, on the other hand, would not be able to trade for themselves but would have to deal for clients on an agency basis through the specialist trading firms or electronic order books.

The consequence of this would be that everyone would know where everyone else stood. Investors would know that brokers were giving honest advice and not seeking to protect their trading books. They would be able to judge whether excess returns were being made by looking at the published results. Brokers would know that their only duty was to give their clients best advice and find best execution for them. There would be no question of tipping the wink to in-house traders. Traders would know that their job was to make a profit and could turn a deaf ear to pleas for favoured treatment of 'special' clients. This system would need to apply to all asset classes – stocks, bonds, commodities and derivatives.

Separation of Broking and Investment Banking

A similar segregated approach is advocated for capital markets issues.[39] Under the current system the same investment bank advises the issuer and arranges distribution through its broking arm. The new rules and regulations have done nothing to address the fundamental problem: that it is very difficult for a single institution simultaneously to advise both the buyer and the seller in a single transaction. Breaking the link with analysts is not enough when the investment bank advising a corporate issuer uses its own broker to distribute the securities. The banks are still working on both sides of the deal, in that advice is still being given to potential investors by broking salesmen who are getting paid by investment banking through an internal transfer from the spread earned in the deal.

The pure solution would be for origination and distribution to be handled by separate firms. The relationship with the issuer would be with the investment bank and the bank would invite independent brokers to pitch for distribution rights to the deal. Brokers would only pitch if they felt that the deal was right for their clients, namely the investors. They would be in the deal because they liked it, because they thought it would be good for their clients, and everything would be open and above board. The investment bank's in-house broker would not be involved in distribution of the deal.

The Segregated Model

Separating the functions in this way would minimize the cross-subsidies that exist at present and increase the transparency of prices and profits. Brokers would have to make their money from commission. They would need to sharpen up their services to investors, pay their staff less and accept lower profits. More money would stick with the end investor and portfolio performance might improve if everyone had an equal opportunity to exploit market inefficiencies. The new trading firms would be measured on their price and size competitiveness; the market would decide which of them would flourish on straightforward criteria.

Without the ability to cross-subsidize and raise barriers to entry, the power of the big firms would be reduced and new entrants – including small and medium sized independents – would find it easier to break in, thus offering wider customer choice. Reducing the power of the investment banks would change the balance between the customer and the investment banker. That might persuade the clients to look more carefully at what it is that they get from their investment banks. It might even persuade them to think twice before they transact. CEOs, independent directors and shareholders and their representatives need to resist the hidden price escalator of basis point charging and seek negotiated fees, to adopt a much more sceptical approach to investment bankers' presentations and to challenge CEOs in a hurry.

Here's to the Next Time

This book has suggested that inequality lies at the heart of the modern free market. In the past twenty-five years economic performance has probably suffered from so much capital being diverted from productive areas of the economy into the relatively few hands of the investment banks' shareholders and employees. At the margin, some of this is recycled into the economy, especially in the areas around New York City and London, and some flows back to ordinary people if their mutual and pension funds hold investment banking shares; but this is a bizarre and inefficient way to recycle capital.*

Market forces will not sort this out until the market is set free. It is not enough to rely on the regulators to make the present structure work, for the regulators will always struggle to keep up with the pace of change in the modern financial services industry. The only real solution is to change the model so that infringements and market abuses are easier to spot. By making prices and profits transparent and by reducing the power of the investment banks, the efficiency of capital allocation would be improved. Capital would be redirected away from the intermediaries back to the end users. Headline fees might rise in some areas but the true cost of capital would almost inevitably fall because investment banking profits – both published and hidden in the form of excessive compensation – would fall.

The emergence of less powerful financial services institutions and a bigger role for small and medium sized firms runs counter to the prevailing doctrines of globalization and scale. Such developments

* Most investors are likely to be underweight in shares held in the independent investment banks on account of the high proportion of shares owned by the employees.

would be highly inconvenient for the financial services conglomerates that have grown or bought integrated investment banks. But precedents for breaking up big industries exist in other sectors, such as America's telecommunications industry and the privatized British utilities. Other professions, such as law, that are built around smaller organizations function well, and some commentators expect the consequence of market concentration in auditing to be the revival of medium sized firms.

In medicine there are no integrated global hospital brands. Indeed one wonders how ready patients would be to commit themselves to the Bulge Bracket Hospital if they knew that the agenda of the doctors and nurses was to push medicines and treatments in which the hospitals' shareholders had a direct financial interest.

There are potential social as well as economic consequences of change. If all market users had broadly equal access to information, the market could become what it is meant to be: free and open, and one in which no participant enjoys an unfair advantage and protected status. This might then trickle down into business, the professions and society at large. The coronation of a group of privileged insiders has gone hand in glove with the triumph of the market culture. Both have had a large impact on the nature of American and British society, contributing to the 'I want it now' culture and weakening egalitarianism, fairness and care. Survival of the fittest is all very well provided that you are fit.

It seems very hard to believe all that has happened in recent years. Scandal has touched most parts of the financial services industry – investment banks, brokers and the exchanges – and clearly investors have ended up footing the bill.

Yet the authorities' response has been very tame. It has consisted of little more than a slap across the wrists and the introduction of new rules – a weak response that surely invites more of the same.

One of the problems in analysing markets, as in analysing many other things, is that it is difficult to imagine that present circumstances will change. Right now, investment banks, regulators and their clients are so compliance-aware that it is hard to believe that they were ever naughty or ever will be again. It was the same last time I wrote about the markets in 1999. Business was strong, recession, bear markets and investment banking lay-offs seemed unimaginable. I felt then as I feel now and close this book with the same words: 'Here's to the next time.'[40]

Notes

Epigraph

1. Galbraith, J. K., *The Great Crash 1929* (Penguin Books edition, 1992), p. 27.

Preface

1. Augar, Philip, *The Death of Gentlemanly Capitalism* (Allen Lane, 2000).

Chapter 1

1. Mahar, Maggie, *Bull!* (HarperBusiness, 2003), p. 315.
2. Morgan Stanley Annual Report, 1999.
3. *Newsweek* (1 January 2000).
4. J. P. Morgan Annual Report, quoted in Smith, Roy, *Comeback* (Harvard Business School Press, 1993), p. 109.
5. Sobel, Robert, *The New Game on Wall Street* (John Wiley, 1987), p. 13.
6. Kaufman, Henry, *On Money and Markets* (McGraw-Hill, 2000), p. 361.
7. Pecora, Ferdinand, *Wall Street Under Oath* (Cresset Press, 1939), p. 75.
8. Ibid., p. 91.
9. Ibid., pp. 84–7.
10. Geisst, Charles R., *Wall Street* (Oxford University Press, 1997), pp. 269–71.
11. Roberts, Richard, *Wall Street* (Profile Books, 2002), p. 31.
12. Packard, Vance, *The Status Seekers* (Longman edition, 1960), p. 112.
13. Stiglitz, Joseph, *The Roaring Nineties* (Allen Lane, 2003), pp. 87–114; Krugman, Paul, *The Great Unravelling* (Penguin Books, 2004), pp. 295–325.

14. Augar, Philip, and Palmer, Joy, *The Rise of the Player Manager* (Penguin Books, 2002), p. 12.
15. Lowenstein, Roger, *Origins of the Crash* (Penguin Press, 2004), pp. 24–5.
16. Wolfe, Tom, *The Bonfire of the Vanities* (Farrar, Straus & Giroux, 1987); *Wall Street* (American Entertainment/20th Century Fox, 1987); Lewis, Michael, *Liar's Poker* (Hodder & Stoughton, 1989).
17. Bruck, Connie, *The Predators' Ball* (Penguin Books, 1989); Stewart, James B., *Den of Thieves* (Simon & Schuster, 1991); Kochan, Nick, and Pym, Hugh, *The Guinness Affair* (Christopher Helm, 1987).
18. For the classic account see James B. Stewart, *Den of Thieves*, op. cit.
19. Bruck, Connie, op. cit., pp. 369–72.
20. Burrough, Bryan, and Helyar, John, *Barbarians at the Gate* (Random House, 2001), p. 622.
21. Geisst, Charles R., *Wall Street*, op. cit., pp. 357–9; Roberts, Richard, *Wall Street*, op. cit., p. 79; Stiglitz, Joseph, *The Roaring Nineties*, op. cit., pp. 37–8.
22. Kochan and Pym, *The Guinness Affair*, op. cit.; Kynaston, David, *The City of London* (Chatto & Windus, 2001), vol. 4, pp. 673–81, 725–6 and 743–4.
23. Endlich, Lisa, *Goldman Sachs* (Alfred A. Knopf, 1999), p. 118.
24. Eichenwald, Kurt, *Serpent on the Rock* (HarperBusiness, 1995); *Business Week* (18 December 1995).
25. Endlich, Lisa, *Goldman Sachs*, op. cit., p. 197.
26. Fay, Stephen, *The Collapse of Barings* (Arrow Books, 1996); Gapper, John, and Denton, Nicholas, *All that Glitters* (Penguin Books, 1997).
27. Partnoy, Frank, *Infectious Greed* (Profile Books, 2003), p. 121.
28. *Washington Post* (11 June 1995), quoted in Partnoy, ibid., p. 55.
29. *Securities Industry Association Factbook 2004*, pp. 60–68.
30. *The Beardstown Ladies Common Sense Investment Guide* (Hyperion Books, 1995).
31. Stiglitz, Joseph, op. cit., p. 275.
32. Jim Ledbetter, *News Hour* with Jim Lehrer, www.pbs.org/newshour (10 January 2000).
33. Stiglitz, op. cit., p. 58.
34. Plender, John, *Going Off the Rails* (John Wiley, 2003), p. 234.
35. This account is based on 'The Investigation' by John Cassidy, *The New Yorker* (7 April 2003).
36. www.sec.gov; *Financial Times* (29 April 2003).
37. Stiglitz, op. cit., p. 92.
38. Class Action Complaint of Lead Plaintiff H. Carl McCall, US District Court, Southern District of New York, p. 76. A class action is a lawsuit in

which a person or a small group represents the interests of an entire class of people.
39. Kessler, Andy, *Wall Street Meat* (HarperBusiness, 2003), p. 189.
40. *Business Week* (13 May 2002).
41. O'Brien, Justin, *Wall Street on Trial: A Corrupted State* (John Wiley, 2003).
42. Speech to the Association for a Better New York, *Wall Street Journal* (10 July 2002).
43. Mahar, op. cit., p. 28.
44. *Financial Times* (4 May, 9 and 10 September 2004).
45. *The Economist* (15 May 2004). All references to *The Economist* copyright © The Economist Newspapers Ltd, London.

Chapter 2

1. Kessler, Andy, *Wall Street Meat* (HarperBusiness, 2003), pp. 198–9.
2. Philip Purcell, speech to the SIA annual conference, 2003 (www.sia.com).
3. *The Economist* (12 August 2004).
4. Speech at conference organized by UBS, *Financial Times* (2 May 2003).
5. *Wall Street Journal* (24 April 2003).
6. *Financial Times* (2 May 2003).
7. Author interview, 2004.
8. Kessler, op. cit., p. 230.
9. Office for National Statistics, *Financial Times* (18 August 2004).
10. It is the acting together that makes the cartel: 'Anti-competitive behaviour does not necessarily involve cartel activity.' Smith, David, *Free Lunch* (Profile Books, 2003), p. 100.
11. Securities Industry Association Antitrust Compliance Booklet, pp. 2–5 (www.sia.com).

Chapter 3

1. Lehman Brothers Annual Report 2002, p. 22.
2. Endlich, Lisa, *Goldman Sachs* (Alfred A. Knopf, 1999), p. 80.
3. Geisst, Charles R., *Wall Street* (Oxford University Press, 1997), pp. 318–19.
4. Hayes III, Samuel L., and Hubbard, Philip M., *Investment Banking* (Harvard Business School Press, 1990), pp. 299–301.

5. Author interview, 2004.
6. Author interview, 2004.
7. www.ml.com, timeline.
8. Partnoy, Frank, *Infectious Greed* (Profile Books, 2003), pp. 107–9.
9. Ibid., p. 86.
10. Author interview, 2003.
11. Rubin, Robert E., *In an Uncertain World* (Texere Publishing, 2003), p. 308.
12. Partnoy, Frank, op. cit., pp. 62–3.
13. SEC Litigation Release 18110 (28 April 2003).
14. 'That Was Then', *The Economist* (26 January 2002).
15. www.thestreet.com (12 July 2000).
16. Freeman & Co., *Back to Basics* (2002) (www.freeman-co.com).
17. Greenberg, Alan C., *Memos from the Chairman* (Workman Publishing, 1996), p. 32.
18. *Financial Times* (27 May 2004).
19. Hintz, Brad, *Large Investment Bank Margin and ROE Trends*, Securities Industry Association Research Reports, vol. 3, no. 2 (11 March 2002), p. 23.
20. Freeman & Co., *2002 and Beyond*, p. 12 (www.freeman-co.com).
21. *The American Lawyer* (July 2003).
22. *Financial Times* (21 May 2004).
23. Research by NYU Salomon Center; 'Per ardua ad astra', *The Economist* (15 April 1999).
24. Author interview, 2003.

Chapter 4

1. John Cleese as the City Gent, 'The Merchant Banker's sketch' (1972).
2. Hintz, Brad, 'Large Investment Bank Margin and ROE Trends', Securities Industry Association Research Reports, vol. 3, no. 2 (11 March 2002), p. 10.
3. *Wall Street Journal* (18 May 2004).
4. Freeman & Co., *2002 and Beyond* (www.freeman-co.com), p. 4.
5. *Financial Times* (20 January 2004).
6. 'The Coming Storm', *The Economist* (21 February 2004), p. 83.
7. Goldman Sachs IPO prospectus, p. 18.
8. Author interview, head of equities, investment bank, 2004.
9. Graham, Benjamin, and Dodd, David L., *Security Analysis* (McGraw-Hill Education, 1951 edition), p. 413.
10. Following Hintz, op. cit. Data collected by the SIA for the securities industry is used in this book as a proxy for the investment banking industry.

11. *SIA Fact Book 2004*, p. 28.
12. The SIA's definition of LIBs is a representative group of the major firms: Bear Stearns, CSFB, Goldman Sachs, Lehman Brothers, J. P. Morgan Securities and Morgan Stanley: Hintz, op. cit., p. 10.
13. Hintz, ibid.
14. Hintz, op. cit., p. 11 for 1980–2000; author calculations for 1990–2003 trend line; *SIA Fact Book 2003*, p. 31, 'Major Firms', for 2001–3 margins.
15. www.sternstewart.com, 'About EVA'.
16. Author interview, 2003,
17. Morgan Stanley Annual Report 2002, p. 3.
18. *SIA Fact Book 2003*, p. 36.
19. *SIA Fact Book 2003*, pp. 36 and 109; *2004*, pp. 32 and 105.
20. Hintz, op. cit., p. 10.
21. Under the CAPM cost of equity is calculated by adding the risk free rate of return (the yield on ten-year Treasuries, say 4 per cent) to the equity risk premium (the amount equity investors require to compensate for the extra risk they accept, a number calculated by academics, say 3 per cent) and multiplying the total by a factor known as beta. Beta measures the volatility of a company's share price and its correlation with the market as a whole. Richard Barker, *Determining Value* (Pearson Education, 2001), pp. 45–8; Wasserstein, Bruce, *Big Deal* (Warner Books, 2000), pp. 609–11.
22. Roger Lowenstein, *Origins of the Crash* (Penguin Press, 2004), p. 230.
23. Hintz, op. cit., p. 20.
24. *Daily Telegraph* (6 June 1998).
25. *American Lawyer* (July 2003), p. 147; Freeman & Co., *2002 and Beyond*, p. 6 (www.freeman-co.com).
26. Freeman & Co., *2001 and Beyond* www.freeman-co.com), p. 27.
27. Calculations from *SIA Fact Book 2004*.

Chapter 5

1. Martin Wolf, *Why Globalization Works* (Yale University Press, 2004). Quote from *Financial Times* (5 May 2004).
2. Lawrence Summers, former US Treasury Secretary, 2001, quoted in Plender, John, *Going Off the Rails* (John Wiley, 2003), p. 7.
3. Industry data in this chapter from *Securities Industry Association Fact Book 2004*.
4. Stiglitz, Joseph, *The Roaring Nineties* (Allen Lane, 2003), p. 275.
5. *The Economist* (16 May 2002).

6. *Financial Times* (14 November 2002); www.oag.state.ny.us
7. Author interview with hedge fund manager, 2003.
8. Author interview with broker at leading investment bank, 2003.
9. *SIA Research Report*, vol ii, no. 7 (August 2001): 'The Roles and Responsibilities of Analysts', footnote 9, p. 10.
10. Taffler, Richard, and Ryan, Paul, Cranfield School of Management Working Paper, 2001.
11. *Financial Times* (14 August 2004).
12. Ibid.
13. Survey by Russell/Mellon CAPS, the US-owned performance measurement consultancy, *Financial Times* (27 January 2003).
14. Fung, Hung-gay, Xu, Eleanor, and Yau, Jot, 'Do hedge fund managers display skill?', *Financial News* (14 June 2004); research by Professor Harry Kat, Cass Business School, *Financial Times* (18 October 2004). CSFB Tremont Index LLC www.hedgeindex.com.
15. Ellis, Charles D., *Capital: The Story of Long-Term Investment Excellence* (John Wiley, 2004).
16. *Financial Times* (24 March 2004); Kay, John, *The Truth About Markets* (Penguin Books edition, 2004), pp, 144–6, 156–7.
17. Ritter, Jay, and Welch, Ivo, 'A Review of IPO Activity, Pricing and Allocations', *Journal of Finance*, vol. 57, no. 4 (August 2002), pp. 1795–6.
18. Author interview, 2003.
19. Ritter and Welch, op. cit., p. 1808.
20. Bradley, Dan, Jordan, Brad, and Ritter, Jay, 'The Quiet Period Goes Out With a Bang', *Journal of Finance*, vol. 58, no. 1 (February 2003), p. 12.
21. Author interview, head of research, investment bank, 2003.
22. Ritter and Welch, op. cit., p. 1797.
23. Plender, John, *Going Off the Rails*, op. cit., p. 17.
24. Lowry, Michelle, 'Why Does IPO Volume Fluctuate So Much?', *Journal of Financial Economics*, vol. 67, no. 1 (2003), pp. 3–40.
25. *Financial Times* (18 February 2004).
26. Geoffrey Boisi, quoted in Endlich, Lisa, *Goldman Sachs* (Alfred A. Knopf, 1999), p. 80.
27. Hayes III, Samuel L., Spence, A. Michael, and Marks, David Van P., *Competition in the Investment Banking Industry* (Harvard University Press, 1983), p. 127.
28. *Financial Times* (24 August 2004).
29. Sudarsanam, Sudi, *Creating Value from Mergers and Acquisitions* (Prentice Hall, 2003), pp. 1–2.
30. *The Economist* (21 February 2004); Moeller, Sara B., Schlingemann,

Frederik P., and Stulz, Rene M., 'Wealth Destruction on a Massive Scale?', *Journal of Finance*, forthcoming paper.

31. Sudarsanam, op. cit., pp. 2–3.
32. Wasserstein, Bruce, *Big Deal* (Warner Books, 2000), p. 179.
33. Author interview, 2004.
34. Partnoy, Frank *Infectious Greed* (Profile Books, 2003), p. 68.
35. International Swaps and Derivatives Association news release.
36. *Financial Times* (30 June 2004).
37. 'A Survey of Risk', *The Economist* (24 January 2004), p. 19.
38. *Business Week* (7 July 2003).
39. *Financial Times* (10 March 2004).
40. *Financial Times* (27 September 2004); *The Economist* (2 October 2004).
41. Partnoy, Frank, *Infectious Greed*, op. cit., pp. 300–301, 351, 390.
42. Ibid., pp. 374–8.
43. United States General Accounting Office, GAO-03-511, *Investment Banks: The Role of Firms and their Analysts with Enron and Global Crossing* (March 2003).
44. Partnoy, op. cit., p. 346.
45. Plender, John, *Going Off the Rails*, op. cit., p. 166.
46. *Wall Street Journal* (14 January 2002).
47. Plender, op. cit., p. 167.
48. *Financial Times* (13 April 2004).
49. Ibid. (30 June 2004).
50. Ibid. (8 January 2004).
51. Ibid. (20 August 2004).
52. Kay, John, *Financial Times* (16 June 2004).
53. *Financial News* (19 April 2004).
54. Pecora, Ferdinand, *Wall Street Under Oath* (Cresset Press, 1939), p. 119.

Chapter 6

1. Smith, Adam, *The Wealth of Nations* (Modern Library edition, 2000), page 148; Smith, Roy, *Adam Smith and the Origins of American Enterprise* (Truman Tulley Books, 2002); Glahe, Fred (ed.), *Adam Smith and the Wealth of Nations: Bicentennial Essays* (University of Chicago Press, 1976).
2. Hintz, Brad, *Large Investment Bank Margins and ROE Trends*, Securities Industry Association Research Reports, vol. 3, no. 2 (March 2002), p. 10.
3. Goldman Sachs IPO prospectus, p. 18.
4. *Wall Street Journal* (18 May 2004).

5. *Financial Times* (24 October 2003).
6. Geisst, Charles R., *Wall Street* (Oxford University Press, 1997), p. 306.
7. Hintz, op. cit., p. 15 ; Freeman & Co., *2001 and Beyond* (www.freeman-co.com), p. 25.
8. *Wall Street Journal* (18 May 2004).
9. Hintz, op. cit., p. 12.
10. Ibid., p. 16.
11. Author interview, head of trading, asset management firm.
12. Author interview, head of trading, asset management firm.
13. Author interview, head of risk, large investment bank.
14. Chen, Hsuan-Chi, and Ritter, Jay, 'The Seven Per Cent Solution', *Journal of Finance*, vol. 55, no.3 (June 2000), p. 1105.
15. Ljungqvist, Alexander, Jenkinson, Tim, and Wilhelm, William, 'Global Integration in Primary Equity Markets', *Review of Financial Studies*, vol. 16, no. 1 (2003), pp. 63–9; *Financial Times* (24 September 2004).
16. Freeman & Co., *Trends in Investment Banking*, p. 15; *2002 and Beyond* (www.freeman-co.com), p. 9.
17. Freeman & Co., *Under Siege* (www.freeman-co.com), p. 7.
18. Freeman & Co., *2002 and Beyond* (www.freeman-co.com), p. 9.
19. Ibid., p. 10.
20. Author interview, former head of investment banking, 2004.
21. *Wall Street Journal* (18 May 2004).
22. *Financial Times* (18 September 2004).
23. Chen and Ritter, op. cit., p. 1129.
24. *Financial Times* (29 January 2004).
25. Chen and Ritter, op. cit., p. 1124.
26. Ibid., p. 1125.
27. Ibid., pp. 1105–6; this quote from a head of underwriting at an investment bank originally appeared in Roger Lowenstein's column in the *Wall Street Journal* (10 April 1997).
28. Author interview, partner in private equity firm, 2004.
29. Author interview, CEO technology firm, 2004.
30. Author interview, 2003.
31. Author interview, 2003.
32. Hintz, op. cit., p. 23.
33. www.economist.com/research/economics
34. Ibid.
35. Freeman & Co., *Trends in Investment Banking* (www.freeman-co.com), p.10.
36. Lecture at Cranfield School of Management, 2004.

Chapter 7

1. Stewart, James, *Den of Thieves* (Simon & Schuster, 1991), p. 352.
2. Research note (26 April 2002).
3. *Securities Industry Association Fact Book* 2004, p. 36.
4. Lowenstein, Roger, *When Genius Failed* (Fourth Estate, 2002), p. 175.
5. Glenn Bedwin, International Research Director, Thomson Financial, Trading for Investors Forum, *Financial News* supplement (2004), p. 14.
6. *Financial Times* (24 May 2004).
7. Morgan Stanley Form 10-K, 2002, p. 62.
8. Bear Stearns Annual Report 2002, p. 44.
9. Lehman Brothers Annual Report 2002, pp. 52–3.
10. Merrill Lynch Annual Report 2004, p. 37.
11. Endlich, Lisa, *Goldman Sachs* (Alfred A. Knopf, 1999), p. 225.
12. Author interview, 2004.
13. Endlich, op. cit., p. 164–5.
14. Ibid., pp. 224–5.
15. Ibid., p. 304.
16. Lowenstein, op. cit., p. 96.
17. Levitt, Arthur, *Take on the Street* (Pantheon Books, 2002), p. 179.
18. Survey by Radley & Associates, *Financial Times* (18 August 2004).
19. Morgan Stanley, Form 10-K, 2002, p. 100.
20. Morgan Stanley Annual Report 2003. There is one reference to 'principal investing' on the penultimate page of full text and a heading 'Principal transactions-trading' in the Selected Financial Data.
21. Goldman Sachs Annual Report 2003, pp. 56–7; Bear Stearns Annual Report 2003, p. 49, year-end figure.
22. Lehman Brothers Annual Report 2002, pp. 6–7.
23. Merrill Lynch Annual Report 2002, p. 27.
24. *Financial Times* (23 June 2004).
25. Author interview, 2003.
26. *Financial Times* (2 February 2004).
27. Ibid. (12 March 2004).
28. Instinet advertisement, *Financial News* supplement, Trading for Investors Forum, 2004 p. 9.
29. Kaufman, Henry, *On Money and Markets* (McGraw-Hill, 2000), pp. 78–9.
30. Author interview, 2003.
31. Author interview, 2004.

32. *New York Times* (16 May 2004); *Financial Times* (2 December 2003).
33. *Financial Times* (4 October 2004); *The Guardian* (8 September 2004).
34. *Financial Times* (22 September 2004).
35. Ibid. (30 June 2004).

Chapter 8

1. *The Economist* (14 November 2002).
2. Greenberg, Alan C., *Memos from the Chairman* (Workman Publishing, 1996).
3. *Financial Times* (16 June 2004).
4. Kaufman, Henry, *On Money and Markets* (McGraw-Hill, 2000), p. 272.
5. Augar, Philip, *The Death of Gentlemanly Capitalism* (Penguin Books, 2001), p. 121.
6. Greenberg, Alan C., op. cit., p. 62.
7. Partnoy, Frank, *Infectious Greed* (Profile Books, 2003), pp. 134–5.
8. *Securities Industry Association Fact Book 2004*, p. 30.
9. *Wall Street Journal* (20 May 1994); Lowenstein, Roger, *When Genius Failed* (Fourth Estate, 2002), p. 42.
10. Endlich, Lisa, *Goldman Sachs* (Alfred A. Knopf, 1999), p. 199.
11. Endlich, ibid., p. 199.
12. Glyn A. Holton, www.riskglossary.com
13. Bear Stearns Annual Report 2002, p. 5.
14. Author interview, 2003.
15. Hayes III, Samuel L., and Hubbard, Philip M., *Investment Banking* (Harvard Business School Press, 1990).
16. Author interview, 2004.
17. Author interview, 2004.
18. Ian Kerr, *Financial News* (15 September 2003).
19. CSFB research quoted in *Financial News* (26 July 2004).
20. Freeman & Co., *Back to Basics* (www.freeman-co.com), p. 5.
21. *Financial Times* (31 October 2003, 2 July 2004).
22. Ibid. (31 October 2003).
23. *Fortune* (1 September 2003); *Business Week* (30 July 2001); Kessler, Andy, *Wall Street Meat* (HarperBusiness, 2004), p. 179.
24. *Financial Times* (28 September 2004).

Chapter 9

1. *Securities Industry Association Fact Book 2004*, p. 36.
2. Judy Bollinger quotes taken from author interview, 2004.
3. Lewis, Michael, *Liar's Poker* (Coronet edition, 1990), pp. 24–6.
4. Hayes III, Samuel L., and Hubbard, Philip M., *Investment Banking* (Harvard Business School Press, 1990), p. 393.
5. Author interview, 2003.
6. www.bankstocks.com/aboutus/howigottowhereiam
7. *Wall Street Journal* (14 July 1992).
8. Author interview, 2003.
9. Chen, Hsuan-Chi, and Ritter, Jay, 'The Seven Per Cent Solution', *Journal of Finance*, vol. 55, no. 3 (June 2000), p. 1129.
10. Hayes III and Hubbard, op. cit., p. 392.
11. Freeman & Co., *Back to Basics 2002*, p. 10 (www.freeman-co.com).
12. Augar, Philip, *The Death of Gentlemanly Capitalism* (Penguin Books, 2001).
13. Author interview, 2004.
14. Author interview, 2004.
15. Courtney, Cathy, and Thompson, Paul, *City Lives* (Methuen, 1996), p. 214.
16. *Financial Times* (16 August 2004).
17. Author interview, 2003.
18. The account of Citigroup and WorldCom is based on an article in the *New York Times* (16 May 2004).
19. *Financial Times* (14 October 2003).
20. Ibid.
21. Lewis, Michael, *Liar's Poker*, op. cit., pp. 196–7.
22. Partnoy, Frank, *FIASCO* (Profile Books, 1998), pp. 48–9.
23. Kaufman, Henry, *On Money and Markets* (McGraw-Hill, 2000), p. 97.
24. Lewis, Michael, op. cit., pp. 196–7.
25. Kaufman, op. cit., p. 339.
26. Goldman Sachs IPO prospectus 1999, p. 2.

Chapter 10

1. *The Economist* (28 June 2003); *The Guardian* (10 March 2004); *New York Times* (15 September 2004).
2. *Financial Times* (6 March 2004); *New York Times* (27 October 2002).
3. *The Economist* (28 June 2003).
4. *New York Times* (27 October 2002).
5. Kessler, Andy, *Wall Street Meat* (HarperBusiness, 2003), pp. 167–8.
6. United States General Accounting Office, GAO-03-511, *Investment Banks: The Role of Firms and their Analysts with Enron and Global Crossing* (March 2003), p. 24.
7. Financial Services Authority, 'Financial Risk Outlook', *Financial Times* (21 January 2004).
8. Author interview, 2004.
9. Plender, John, *Going Off the Rails* (John Wiley, 2003), p. 147.
10. The earnings of big technology companies would have been cut by a third if they had been forced to deduct options costs and S&P 500 company earnings would have been 5–6 per cent lower: research by CSFB and Citigroup Global Markets, *Financial Times* (22 June 2004).
11. *The Economist* (28 June 2003); *Financial Times* (17 January 2004).
12. Title of NBC programme, 1984.
13. *Financial Times* (11 October 2004).
14. Plender, John, op. cit., pp. 124–36.
15. *Financial News* (12 July 2004).
16. Author interview, 2003.
17. Smith, Adam, *The Wealth of Nations* (Modern Library edition, 2000), p. 485.
18. David Smith, *Free Lunch* (Profile Books, 2003), p. 49.
19. *The Economist* (16 November 2002).

Chapter 11

1. *Wall Street* (American Entertainment/20th Century Fox, 1987).
2. Galbraith, J. K., *The Great Crash 1929* (Penguin edition, 1992), p. 153.
3. *Financial Times* (22 September 2003).
4. Gary Silverman, *Financial Times* (27 December 2003).
5. Author interview, Fortune 500 company senior executive, 2004.
6. Author interview, 2004.

7. Author interview, 2004.
8. Author interview, 2004.
9. *Financial Times* (19 September 2003, 5 May 2003).
10. Stiglitz, Joseph, *The Roaring Nineties* (Allen Lane, 2003), p. 126.
11. Author interview, 2003.
12. Author interview, 2003.
13. Author interview, 2003.
14. Author interview, 2004.
15. Author interview, 2003.
16. Author interview, 2003.
17. Author interview, 2004
18. Author interview, 2004.
19. *The Economist* (11 October 2003).
20. *Financial Times* (24 June 2004).
21. Author interview, 2003.
22. Loughran, Tim, and Ritter, Jay, 'Why Don't Issuers Get Upset About Leaving Money on the Table in IPOs?' *Review of Financial Studies*, vol. 15, no. 2 (2002), pp. 413–43. By permission of Oxford University Press.
23. *The Economist* (16 November 2002).
24. Center for Responsive Politics (www.opensecrets.org).
25. *Financial News* (1 July 2004).
26. *Financial Times* (16 June 2004).
27. Ibid. (14 June 2004).
28. Ibid. (9 September 2003).
29. Stiglitz, Joseph, op. cit., p. 267.
30. Rubin, Robert E., *In an Uncertain World* (Texere Publishing, 2003), p. 339.
31. *Financial Times* (8 October 2002).
32. Levitt, Arthur, *Take on the Street* (Pantheon Books, 2002), p. 249.
33. Stiglitz, op. cit., p. 154; Levitt, op. cit., pp. 87–104.
34. *Financial Times* (23 March 2004).
35. Securities Institute press release (2 April 2004).
36. *Financial Times* (9 December 2003)
37. United States General Accounting Office, GAO-02-302, *SEC Operations: Increased Workload Creates Challenges* (March 2002).
38. *The Economist* (10 May 2001).
39. *Wall Street Journal* (25 May 2004).
40. *Financial Times* (25 May 2004).
41. Ibid. (15 January 2004).
42. Levitt, Arthur, op. cit., p. 67.

43. *Washington Post* (11 November 2002), one of six articles, 'Bubble: The Root of the 90s Boom and Bust'.
44. *Financial Times* (1 December 2003).
45. Ibid. (8 January 2004).
46. *Financial Times* and *The Guardian* (16 March 2004).
47. *Financial Times* (8 January 2004).
48. Ibid. (24 February, 13 April 2004).
49. *Private Eye* (23 January 2004).
50. Morgan Stanley Annual Report 2003, p. 13.
51. Morgan Stanley press release (8 January 2004).
52. *Financial Times* (21 November 2003).
53. Aggarwal, R., Prabhala, N. P., and Puri, M., 'Institutional Allocation in IPO Offering', *Journal of Finance*, vol. 57 (2002), pp. 1421–42.
54. *Financial Times* (30 January 2004).
55. Ibid. (21 November 2003).
56. *Institutional Investment in the UK: A Review* (HM Treasury, 2001), p. 186.
57. Author interview, 2004.
58. *Financial Times* (17 December 2003 and 15 January 2004).
59. *Institutional Investment in the UK: A Review*, op. cit.
60. *Financial Times* (7 January, 8 May 2004).
61. Letter dated 2 March 2004 from Fidelity to SEC on SEC web site (www.sec.gov).
62. *Wall Street Journal* (16 March 2004).
63. *Financial Times* (16 June 2004).
64. *Financial News* (13 September 2004).
65. *Financial Times* (21 July 2003).
66. Ibid. (15 July 2002).
67. Author interview, 2004.
68. Author interview, 2003.
69. Author interview, 2004.
70. Author interview, 2003.
71. *Financial Times* (13 November 2001).
72. Stein, Mark, 'Unbounded Rationality: Risk and Organizational Narcissism at Long Term Capital Management', *Human Relations*, vol. 56, no. 5 (2003), pp. 523–40.
73. Merrill Lynch Annual Report 1999, p. 3.
74. Morgan Stanley Annual Report 1999, p. 1.
75. Goldman Sachs Annual Report 2000, p. 3.

76. Miller, Danny, *The Icarus Paradox* (Random House, 1993); Janis, Irving L., *Groupthink* (Houghton Mifflin, 1982).

Chapter 12

1. *The Economist* (26 July 2003).
2. Ibid. (28 February 2004).
3. *Financial Times* (30 July 2004).
4. Ibid. (7 September 2004).
5. Ibid. (22 June 2004).
6. Skiles, Marilyn E., SIA Research Report, *After the Bubble has Burst: New Regulations for Research Analysts in the USA* (May 2003).
7. *Financial Times* (13 April 2004).
8. Ibid. (3 June 2004).
9. Ibid. (14 July 2004).
10. Ibid. (17 May 2004).
11. Author interview, 2004.
12. *Financial Times* (24 July 2003).
13. *Financial News* (7 June 2004), research by Greenwich Associates.
14. Ellis, Charles D., *Capital: The Story of Long-Term Investment Excellence* (Wiley, 2004).
15. William Donaldson at the Senate Banking Committee, 9 March 2005, www.sec.gov
16. Ibid. (17 May 2004).
17. Ibid. (8 November 2003).
18. Ibid. (17 February 2004).
19. 'About the NYSE' (www.nyse.com).
20. Speech at the SIA conference, November 2003 (www.sia.com).
21. Author interview, 2004.
22. Speech at the National Press Club, June 2002.
23. *Financial Times* (13 April 2004).
24. SEC notice, November 2003.
25. SEC Litigation Release 18115 (28 April 2003).
26. Ibid. (16 August 2004).
27. *New York Times* and *Financial Times* (15 September 2004).
28. *The Economist* and *Financial Times* (25 September 2004).
29. Author interview, 2003.
30. *Financial Times* (14 June and 27 August 2004); *The Economist* (4 September 2004).

31. *Financial Times* (22 June 2004).
32. Ibid. (19 March 2004).
33. Ibid. (14 June 2004).
34. Ibid. (10 and 20 September 2004).
35. *Bank Credit Analyst* (August 2004), pp. 20–32.
36. *Financial Times* (17 April 2004).
37. Ibid. (16 June 2004).
38. *The Economist* (16 November 2002).
39. Irwin Stelzer, director of economic policy at the Hudson Institute, quoted in Moneypenny, *Financial News* (26 July 2004); Howard Jones, 'Breaking up the banks', *Financial Times* (28 August 2002).
40. Augar Philip, *The Death of Gentlemanly Capitalism* (Penguin Books, 2001), p. 343.

Index